Charles Allen was bor[n] ...
his family served under ...
years of his childhood he ... Assam, where his father
was a Political Officer on the North-West Frontier until
1953. After being educated in England he returned to the
Indian sub-continent in 1966 to work with Voluntary
Service Overseas in Nepal. He ended his service with a long
walk through the Himalayas that won him the *Sunday
Telegraph* Traveller of the Year trophy in 1967. Since then
he has trekked and climbed extensively in the Himalayas and
in other corners of the world.

A writer and oral historian specialising in colonial and
military subjects, Charles Allen is the author of several other
books including *Tales from the Dark Continent*, *Tales from the
South China Seas* and *Plain Tales from the Raj*. He is married
with three children and lives in North London.

Also by Charles Allen

Plain Tales from the Raj
Tales from the Dark Continent
Tales from the South China Seas
Raj Scrapbook
The Savage Wars of Peace
Thunder and Lightning
Lives of the Indian Princes
A Soldier of the Company
A Glimpse of the Burning Plain
Kipling's Kingdom
A Mountain in Tibet
The Buddha and the Sahibs
Soldier Sahibs
Duel in the Snows
God's Terrorists
Kipling Sahib

The Search for Shangri-La

A Journey into Tibetan History

CHARLES ALLEN

Photography by Richard Davies

ABACUS

First published in Great Britain in 1999
by Little, Brown and Company
This edition published in 2000 by Abacus
Reprinted 2001, 2007 (twice)

A CIP catalogue record for this book
is available from the British Library.

ISBN 978-0-349-11142-1

Maps by M Rules

Typeset in Fournier by M Rules
Printed and bound in Great Britain by
Clays Ltd, St Ives plc

Abacus
An imprint of
Little, Brown Book Group
100 Victoria Embankment
London EC4Y 0DY

An Hachette Livre UK Company

www.littlebrown.co.uk

For Dick, whose sleeping habits I now know almost as well as Celia does, the others of the Six Proud Walkers — Terry, Barney, Chris and Mel — and those we love. With special thanks to Binod and to Dr Kidwai for giving me a second chance.

Contents

A NOTE ON TIBETAN SPELLING

Written Tibetan was adapted from a form of Sanskrit in the seventh century of the Christian era (here referred to as CE, with the pre-Christian era being referred to as BCE – before the Christian era). Tibetan pronunciation has changed very significantly since then, but written Tibetan has not. This creates difficulties when it comes to transcribing ancient Tibetan names and words into Roman form; what works for scholars becomes unpronounceable and incomprehensible to the layman. Wherever possible, I have stuck to the path followed by most non-academics, setting down the Tibetan word in Roman letters as it sounds today, rather than as it is written.

Acknowledgements

My special thanks go to those in Kathmandu who helped me along the way, in particular Binod, Jagdish and Philemon Rai, Colonel Mike Allen, Lisa and Tenzin Choegyal, the Venerable Yongdzin Rinpoche and Tenpa Yungdrung at the Tritan Norbutse Gompa, Charles Ramble, Mohun Basnet, Sangay, Kaji and Bagbir Tamang, and Surendra of Surendra's Tibetan Thanka Treasure. I should also like to thank Anthony Aris of Serindia Publications, and Professor David Snellgrove, Samten Karmay, Per Kvaerne, Roberto Vitali, Dan Martin, Martin Brauen and Gyurme Dorje for permission to quote from their work. All the photographs in the book were taken by Richard Davies, with the exception of the illustration of the Shambhala Thanka, which is reproduced by kind permission of the Musée National des Arts Asiatiques in Paris. All the line drawings other than the Tibetan woodblocks are by Terry Cockerell.

My thanks, too, to Lama Khemsar Rinpoche, Director of the Yungdrung Bon Study Centre, Tring, for his prayers and blessings, and to Dr Paul Wiseman, Patsy Maddock and C. D. Mistry for their medical advice and support.

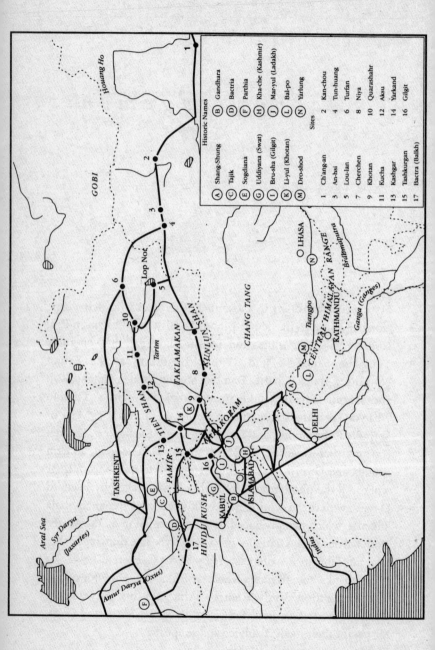

Historic Names

(A) Shang-Shung (B) Gandhara
(C) Tajik (D) Bactria
(E) Sogdiana (F) Parthia
(G) Uddiyana (Swat) (H) Kha-che (Kashmir)
(I) Bru-sha (Gilgit) (J) Mar-yul (Ladakh)
(K) Li-yul (Khotan) (L) Bal-po
(M) Dro-shod (N) Yarlung

Sites

1 Ch'ang-an 2 Kan-chou
3 An-hsi 4 Tun-huang
5 Lou-lan 6 Turfan
7 Cherchen 8 Niya
9 Khotan 10 Quarashahr
11 Kucha 12 Aksu
13 Kashgar 14 Yarkand
15 Tashkurgan 16 Gilgit
17 Bactra (Balkh)

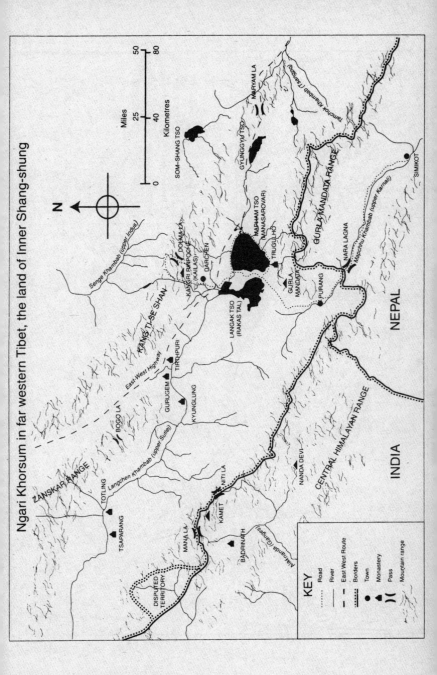

Ngari Khorsum in far western Tibet, the land of Inner Shang-shung

Introduction: The Long Road

How long is the road to the weary. How long is the wandering of the fool who cannot find the path.

From the Dhammapada, 'The Footsteps of the Law', the collected sayings of Buddha Shakyamuni

It cannot be often that an author writes a book based on solid historical research and then discovers some years down the road that he has got it all wrong. But it happens. In 1981 I wrote a book called *A Mountain in Tibet: The Search for Mount Kailas and the Sources of the Great Rivers of India*. It enjoyed considerable success over the years and I like to think that it still has a cult following among a certain kind of traveller. But the more I read and the more I travelled, the more obvious it became that in writing *A Mountain in Tibet* I had actually missed the main point. I had written about a holy mountain sacred to Hindus, Buddhists and Jains as the centre of the world, but without grasping *why* this should be so. I had, as it were, felt and accurately described the elephant's tail and rump but missed the trunk, head, tusks and ears. I had overlooked a civilisation centred on that mountain which had preceded Hinduism, Buddhism and Jainism and which had laid the foundations upon which Tibetan Buddhism was built. In doing so, I had missed a quite extraordinary story. So, to begin again at the beginning.

Paradise lost, the underlying theme of this book, is the leitmotif of many a childhood. As it was of mine. My first, blissful summers were spent at a hill station called Shillong in the Khasi Hills of Assam. I swear that on a clear day you could look north from the peak above the town out over the expanse of the Brahmaputra valley and see the snows of Bhutan shimmering 150 miles away.

The Himalayan ranges came closer when my father was posted to Sadiya, right up in the extreme north-east corner of Assam, where the Tsangpo river forces a passage between the breasts of the sow goddess Dorje Phagma – the mountain peaks of Namche Barwa and Gyala Peri – and breaks out on to the plains of India as the Brahmaputra. The town of Sadiya stood then at the confluence of two rivers, at one of those power-points which the Hindus call prayag (which did not prevent it being entirely washed away in later years).

This was where I met my first Tibetans. In the bestiary of a five-year-old child they fell somewhere between ogres and bears: swaggering, shambling, woolly creatures, dressed in felt boots tied at the knees and black, hairy pelts of yak's wool gathered up by a waistbelt and worn with one long sleeve loose and flapping at the back. Tibetans glittered: gold thread in their fur hats, gold in their teeth, chunks of turquoise set in gold earrings, gold and silver amulets round their necks, swords in silver sheaths dangling from their waists. They carried gems, amber, musk and borax, brought from the far side of the Himalayas to be traded at market in Sadiya.

They made a lasting impression, not least because summer sun bearing down on yak-butter-smeared bodies produces a particularly rancid stench that lingers in the air for hours. But one Tibetan I remember in particular: a jadhu-wallah or magic-maker who carried the narrow-sided rattledrum on a stick known as the damaru. My elder brother and I first came upon him holding court with the household servants on the back verandah of my parents' bungalow. As honorary members of this circle, we stayed to hear him tell fortunes by throwing bones in the dust.

My parents only learned of this when I came to them in a rage: the jadhu-wallah had promised my brother success as a warrior (he eventually made it to full colonel in the Gurkhas) and a ripe old age, but for me he foretold a life of austerity as a scholar – and ill health. I also carry with me from that osteomancy a blurred memory of a dove being sacrificed: the magician cuts its head off with a sharp knife, briefly holds apart the two sections of the bird and then reunites them – and then throws the creature into the air. It flies about before settling on a rafter, and I have a distinct image of a ring of blood round its neck. I have to add that my brother remembers nothing of this.

Many years later – in the summer of 1966 – I was sent to Kathmandu as an English teacher with Voluntary Service Overseas. Every morning I washed myself under a standpipe in the school yard under the all-seeing eyes of the Swayambunath stupa that looks down on the Kathmandu valley from its hilltop. If time allowed I would bike over as the sun was coming up, climb the 300 or so steps and join the monks of the Gelugpa school of Tibetan Buddhism at their morning prayers. The content meant nothing; the sound was everything.

About two dozen gelong (monks; the term lama is more properly used to describe a spiritual teacher) would sit cross-legged and facing each other in two rows before a great gilt image of the Buddha. Their prayers followed a regular pattern: a solo recitation by a senior monk; a response; a sing-song chant in which the older men supplied a deep bass growl; then the chant gathered pace and was reinforced by the clashing of cymbals, the blowing of conches, the trumpeting of horns; and, finally, a curiously crooked stick would be banged on a large flat drum, a slow measured tap, at first, but quickly speeding up to a loud climax. After a moment or two of silence the whole cycle was repeated.

It was – and remains still – a wondrous sound. It seemed to throb both within the prayer hall and my own skull. It carries within it that archetypal resonation that comes from the pit of the stomach and which in both Hindu and Buddhist mantras represents the universal sound of creation – *Om*.

The monks of Swayambu were cheerful souls. Many were youngsters, as chirpy as any other boys of their age. At their prayers they yawned, scratched themselves, twiddled their ears with their little fingers and often nodded off. Whenever this happened an adult would lean forward and slap them hard around the face.

A small community of Tibetan refugees had settled near the base of Swayambu hill and from among them I recruited a Tibetan named Nawang Dorje to cook and teach me Tibetan. Nawang's culinary skills were nil but most evenings he would come to my room and knock up a meal on my primus stove. One night he asked if I could help a friend of his. He took me back to his home, and there I met a burly young man who appeared to have breathing trouble. I suggested he go to the local hospital but Nawang said that this would be impossible. He then lifted the back of his friend's shirt and there, just under the right shoulder blade, was a bullet entry wound like a pink rose. There was no exit wound.

Nawang Dorje and his friend were Khampas, men from the Kham district of eastern Tibet celebrated as warriors and notorious as brigands. The Khampas had played a leading role in the uprising against the occupying Chinese which had started in Lhasa in 1959, eight years after the Chinese People's Liberation Army (PLA) had occupied Tibet in order to restore it to the bosom of the Chinese motherland (a claim of sovereignty that no international court of law would uphold, based chiefly on the grounds that the Manchu emperors actively intervened in Tibetan affairs for almost two centuries until all Chinese representatives were expelled from Lhasa in 1912. Tibet was first declared to be part of China in 1931, but when the Chinese government attempted to exercise control it was rebuffed. Tibet remained fully independent until October 1950, when Chinese 'liberation forces' advanced into Tibet to 'liberate 3 million Tibetans from imperialist aggression'. In April 1951 a fatal 17-Point Agreement was concluded between the two governments, by which Tibet agreed to 'return to the big family of the Motherland' in return for certain guarantees, including internal autonomy in matters of custom and religion and the continuance of the existing political system). Nawang and his friend had fought with the Khampas against the Chinese until they were forced to retreat across the border into Nepal. With support from the CIA and the Indian government, the Khampas had then set themselves up in Mustang, a little chunk of Nepal jutting into the Tibetan plateau. Pressured by the Americans and the Indians on the one hand and by the Chinese on the other, the Nepalese government had been placed in a very awkward position. Finally, it acted against the Khampas.

The bullet rattling around inside the chest of Nawang's friend came not from a Chinese but a Nepalese rifle. His band of Khampas had been chased out of Mustang by the Nepalese Army, then caught in an ambush and broken up. This was in the spring of 1967.

That year was the worst in Tibet's history. In the previous autumn we three VSOs in Kathmandu had cycled to the Chinese Embassy to watch its entire staff gather outside its corrugated tin gates for spontaneous demonstrations of support for the Great Helmsman. All wore blue Mao caps and blue Mao suits with red Mao badges in their lapels, and waved their copies of *The Thoughts of Chairman Mao* in red plastic folders while they screamed and stamped and waved themselves into mass hysteria. It was comic yet chilling.

But there was nothing remotely funny about what the Chinese were doing next door in Tibet. The Cultural Revolution unleashed by the Great Leader in the autumn of 1966 had started to thrash its way across the Tibetan plateau like some insane cyclone. It reached its apogee in 1967, when thousands of monasteries, hermitages, shrines, chortens (stupas), mane (prayer) stones, mane walls and rock carvings were dynamited or torn down stone by stone. Thousands of statues were smashed, thousands of wall paintings defaced, thousands of sacred texts thrown on to bonfires along with thanka, religious paintings on cloth. No effort was spared in grinding into dust every trace of Tibetan religion.

It took a little longer for the Cultural Revolution to reach western Tibet. But here the banning of religious worship and the private ownership of livestock pushed the nomads into open rebellion. At first they succeeded in expelling the revolutionary cadres but their victory was short-lived. Soldiers from the PLA were trucked in and the insurgents were disarmed of their ancient flintlocks and relocated in communes. It is said that in that winter of 1967–8 more than half a million Tibetan nomads – somewhere between a tenth and a fifth of the entire Tibetan population – perished from hunger, hardship or disease, the direct result of resettlement programmes that left them without any means to feed themselves. This was a winter of genocide that very few outside Tibet ever heard about. A nightmare period of Red Guard denunciation of class enemies and reactionary habits followed in which the 'four olds' – old ideas, old culture, old customs and old habits – were relentlessly done away with.

If the outside world had been able to see events in Tibet on its television screens the Chinese might have been shamed into moderating their behaviour. But even in Kathmandu – only 50 miles from the border by the new Friendship Highway the Chinese were then building – the news from Tibet was patchy at best. It arrived mostly in the form of waves of refugees who provided rich pickings for the art houses of the West. There was a glut on the Tibetan curio market.

But, as with the fall of Byzantium, one culture's loss is another's gain. For what brought about the extraordinary diffusion of Tibetan Buddhism in recent years throughout the West, if not the Tibetan diaspora? In my own case, karma brought me face to face with an old Tibetan woman begging at the gates of the Royal Hotel in Kathmandu. She sold me the only thanka I could then afford. Because it was burned along both sides and all its paint had flaked off in the heat of the fire it was mine for 16 rupees. It portrays the medicine Buddha, Sangye Menla, one of eight such Buddhas who together form a sub-group within the Tibetan Buddhist pantheon of deities and saints at the level of enlightenment achieved by bodhisattvas. His ears have long pendulous lobes, which denote wisdom, and he sits cross-legged on a lotus in the lotus position, holding in his left hand a bowl containing the universal panacea known as myrobalan. Lesser bodhisattvas hover in the air around him. The colours have gone, the underlying lines are faded and the surrounding maroon cloth has been patched and stitched time and again. For thirty years now Sangye Menla has watched over my bed. But for perhaps ten or twenty times that long he has watched over other sleepers, probably hanging in the corner of the black yak-wool tent of some nomad family, as it followed the cycle of transhumance year after year, generation after generation.

The Chinese occupation of Tibet merely continued the policy of isolation that had for so long preserved Tibet's image as a country out of bounds. The Indian government, still smarting from its hammering from the Chinese in their border war of 1962, also played its part by refusing to let foreigners anywhere near its northern borders. Unable to enter Tibet myself, I began to study the explorers and adventurers who had tried to penetrate its mysteries and the reasons why they had felt impelled to try. Some of these had been players of the Great Game, the covert political struggle between the British and Russian Empires in the nineteenth century, which was played out in Tibet and central Asia. But far more interesting were those drawn by a quest, those who, in Kipling's words, went looking for 'something lost beyond the ranges, lost and waiting to be found'.

My own questing started in 1979 when the pilgrim trail to the traditional source of the Ganges in the Garhwal Himalayas was first opened to foreigners by the Indian authorities. I travelled with the photographer Richard Cooke and as the first Westerners allowed to visit those parts for many years we aroused some suspicion. A permit was required from New Delhi and we had to inscribe our names in a spanking new register at the Uttarkashi checkpost. Here an unspeakable government official, whom we named the Purple Brahmin because of his caste and his ridiculous beret, informed us that he would honour us with his company. Over the next two days he drove us to the point of distraction with his ceaseless extolling of the virtues of Brahminical culture compared to the moral depravity of the West. By the third day we were desperate to get rid of him, but the faster we walked the harder he talked. He matched us stride for stride as we came through the deep cleft which the Bhagirathi has carved through the central Himalayan range, and he was still chattering away as we rounded the bend in the river that brought us east into the upper Gangotri valley. But just below a village called Harsil we gave the Purple Brahmin the slip, quietly packing up and tiptoeing away while he dozed after tiffin.

One of the aims of this trip was to examine the viability of slipping into Tibet at the head of a valley off to the north of the one we were following, via the Tsang Choka La ('la' means 'pass'). It was this pass that Heinrich Harrer, author of *Seven Years in Tibet*, and his companion Peter Aufschnaiter had crossed to enter Tibet after escaping from their internment camp in India in 1944. But the pass and the valley leading up it were now disputed territory, claimed by both the Indian and Chinese governments. It was a highly sensitive area from the Indian point of view, as Richard and I discovered when we were arrested at the instigation of the Purple Brahmin. The local police treated us very decently and we were soon freed, but it put paid to any ideas of further exploring Heinrich Harrer's escape route.

At about this time – I fudge the date deliberately – I went to look at the other main tributary of the Ganges to weigh up the prospects of crossing into Tibet by way of the Mana La beyond Badrinath, or the Niti La further east. After being caught napping by the PLA in 1962 the Indian government had embarked on a crash programme of road-building in the Himalayas so that reinforcements could be quickly moved up to any threatened frontier post. That meant it was now possible to drive all the way by bus from the plains of India to the famous temple of Vishnu at Badrinath, one of the most ancient and important pilgrimage sites in India – and, formerly, one of the hardest to reach.

For a thousand years and more pilgrims from the plains of India have been making their way here on foot: first to Hardwar, where the Ganges breaks out through the Siwalik foothills; then to the confluence of the Bhagirathi and Alaknanda Ganga at Rudraprayag. Here you can take the left fork, which leads to Gangotri and Gaumukh, where the Ganges emerges from the 'cow's mouth' of a glacier, or you can fork right and follow the Alaknanda to Badrinath.

One of the first Hindu shrines in the Himalayas was built here at Badrinath. The sacred Hindu text known as the *Skanda purana* states that, at the time of the Hindu revival in the eighth century of the Christian era (CE), the reformer Adiguru Shankaracharya threw out a Buddhist statue from the temple and replaced it with an image of Vishnu, which itself had been thrown out by the Buddhists a thousand years earlier. But look carefully at the weathered black stone statue now enthroned in the temple at Badrinath, and you will see a figure seated in the padmasan posture of meditation, far more characteristic of Buddhist statuary than Hindu. Whatever Hindu orthodoxy may say, the fact is that the Himalayas were never 'Hindu' as we would understand the term before the eighth century. Indeed, the first deities which were worshipped here almost certainly belonged neither to Buddhism nor to Hinduism. The probability is that they belonged to the faith which preceded Buddhism in Tibet, the mysterious, much-maligned religion which was once practised throughout the Tibetan plateau – and which is the main subject of this book.

Badrinath is today one of Hinduism's most important shrines. This is partly because of its proximity to the source of one of the main headwaters of the sacred Ganges, but also because it stands at the threshold of the most important pilgrimage site in Hinduism: the holy mountain Kailas, abode of the tantric god Shiva, and the holy lake at its foot, Manasarovar, the lake conceived in the mind of the great god Brahma. But to reach Kailas you have first to cross the Mana La into Tibet.

The Mana La is about 25 miles beyond and 8,000 feet higher than Badrinath. The local village of Mana was as far as I was allowed to go, so I turned round and caught the bus back to Joshinath. Here I got off the bus and, finding no one there to stop me, started yomping along the military road into the Dauli valley, which leads up to the Niti La.

I hadn't gone more than a couple of miles when a jeep drew up beside me. In perfect English a voice asked, 'Can I give you a lift?'

I climbed in and we drove on up the valley. As we proceeded I was questioned with great courtesy by a person whom I shall describe simply as a senior Indian Army officer. Did I know I was in a prohibited area? What was I proposing to do? As we talked we got on to the subject of early Himalayan travellers and the so-called 'pundits' recruited in these same hills and trained by the British as explorer spies. We were driven through two military checkpoints.

'Shall I duck?' I asked, as we approached the first.

'Why? You're with me!'

So we drove on and up until we came to the end of the met-alled road. The Niti La must have been no more than four or miles further on. It was the nearest I had yet come to Tibet. Here the senior officer invited me to share his tiffin in a tent. When the meal was over we shook hands and I was packed off with his driver back to Joshimath. If he should ever read this account of our meeting, I offer him my salaams.

The fruit of these travels and researches was *A Mountain in Tibet*, first published in 1982. In that same year the Indian and Chinese governments – still to this day in a state of ceasefire rather than at peace, and still disputing several sections of the Indo-Tibetan border – reached agreement on cross-border crossings by Hindu pilgrims from India.

Every June and July since, a limited number of these *yatris* have been allowed to cross into Tibet from Garhwal, not by the Mana or Niti passes but by the Unta Dura pass further to the east, which brings them down into far western Tibet near to the regional headquarters of Purang. Here Chinese lorries drive them to their destination, first to the shores of Lake Mana-sarovar and then on to Mount Kailas.

These pilgrims have to be bona fide Hindus and Indian nationals. I was not the only foreigner who tried to get on the list and failed. Of a number of fascinating letters from readers of *A Mountain in Tibet*, the most treasured was received in 1992 from a thirty-two-year-old Welshman christened Stuart but now a Shaivite (follower of Shiva) named Bom Shankar. His experiences mirrored mine, but on a different plane. Bom had visited all the 'upper' shrines in India and then set out to go a little further:

Inspired by the nectar of Shiva – charas [Indian hemp or marijuana] – which I had been consuming with relish in the company of the local sadhus, I set off, but just after skirting the village of Mana I was intercepted by the local peace-keeping force who refused to let me continue, despite my efforts to convince them that I was on a yatra [pilgrimage] and not a tourist. I returned to Badrinath and then to Joshinath before, more carefully, heading straight for Kailas via the Niti route. Sadly, a chance meeting with authority near the Niti pass.

'Why no Tibet visa?'

'Would you have let me in, even with one?'

'No.'

'That's why I didn't bother to get one!'

Even when asked at what stage in history had the law of man superseded the law of God, they refused to let me go on. I shall have to stop asking that question. I asked it last week, too, as Dover HM Customs and Excise were separating me from my one kilogram of charas – no intent to supply, just to dance with Shiva!

Bom Shankar's letter had been written in HM Prison Canterbury. He had been banged up for attempting to import a kilo of Indian hemp into the UK. I wrote to him in jail but my letter was returned unopened; the addressee had been moved to another prison and they were apparently unable to forward it. So if you read this, Bom, *Om namaya Shivaya!*

Other pilgrims had better luck. John, formerly of Twickenham but now Jungli Jaan and residing in the Indian hill station of McLeodganj in Kangra, wrote to say that he had completed more than forty journeys into the Himalayas and western Tibet. Between 1986 and 1992 he had managed to visit the traditional and true sources of the Indus, Tsangpo-Brahmaputra, Sutlej and Karnali-Ganges, the four great rivers of the Indian sub-continent linked to Mount Kailas and Lake Manasarovar in both geographical and mythological terms. This is something that even the great traveller Sven Hedin failed to accomplish (see my two chapters on Sven Hedin in *A Mountain in Tibet* for a potted account of his extraordinary efforts to 'conquer all Asia' or, better still, read his own accounts on his Tibetan travels between 1894 and 1908 in *Southern Tibet, Central Asia and Tibet, Adventures in Tibet* and *Trans-Himalaya*).

These were golden years for independent travellers in Tibet. The authorities seemed to have no system for keeping tabs on those who did it the hard way, wandering round Tibet on foot, hitching rides in lorries where they could. None was more dogged and resourceful than an American physicist named Victor Chan, who over some ten years probably covered as much ground as all the great explorers of Tibet from the 'Chief Pundit' Nain Singh to Professor Giuseppe Tucci put together. Chan's monumental *Tibet: A Pilgrim's Guide* will be the discerning Tibetan traveller's vade mecum for years to come.

Westerners can now travel quite legally and openly within Tibet. There are restrictions – most notably, the requirement to travel as part of a group of five or more and with an accredited Tibetan guide – but the situation has improved dramatically since the years of horror.

For almost two decades the Chinese authorities did all they could to destroy Tibet's identity. The nightmare years ended in China in 1976 with the public scapegoating of the 'Gang of Four' and the admission that 'errors' had been made at the time of the Cultural Revolution, but it took time for these more liberal policies to reach Tibet. Not until 1981 was the communal system of livestock rearing abandoned as an unfortunate experiment. Every surviving adult nomad was then given an equal share of the communal pool, which worked out at five yak, twenty-five sheep and seven goats. To allow the local economy to recover, all local taxes were abandoned until 1990.

The nomads have been allowed to return to their old way of life and once more roam the Chang Tang – the great Tibetan upland – with their herds of yak, goats and sheeps, their mastiffs and black tents. They are currently believed to number about half a million in all, far and away the largest single element of the Tibetan population within Tibet, which numbers about 2 million. However, there are also believed to be as many as

400,000 khaki-clad representatives of the PLA stationed within Tibet's borders, the spearhead of a Han mass migration from China which in eastern Tibet now far outnumbers native Tibetans.

Freedom to worship has also been restored and with it the freedom to go on pilgrimage. All over Tibet the ruins of monasteries, temples, shrines, chortens and mane walls are slowly and lovingly being restored. Mane stones are being recarved and frescos repainted. Terrible things were done to the Tibetans and the outward manifestations of their faith and – on a greatly reduced scale – injustices, oppression and tragedies continue, but the spirit of Tibet, the shared inner life-force which gives its people their own special grace, remains as vital as ever.

Greater access to Tibet, coupled with the spread of Tibetan scholarship outside its borders, has given Tibetan studies an enormous boost in the last few years. As new sources and texts become available for study and translation in the West, our understanding of Tibetan culture is being transformed. Tibet's history is now having to be totally reassessed. In that process the part played by the pre-Buddhist religion of Tibet has suddenly taken on a new significance.

This most curious and misrepresented of religions goes by the name of Bon. It adherents are known as Bonpo, 'followers of Bon'. Its homeland on the Tibetan plateau was a mysterious kingdom called Shang-shung. Together, these three elements – a religion, a people and a kingdom – provide much of the subject-matter for what follows.

Virtually nothing was known about Bon in the West until refugees began to flow into India and Nepal from 1959 onwards. David Snellgrove's pioneering study *The Nine Ways of Bon* appeared in print in 1967, followed by the publication in 1972 of Samten Karmay's *The Treasury of Good Sayings*, both containing part-translations of major Bonpo historical texts. Since then it has become increasingly apparent that Tibet's early history has been seriously, even grossly, misrepresented. The main culprits have been the scholars of the Gelugpa school, popularly known as the 'yellow hats'. This monastic sect became the most powerful of the four main Tibetan Buddhist schools in the early fifteenth century mainly as a result of the patronage of the Mongol emperors. Through the authority of their spiritual leaders, the Dalai Lamas and Panchen Lamas, the Gelugpas were able to impose their own orthodoxy over much of Tibet. This led to the Bonpo, along with followers of the two oldest schools of Tibetan Buddhism, the Nyingmapa and Kagyupa sects, being persecuted in very much the same manner (and at more or less the same time) as were non-Catholics in Europe in the hands of the Inquisition in the years of the Counter-Reformation. The curious Tibetan custom of sticking out one's tongue as a gesture of respect is said to originate from this persecution. It was believed that constant repetition of 'black' mantras by the Bonpo and others of the heretical faiths turned their tongues black or brown, so to prove your innocence you stuck out your tongue whenever you met someone of high rank.

As part of the process of eliminating heresy, Tibetan historical texts were revised to expunge or downplay Tibet's Bon heritage. From the eleventh century onwards the Bon tradition was presented as a false or 'black' religion which had shamelessly modelled itself on Buddhism and plagiarised Buddhist religious texts. This calumny stuck and was taken up by the first generations of Tibetologists from the West. As recently as 1964 it was still possible to find an American anthroplogist – who should be thoroughly ashamed of himself – describing Bon rituals as 'patently a wilful distortion or perversion of Buddhist ritual . . . which brings to mind the Black Mass of Satanic cults'.

After much painstaking research – by Per Kvaerne in Sweden, R. A. Stein and Samten Gyaltse Karmay in Paris, Dan Martin in the United States, Namkhai Norbu and Roberto Vitali in Rome, Charles Ramble in Kathmandu, and others – only now in the 1990s is a more balanced picture of Bon's place in Tibetan history and culture beginning to emerge.

At the same time, the present (Fourteenth) Dalai Lama and his advisers in exile at Dharmsala in India have made real efforts to redress the injustices of the past. The Bon religion is once more recognised as an integral part of Tibetan culture and support has been given to the rebuilding of its institutions, both within Tibet itself and at Dolanji in India, where Gyalwa Menriwa, the present leader of the Bon church, has his headquarters.

Yet Bon remains a great mystery and the original Bonpo remain the Etruscans of Tibet: nobody quite knows who they were, where they came from or what their original religion was. This mystery is neatly summed up by Dan Martin in his recent book, *Mandala Cosmogony*, as follows:

> We do not know how it originated. The statements usually supplied in answer to the question of origins, while various, may be reduced to a few types. The first basically says, 'We know that Bon is the pre-Buddhist primitive shamanism of Tibet.' The second says, 'Bon equals Tibetan folk religion.' A third group, basically agreeing with Tibetan polemical traditions, says, 'Bon, as it existed during the last millennium, is little more than a deceitful appropriation of Chos [Tibetan Buddhist] scriptures and practices.' A fourth group, which includes most of the adherents themselves, believes Bon is the original Buddhism, predating Sakyamuni Buddha by thousands of years. The fifth view . . . is this, 'Bon as it existed during the last millennium represents an unusual, yet quite legitimate, transmission of Buddhist teachings ultimately based on little-known Central Asian Buddhist teachings.'

This book presents a sixth view. To summarise it here would be to spoil the fun, but it sets out to tell what I believe to be the *real* story of far western Tibet and Mount Kailas – or rather, Kangri Rinpoche, the 'Precious Snow Mountain', since 'Kailas' is nothing more than a garbled Sanskrit rendering of the Tibetan

Kangri. I have approached the subject rather as an archaeologist with limited resources might do when confronted by a large site which contains a number of tantalising mounds. I have dug a limited number of trial trenches to various levels at a number of promising points around the site, and reported on each of these trenches in turn. Only when all my trial trenches have been dug have I drawn conclusions about the site as a whole. Some of these trenches may, at first sight, appear misplaced. One, for example (see Chapter 5, 'The Kingdom of Prester John') sheds light on the medieval legend of the priest-king of inner Asia but tells us precious little about the Bon religion or Shang-shung. Having read it, the reader might feel justified in asking what this has to do with my 'sixth view'. But read on, because it has a great deal to say about the spread of Nestorian Christianity through inner Asia and about the Western view of Tibet as a place of hidden mysteries.

So this is not the full story. It is only a beginning; an enormous amount of digging has still to be done. It is bound to contain errors of fact, since I have made a number of assumptions based on still far from conclusive evidence. And it is most certainly going to infuriate those Tibetologists who belong to what might be termed the sentimental school of Tibetan Buddhist scholarship. But I hope I have done enough to show that long ago something quite extraordinary took place in far western Tibet in the shadow of the Precious Snow Mountain. It is the stuff of legend – and that, as we shall see, is precisely what it became. Out of the ruins of the Bon kingdom of Shang-Shung came the story of Shambhala – the mystical, hidden land beyond the Himalayas – and from Shambhala came the more mundane ideal of an earthly paradise which we know of in the West as 'Shangri-La'.

Literary research has its limitations. A time comes when you have to push back your chair, close the books, shut down the computer and get your boots on. The grand theories must be put to the test.

For years I had tried and failed to get access to far western Tibet by way of the ancient pilgrim trails over the Himalayas. But in May 1996 the way was at last opened for me to enter Tibet – though not from the plains of India, as I had wanted, but from western Nepal. I gathered together five friends and off we went.

1 *Lost Horizon*

'Lama, how does it happen that Shambhala on earth is still undiscovered by travellers? On maps you may see many routes of expeditions. It appears that all heights are already marked and all valleys and rivers explored.'

'Verily, there is much gold on the earth, and many diamonds and rubies in the mountains, and everyone is so eager to possess them! And so many people try to find them! But as yet these people have not found all things – so, let a man try to reach Shambhala without a call . . . Many people try to reach Shambhala uncalled. Some of them have disappeared forever. Only few of them reach the holy place, and only if their karma is ready.'

Nicholas Roerich, 'Shambhala the Resplendent',
published in *Talai-Pho-Brang*, 1928

MID-MAY 1996

Gatwick Airport North Terminal on a mild Sunday afternoon, in the fourth month of the Year of the Iron-Mouse. There are six of us; all male, five of us North Londoners, the sixth formerly from North London but now living in Hollywood: Chris, a movie actor who plays baddies with smooth upper-class British accents. He works out and has an impressive physique. He has prepared for this as carefully as for any role, but my main concern at this stage is that he has brought far too much baggage. He is to be partnered by Mel, on the theory that opposites attract. Mel describes himself as 'just an ordinary Jewish boy from North Willesden'; he's dark, lean, wiry, horribly fit, tough as nails, and the country's leading sports injury physio. That's one reason why I've invited him along; the other is that he's climbed in the Himalayas. Chris and Mel are the outsiders. The rest of us have known each other since the days when our kids first started going to the same local schools. Three of us – myself, Dick and Terry – are all teetering close to or over the fifty-year mark; the fourth – Barney – is Terry's eldest son, probably the most mature and self-composed member of the party, even if he is only twenty-one. I would go so far as to describe Dick and Terry as my 'best mates' and that is chiefly why I invited them to join me. But it helps that Dick is a highly rated professional photographer and Terry an artist.

The six of us stand and marvel as the space in front of the Royal Nepalese Airlines check-in counter fills with men and women clad in the purple robes and saffron vests of Tibetan monks. Only they're not Tibetan monks. They have shaven heads and sport all the right trappings in the way of rosary beads and prayer wheels, but something jars. They have pink and white skins. Their bare shoulders and pates are too pale and the skull shapes are wrong: dolichocephalic when they should be neatly brachycephalic. Their ears stick out. Some even sport tattoos.

But we take this collective contemplation of monks to be prime karma. We make our farewells and board the plane in good spirits; jumbos packed with so much faith don't fragment at 35,000 feet. The Buddhists fill the first four rows of the main cabin. From behind they resemble rows of Humpty Dumpties sitting on walls.

Young Barney discovers that I have brought four pairs of footwear: walking boots, trainers, flip-flops and après-ski snow boots. This after I have badgered everyone to travel very light. He names me the Imelda Marcos of the expedition. Having also suggested that we confine ourselves to one book each, I have again played foul by bringing Simon Schama's doorstopping *Landscape and Memory*. This will prove to be my Pilgrim's Burden, growing increasingly heavy and hateful, until finally Dick covers it with urine one night in a failed attempt to follow Lyndon Johnson's well-known advice about peeing out of tents.

This will allow me to give it an honourable burial up on the Tibetan steppe (perhaps one day it will be found as a terma, a text deliberately hidden in order to be rediscovered in the future, and so add a further footnote of confusion to Tibetan history).

On the final leg of the flight, from Dubai to Kathmandu, I get talking with one of the Buddhist monks on the plane. He is a Mancunian named Tashi and a member of the Samye Ling Tibetan monastery at Eskdalemuir in Dumfriesshire. Their party is led by two Tibetans: Lama Yeshe Losal, the Retreat Master of Samye Ling; and his brother the abbot, Lama Akang Rinpoche. They plan to fly on from Kathmandu to Lhasa and then visit Tsurphu monastery, about eighty miles west of Lhasa, the historic seat of the Karma Kagyupa school of Tibetan Buddhism. The monastery was founded in the twelfth century by Karmapa Dusum Khyenpa, a renowned ascetic and yogi who is credited with the inception into Tibetan Buddhism of tulku: the institution of the reincarnated lama which became a very important feature in Tibetan politico-religious life. Before his death the first Karmapa predicted the circumstances of his rebirth, so making it possible for his reincarnated self to be found and installed as his successor. Since that time seventeen Karmapa reincarnations have presided over the monastic life of Tsurphu. For several centuries they dominated the political life of Tibet, as well as providing spiritual leadership first to the Mongols and then subsequently to the Ming emperors of China, before giving way in the mid-seventeenth century to the increasingly powerful Dalai Lama reincarnates of the Gelugpa sect. From then until 1951 and the arrival of the Chinese it was the Dalai Lamas who called all the shots in Tibet, while the Karmapas returned to the role of spiritual heads of their order.

Talking with Abbot Akang Rinpoche, I learn how he served the Sixteenth Karmapa until his death as an exile in 1981. He had then taken part in the search for his successor, who was found in Tibet as a small child of four in 1990. After passing tests, which included picking out his previous incarnation's rosary beads, drinking bowl and other personal items, the boy was recognised as the Seventeenth Karmapa. He was allowed to return to Tsurphu by the Chinese governing powers to preside over the rebuilding of his monastery and the restoration of its monastic community. Now the abbot is on his way to revisit someone whom he regards as an old friend and mentor, and whose identity he recognises in the person of a small boy.

Our hotel is within the bounds of the mediaeval city of wooden temples. When I first came here thirty years ago it was very different: ownership of private motor cars restricted to members of the Nepalese Royal Family and a privileged inner circle, no taxis other than pedal-rickshaws, a curfew at night and just one set of traffic lights. Now the old Kathmandu narrow toles are packed with vehicles, as noisy and polluted as any other city on the sub-continent. Cow killing still tops Nepal's criminal statute book but now plastic is performing the slaughter. Every mendicant cow I meet has scraps of plastic bags sticking out of the corner of its mouth. I drift off to sleep to the barking of dogs. What once drove me to distraction now fills me with nostalgia.

We need several days to sort out permits and logistics before flying out west to Simikot. The sights still enthral: the great Durbar square with its pagodas; Pashupatinath and its burning dead; Swayambunath with its golden eyes; Bodnath, where the circular ambulatory enclosing the great white stupa is packed thick with tourists and now lined with booths selling Tibetan trinkets. We buy several rolls of brightly coloured prayer flags. We also buy some pot.

Cannabis resin in the form of ganja plays a big part in Hindu ritual, particularly in northern India and the hills. Since the '60s it has also loomed large in the lives of Western travellers and hippies in Kathmandu, so the heart gives a little jig of recognition when a shifty little man sidles up as we leave the Bodnath complex and hisses: 'Wanna buy some hash, man?' Echoes of 'We are stardust' and 'Be sure to wear some flowers in your hair'. Thrilling with guilt, we pile into a nearby café to make the deal. The ganja man stage-whispers, ducks, weaves and slides his eyes so dramatically that I start to wonder if this isn't a set-up. Paranoia – a classic element in the pot experience. Then we spot the real dealer, a Westerner seated in a corner trying to smother his giggles. The price is settled and now a further pantomime of oh-so-furtive drop and pick-up has to be played out before 10 grams of resin can change hands for 850 Nepalese rupees, about $15. 'I can't think what all the fuss was about,' I tell the others. 'It's all quite legal here.'

But when I tell Binod Rai, who's coming with us as guide leader, and his father Jagdish, who's organised the trek for us, their bronze Gurkha faces blanche under their smiles. Scene's changed, man. In Kathmandu jail there's a lad from Kentish Town who's serving six years just for possession. Not only is pot now illegal but so is alcohol where we're going – as well as meat, once we cross the border. Mortification. The ganja is dumped and the liquor stored for our return.

The morning before our flight to the west I slip out while it's still dark and take a scooter-rickshaw to Bodnath. How different at half past five in the morning! All the booths are shut and the courtyard silent but for the shuffle of feet, the click of beads, the creak of spinning prayer wheels and the murmur of prayers. Circling round the stupa are hundreds of Tibetans, walking four and five and six abreast. They stride out, heads down, concentrating their thoughts: a bright swirl of colour.

A curtain has been drawn across the entrance to the main temple. Over it I can just see the top of the shaven head of a Tibetan monk. What is odd is that this head glides along behind the curtain from left to right, then turns and glides back, then turns again, back and forth. When I lift the curtain I see that the monk is skating on two dusters, polishing the central aisle of the temple in a kind of ritual dance. Behind him, morning prayers have already started.

About forty monks are present, seated cross-legged facing

each other across the aisle in two rows. All ages, including boys who could be as young as five or six. The prayers follow their familiar cycle: monotone to choral chant to brazen climax. The yawns and scratching are equally familiar. A boy dozes off, his eyes close and his head drops. An elder catches the eye of a younger boy next to the sleeper and jerks his head in his direction. Without batting an eyelid or missing a note the lad turns, clips his neighbour on the pate, returns to his orisons.

An hour into the service two youngsters trip round with wooden bowls and buns and then return to pour out tea from an elegant copper teapot with a long curved spout. Prayers stop while buns are dipped into bowls; breakfast is taken in silence. Salt-butter tea, the flavour of which has been described as akin to a beggar's armpit, but palatable if taken in small sips. I sip small, dip and nibble contented, privileged to have shared this communion.

I slip out as the service winds down to a close. My joints have seized up; I stagger into the sunshine like a drunk.

Bad weather means we fly to western Nepal a day later than planned. That extra night in Kathmandu I do precisely what I have warned the others not to do: I eat some foul-tasting buffalo meat.

We fly west to Nepalganj early next morning but too late to catch the daily Pilatus flight north, so we check into a local hotel. Nepalganj, down in the Nepalese terai, is as hot as any plains town in north India in late May: that's to say, a fanless oven set at 140 degrees Fahrenheit with the door closed. By mid-morning I am seriously unwell, losing more liquid than I can keep down. By mid-afternoon my body's temperature-control mechanism has started to shut down. I'm going downhill so unbelieveably fast that it's impossible to take it on board myself, let alone convince anyone else that I'm seriously in need of medical attention.

Fortunately for me, young Binod Rai appears and takes a grip.

He lugs me out into a rickshaw and I'm pedalled, semi-conscious, across the open plain for what seems like miles. I am driven to the gates of hell and then dragged up steps into a dark, airless blast furnace, crammed with the sick and dying. I see the name 'Dr M. Kidwai' written on a notice board but my poor tilting mind reads this as 'nilgai', the Indian name for the blue bull *Boselaphus tragocamelus*. I titter at the doctor as he takes my fading pulse. 'You're a blue bull,' I croak.

I writhe on a bed of flames; fire rages in my brain and every cell in my body is burning to cinders. Dark shapes hover round me, fan me, wipe me with wet cloths, hold my hand. I greet the needle biting into my inner elbow with a groan of delight, expecting a rush of glucose to follow. But no relief. The drips slide down like translucent slugs. At times my consciousness divides: I'm inside myself, mind whirling uncontrollably round and around like a wave trapped in a sump hole; but also outside myself so that I observe myself clinically as I am: a pallid middle-aged man spread semi-naked on a rubber mat, whimpering, shaking, panting. To my left lies a little child so stark and still that she must be dead, to my right an old man who has just had his pelvis crushed by a lorry. I am humbled by their company but also indignant at the manner of my going. This isn't how I thought it would end.

An hour stretches like chewing gum. One infusion bag gives way to another and somewhere down the line it dawns on me that I am not going to die today. I drop into shallow pools of sleep and each time I surface Binod is there, bathing me like a mother.

Later that same night I'm stabilised enough to be brought back to our hotel. The others are gathered in one room and look suitably subdued when I appear looking like Banquo's ghost. I tell them there's no question of my going on. It isn't simply a question of not being strong enough; I'm in a funk. If I have another attack like that in Tibet there will be no one to save me with intravenous drips. I was very fit, very healthy, but in half a day I have been reduced to an invalid. I am simply too shit-scared to go on.

So the others fly up to Simikot and Binod's father Jagdish flies out from Kathmandu to look after me. I didn't think it possible to feel so weak. For two days I totter from my room to the verandah and back, while Jagdish coaxes food into me. Looking down at my body I think of those old film clips of newly released British POWs at the end of World War Two. Weeks later, after weighing myself, I realise that in that one day of horrors at Nepalganj I must have shed something close to thirty pounds in weight.

The others have offered to wait two nights in Simikot before starting to walk; officially to acclimatise at just under 10,000 feet, but really to give me a chance to catch up. I clutch at this straw and on the third evening in Nepalganj Dr Kidwai warns me against it but clears me to go. There's a seat for me on the plane next morning and I take it. As the Pilatus taxis to take off I see Jagdish waving goodbye, his face creased with worry.

From Nepalganj the plane flies due north until it reaches the point where the Karnali debouches out through the lower foothills of the Himalayas on to the Indian plains. From then on we follow the twists and turns of the river as the green hills grow into brown mountains and the brown mountains into grey, jagged peaks and ridges and rounded snow summits. Range follows range and perhaps for the first time in my life I can comprehend the enormous depth as well as length of the Himalayan barrier. Standing between the pilots' seats as the nose of the plane dips down towards the landing strip at Simikot, a frisson of fear passes through me: I have crossed into the fourth world where luxuries like doctors and drip-feeds are no longer available on call.

Simikot perches high above a junction of two rivers, with the last great range of the Himalayas at its back. Here the Karnali river turns from its eastward course and grinds its way south down through the ever rising folds of the Central Himalayas.

Heart in mouth, I step down onto the airfield – and there's Mel jumping up and down outside the perimeter fence and grinning like a idiot. Much backslapping and hugging. They waited for me!

The tents have already been struck and the baggage packed, so now it's just a matter of loading up the ponies and going. Fortunately, there's barely 500 feet to be climbed on this first day and the rest is all downhill, so I start walking as soon as is polite and before my body starts to cotton on that it isn't acclimatised. Easy and slowly as she goes, and before long I'm over the ridge above Simikot and scrambling 2,000 feet down into the Sat Thapali, the Valley of the Seven Villages. My heels are chafed and blistered but my spirits are singing. A long lunch of soup and chapatis in the shade of a spreading walnut tree draped with mistletoe. Nearby is the first and what turns out to be the only shop in the valley. In a day or two it will dawn on us that this valley is as Nepal was thirty years ago: no pukka road, no electricity, no tea houses, no hoardings, no litter and – apart from us – no tourists. We are the foot in the door. In five years' time the Sat Thapali will be abuzz with backpackers.

Campsites are few and far between. We pitch our tents on either side of the track, 100 feet above the Karnali river. Two whistling thrushes wheel about singing their hearts out, their liquid sound almost lost in the thunder of the waters. A mountain torrent joins the river just above the camp and I'm standing in it cooling my feet when one of our ponies wheels about and knocks me into the water.

Chris joins me in the stream and performs the first of several wash-downs which leave our porters and the inevitable local spectators agog. Some years ago Chris hit the headlines with the first male frontal on British television. Now he performs a Nepal first, all rippling pecs and six-pack, to a small crowd of bemused bystanders. Chris's greatest virtue is that whatever he does, he does wholeheartedly. Nothing by halves. On the march he carries two adjustable metallic poles and strides out like Roald

Amundsen on his way to the South Pole, which earns him the title of Nanook of the North. He is a great hit when we pass through a village, provoking screams of excitement from the younger women.

Next morning we climb through a narrow gorge where the river plunges spectacularly down a series of falls. The path twists between two hundred-foot waterfalls from side streams and on the far side of the main river, where a third waterfall drops into the Karnali, a troop of Hanuman langur monkeys with long tails and black faces gibber at us from the treetops. The place is called Chachera, which I translate as Gorge of the Three Waterfalls, though its literal meaning is 'place of high water'. The gorge is a gateway: behind and below us the Hindu country of temples, paddy fields, cows and water buffaloes; in front and above the Buddhist world of prayer flags on poles, mane stones on mane walls, barley fields and yaks.

Snow still covers the higher slopes down to about 12,000 feet but at the sharp end of our valley, at about 8,000–8,500 feet, the temperature soars. The day drags out into a long, hot afternoon as we climb diagonally along the northern slope of the valley, first through woods of wild pear and then to the edge of the coniferous forest line where wild strawberries are ripe for picking. The others wait for me at the summit of our first real pass: the 9,800-foot Salli Lagna, the Pass of the Pine Trees, marked by a cairn piled with carved mane stones. A breeze tugs at the bright-coloured prayer flags. From here we can see tonight's campsite in a forest of tall pines about 800 feet below us.

This first rock pile has significance for each of us. I overhear Binod, who is a Christian, mutter the Buddhist mantra '*Om mane padme hom*' under his breath as he replaces a stone that he has dislodged off the cairn. He grins like a schoolboy caught with a stolen sweet when I catch his eye.

Binod's family are from the Rai hill tribe of eastern Nepal, who for generations have supplied first the old Indian Army and subsequently the British Army with recruits for the Gurkhas, reckoned by many to be the finest infantry soldiers in the world. Binod had hoped to follow in the footsteps of his father Jagdish and become an officer in the British Gurkhas, but his eyesight let him down. A cruel blow for him but a blessing for us, because Binod is the best there is, even though he's only in his mid-twenties. He possesses the Gurkha virtue of absolute self-confidence coupled with a modest demeanour. He listens quietly to your argument and then equally quietly puts you right. A great man in a crisis, as I have already discovered. He also has that extra ingredient which might be termed a sixth sense. In the previous summer Binod was taking a party of British Army soldiers on an adventure training holiday round the Annapurna range. It was an out-of-season trek and the summer rains were in full spate. They had come to a tourist lodge close to a mountain stream and were just about to sit down to their evening meal when Binod told the British warrant officer in charge of the group that they should move out. The WO accepted his advice and, despite protestations from the soldiers, they packed up and moved on in the pouring rain. That same night a dam created by an earlier landslide upstream gave way and a wall of water tore through the tourist lodge, killing a number of trekkers and local people.

As well as Binod, we have four Nepalese who constitute a core group of experienced guides. Three of them – Sangay, Kaji and Bagbir – are from the Tamang hill tribe and come from the mountain region that encloses the Kathmandu valley. The fourth, Mohun Basnet, is a Chhetri – a member of the so-called warrior caste which makes up the second of the five Hindu castes found throughout the Indian sub-continent and the foothills of Nepal. He and Sangay share the cooking between them, while the other two look after all the other tasks such as pitching tents and making up loads. Together they comprise the most perfect team one could ever hope to have on such a journey. They don't say much but they do a lot of grinning.

On the third day we're faced with a choice: to stay on a lower path which follows the main river but is said to be dangerously exposed to rockfalls, or to take the safer but much more strenuous high road. We have already been given some idea of what the lower path is like. On one exposed section of the path that took us out far above the river I experienced nothing more menacing than a flock of yellow long-tailed minivets, but Mel and Barney at the front were bracketed by a shower of boulders and the former was lucky to get away with no more than a bruised thigh.

So high road it is: past two picturesque villages, Yalwang and Yangar, each with fifty or sixty tight-packed, flat-roofed dwellings growing up the hillside like stacked playing cards. Three hours on the diagonal brings us to the foot of a rock wall where a crude stairway of boulders zigzags up to the top of a spur another 900 feet or so above us. I'm pleased to see that Dick is also suffering. Together we bring up the rear, leapfrogging each other in short spurts, perhaps one hundred paces at a time, then off with the pack, swig of water, application of sun cream, admire the view, wipe away the sweat, flap the T-shirt, take another swig, buckle on the backpack, another 50 feet. So it goes on, all in the knowledge that if this is what it's like at 11,000 feet, imagine what the body feels at twice that height – and more.

A pair of lammergaiers have been patrolling the valley behind us: small bodies but exceptionally long narrow wings like a glider, perhaps 8–9 feet from wingtip to wingtip. As we reach the saddle of the pass they swoop and wheel round and round the cairn where the others are waiting. Known locally as the Illing La, we rename this the Lammergaier Pass. We still have a long way to go that day, right down to the river and across an ancient twisting bridge to camp at the village of Muchu. The effort is now telling on me. I am so exhausted on this and on succeeding days that I am unable to respond with any enthusiasm to the amazing mountainscapes and vistas that unfold before us. I am on autopilot. Rest and sleep are my prime imperatives.

Day four takes us away from the main river, which now disappears north into a high gorge with sheer cliffs on either side. We march up a side valley which takes us to Yari at 13,800 feet, the jumping-off point for the crossing of the Nara Lagna, the high pass which takes us into Tibet. Now we're meeting more and more of the herds of sheep and goats which have shaped the trading patterns of the trans-Himalayan peoples for centuries.

Each herd is between about fifty and one hundred strong, always with a mix of sheep and goats in roughly equal proportions. All the goats in this valley are rough-haired; only in the highest valleys of the Humla region do they breed the pashmin goat which produces the super-soft underhair known as kulu, the wool from which cashmere shawls and woollens are made. Each flock is herded by two or three men or perhaps a family consisting of a husband, wife and child. Known as bakriwals, these goatherds follow an extraordinary cycle of movement through the short summer months.

As the snows clear on the higher alps a massive migration of livestock gets underway throughout all the valleys of the central Himalayan ranges. This is partly to allow yak, sheep and goats to feed on the new grasses of the uplands, but also for purposes of trade. Here in Humla and in neighbouring Jumla and Dolpo the custom is to use the sheep and goats as pack animals. Each animal is fitted with a double saddle-pack which is strapped on each morning and taken off at night. An intricate trading loop begins with a journey down into the plains where the packs are filled with grain and then sewn up. The sheep and goats then return to Humla and, as soon as the passes are cleared of snow, they continue on into Tibet, where the food is traded for salt gathered from salt pans up on the plateau. This salt, in its turn, is carried down to the plains to be traded for grain.

That, at least, is how it used to be. Talking with an old bakriwal on the trail I learn that it takes him sixty days to get down to Surkhet in the plains, and then another fifteen days to get to Tibet. This allows him to complete two journeys between May and the end of October. But he now carries rice instead of grain and the salt from the salt pans of Tibet is inferior to the iodine-rich salt available to the plainspeople in southern Nepal. So today he sells rather than trades, since the markets across the border at the frontier town of Purang have little else to offer other than Chinese medicines, rubber plimsolls and thermos flasks. In his father's time it was very different. Then they used to roam far into Tibet with their herds of sheep and goats, often with ponies and yak. Then came the Chinese in the 1960s and the closing down of all border crossings; within a decade trans-Himalayan trade that had continued down the centuries had withered away.

The Nara Lagna , the Pass of the Blue Sheep, has been open for about a week. We start climbing at 6.30 a.m. and Dick and I are soon left trailing behind. Dick pauses frequently to photograph what I assume to be alpine flowers beside the trail but whenever I reach the point where he took his photograph I can never find the ones he photographed. Dick is the existentialist of our party. He has the detached retina of the professional photographer. His house is full of unlikely art and objets trouvés. Thus a rug brought from Afghanistan is no antique but a modern one showing Russian tanks, guns and MiG jets. Dick is the cat that walks by himself, observing everything, ignoring the obvious, so it should come as no surprise to find that Dick is not photographing alpine shrubbery but bits of old shoes. He has thought hard about this for several days and concluded that these trails are Nepal's motorways. The sad scraps of rubber and canvas are the equivalent of blow-outs. They have been worn into the ground. A point is reached when they can no longer be held together and their owner simply walks on wearing, one presumes, just the surviving shoe. Dick calls it 'sole searching'. There is no answer to this. I find his shoe-photo fetish enormously irritating.

Each of us prefers his own company on the road. Chris and Mel, whom I asked to share a tent, have become polite enemies, each stretching the nerves of the other. Their tent-sharing lasted only one night. I, who spent so many years dreaming, scheming and planning just such a journey, am now occupying a large part of my waking hours thinking of escape routes. Hilsa, the final

Nepalese village before the frontier, is the last point where a Nepalese Army helicopter could put down to casevac me out. Beyond this point I'm a goner if I fall ill again, so I plan and discuss elaborate opt-outs involving Chinese lorries and days of driving east down the Tsangpo valley. This endless speculating on how to get away from a country we haven't even arrived at ends when Terry, most mild-mannered of men, bawls me out. For a brief, bad-tempered spell our walk comes to resemble one of those movies where a group of carefully assorted stereotypes are trapped – in a mine, an upturned luxury liner, a patrol in the jungle – and start to turn on each other.

Some distance below the Nara Lagna pass I pause, quite by chance, beside a huge spike of rock sticking out of the ground and my eye is caught by indentations under the lichens and moss. The rock has been incised with a large image of a female deity, a meditating Tara. Only an expert could tell how long ago and who by, but this unexpected apparition gives me a big boost. The final climb runs along one side of a V-shaped gully lined at the bottom with a crust of thick ice pocked with holes into which it would be easy to slide and disappear. Here I am overtaken by two local women, both carrying enormous wooden beams across their shoulders like participants in some Easter Passion.

So to the Pass of the Blue Sheep, at just over 15,000 feet one of the easiest crossing points into Tibet in the western Himalayas. The others are all waiting there at the top, urging me up the last few paces, and when I reach the cairn it's hugs all round. From here it's downhill all the way into Tibet. Now I know I'm going to get there. I burst into tears.

From the ridge to the left of the saddle we look out westwards across the upper course of the Karnali river. To the south lies India and the ramparts of the Garhwal Himalaya, with Nanda Devi and Trisul tucked away somewhere among all those snow peaks. To our north, the vast massif of Gurla Mandhata. But directly below us is Tibet.

To be truthful, we can only see a small segment of Tibet: just a crumpled slice of deeply eroded muddy brown moonscape. But it's enough to set the imagination racing.

We are poised on the threshold of what to many millions is holy ground. Not just a land of gods but the home of the gods. Not just a holy lake and a holy mountain, but the navel of the world and the spine of the universe.

I don't see it quite that way, but I do believe that here in far western Tibet lie the bones of Tibet's earliest civilisation still waiting to be uncovered – and that lost somewhere beyond 'that last blue mountain, fringed with snow' are the origins of the legend of Shangri-La.

Again I am quite unable to stop the tears pouring down my cheeks.

A curious, almost forgotten episode in Royal Air Force history began at 3 a.m. on a May morning in 1918 on British India's Northwest Frontier when the 'Old Carthusian', a twin-engined Handley Page V/1500 bomber – the only one of its kind east of Palestine – took off from the landing strip beside the civil lines at Lahore. It circled for half an hour to gain a height of 3,000 feet and then headed northwest towards Peshawar, the Khyber pass and Afghanistan. As it passed over Jelalabad one of the engines developed a water leak. The pilot and the bomb-aimer conferred and decided to carry on.

'Then we came to the Jagdalek Pass which I could see high above me,' later wrote the pilot, Captain 'Jock' Halley, DFC and bar, AFC. 'Chancing all, I hauled back on the stick and just cleared the top, then dropped down on the other side. Below, Villiers could see dozens of camels of a long caravan scattering in all directions, several falling over the edge of the mountain side. On the other side I saw our target ahead spread out on a vast fertile plain.'

They had reached Kabul, where the bomb-aimer lobbed sixteen 20-pound bombs over the side in the general direction of King Amanullah's palace before Halley turned the plane round and headed back to India. Four of the bombs hit their mark and demolished a wall of the Amir's harem. Amanullah was so impressed that he immediately sought an armistice to the war then being waged between Afghanistan and the British, and it was soon followed by the signing of a peace treaty.

Now to a second air flight. It is the summer of 1931. A revolution has broken out in a country – unnamed but clearly Afghanistan – which lies between Persia and India, and foreign nationals are being evacuated from its capital by air. The last plane to fly out carries the British Consul, 'Glory' Conway, his assistant and two other passengers, an English woman missionary and an American businessman. Their destination is Peshawar in northern India but it soon becomes clear to them that they are heading elsewhere: their plane has been hijacked and they are being flown eastwards past the 'icy ramparts' of the Karakoram mountains. They recognise the upper valley of the Indus and snowy flanks of Nanga Parbat and then, as darkness falls, they cross the western Himalayas. For half the night the plane continues to fly eastwards until at last it runs out of fuel and crashlands, fatally wounding its pilot.

The four passengers find themselves stranded on a high plateau 'picked clean as a bone by the roaring winds'. Conway guesses that they have reached the 'loftiest and least hospitable part of the earth's surface, the Tibetan plateau, a vast, uninhabited and largely unexplored region of wind-swept upland'. As they start to digest the implications of being 'marooned in far less comfort than on most desert islands', the moon comes out to reveal their surroundings:

Conway could see the outline of a long valley, with rounded, sad-looking low hills on either side jet-black against the deep electric-blue of the night-sky. But it was to the head of the valley that his eyes were led irresistibly, for there, soaring into the gap, and magnificent in the full shimmer of moonlight, appeared what he took to be the loveliest mountain on earth. It was an almost perfect cone of snow, simple in outline as if a child had drawn it, and impossible to classify as to height, size or nearness. It was so radiant, so serenely poised, that he wondered for a moment if it were real at all.

With his last breath, the pilot — 'he had the typical Mongolian nose and cheekbones, despite his successful impersonation of a British flight lieutenant' — informs Conway that they will find shelter in the valley which lies under the mountain. He names it as Shangri-La.

By now the reader will probably have recognised the plot outline of the opening chapter of James Hilton's romance *Lost Horizon* or the opening scenes of the film of the same name.

Born in 1900 in Leigh, Lancashire, Hilton read history and English at Cambridge and published his first novel while still an undergraduate. But it wasn't until 1933 that he hit the big time with the publication of *Lost Horizon*, written in Woodford Green, in the outer suburbs of northeast London. This was Hilton's third novel but only found a wider audience in the wake of his outrageously sentimental *Goodbye, Mr Chips*, which was written (reportedly, in four days) in that same year and became a surprise bestseller in America. Hollywood transformed both books into motion pictures and the immediate success of *Lost Horizon* on the silver screen in 1937 helped to make Hilton a rich man. He was summoned to Hollywood where he combined script-writing for the movies with the writing of more romances, all long sunk in obscurity. He married and divorced twice and died at his home in Long Beach, California in December 1954. His remains lie buried in Forest Lawn Cemetery. A small, quiet and by all accounts self-effacing man, his two great pleasures in life were mountaineering and reading. Both were put to good use in the writing of *Lost Horizon*.

Directed by Frank Capra and starring Ronald Coleman as the clean-cut Conway, the film version won several Oscars. Two years later *Lost Horizon* was republished as the world's first paperback. President F. D. Roosevelt started a fashion by naming his mountain retreat in Maryland 'Shangri-La', and within a decade of its first appearance in print and on celluloid 'Shangri-La' had entered the English language as a synonym for the ultimate haven. Today it has international currency. In Kathmandu alone half a page in the telephone directory is given over to Shangri-Las of one kind or another, from hotels and restaurants to laundry services and magazine titles.

At the centre of Hilton's novel lies the notion that hidden somewhere beyond the Himalayas in western Tibet, in the shadow of a great white mountain, is a valley inhabited by all-wise lamas who have achieved an ideal human existence. Conway and his fellow passengers are expected. They are escorted along a narrow path across a precipice which leads into a deep gorge:

> The track consisted of a traverse cut along the flank of a
> rock wall whose height above them the mist obscured.
> Perhaps mercifully, it also obscured the abyss on the other
> side . . . Hardly less an enticement was the downward
> prospect, for the mountain wall continued to drop, nearly
> perpendicularly, into a cleft that could only have been the
> result of some cataclysm in the far past. The floor of the
> valley, hazily distant, welcomed the eye with greenness;
> sheltered from winds, and surveyed rather than dominated
> by the lamasery, it looked to Conway a delightfully favoured
> place, though if it were inhabited its community must be
> completely isolated by the lofty and sheerly [sic] unscalable
> ranges on the further side.

Conway asks about the 'dazzling pyramid' which dominates the valley 'like a light-house' and learns that it is named Karakal, which 'in the valley patois, means Blue Moon'.

The travellers are brought to a monastery built on the side of the great mountain where, to their astonishment, they find all the mod cons: twentieth-century plumbing and central heating, a grand piano and a magnificent library stocked with all the world's great literature. Far below the monastery lie rich green fields, where mangoes grow alongside grapes and a contented populace made up of Tibetan peasants goes about its business in harmony with itself and nature.

Many more surprises follow: Shangri-La is revealed as a haven of civilisation ruled over by a benevolent élite of long-lived sages whose philosophy – a mix of Buddhism, Confucianism and Taoism leavened by Western pragmatism – is summed up as moderation in all things.

Conway eventually meets the High Lama, who discloses he is an extremely ancient Capuchin monk named Father Perrault. It seems that in 1719 four such Capuchins set out from Peking in search of outposts of Nestorian Christianity in central Asia. Perrault, the only survivor, stumbled upon the Shangri-La valley, where he was nursed back to health by its inhabitants. Eventually he became their leader and the head lama of a monastery which he himself helped to build. Through a combination of mildly narcotic berries and a rigorous regime of yogic exercises and meditation, he discovered the secret of more or less eternal youth. With mankind seemingly bent on self-destruction, the High Lama and his colleagues have set out to bring together and preserve the fruits of the world's learning and culture, together with a chosen few, so that after the great holocaust to come they can emerge to inherit the earth. 'The Dark Ages that are to come will cover the whole earth,' prophesies the High Lama. 'There will be neither escape nor sanctuary, save such as are too secret to be found or too humble to be noticed. And Shangri-La may hope to be both of these . . . I see, at a great distance, a new world stirring in the ruins, stirring clumsily but in hopefulness, seeking its lost and legendary treasures. And they will all be here, my son, hidden behind the mountains . . .'

Love interest is provided by an exquisitely beautiful Manchu princess, who was on her way to Kashgar in 1884 to marry a Turkish prince when her party wandered off the Silk Road. Both Brits fall in love with her.

All who enter Shangri-La have to remain there in order to preserve its secret. Conway, the American and the missionary are happy to stay but Conway's younger rival in love is determined to flee. When he and the Manchu princess make a bid to escape Conway feels obliged to help them. Only Conway survives the attempt. He is found in China sick and suffering from loss of memory. As his health improves his memory begins to return. He recounts his experiences to the narrator of the story – and then disappears. We are led to assume that Conway has decided to return to Tibet to rediscover his lost paradise and to take over the role of High Lama.

Lost Horizon falls a long way short of being a literary masterpiece but its author undoubtedly succeeded in catching the mood of the times. He reflects the fears of a generation which had survived the Great War and the Depression, had seen the failure of the League of Nations and was now once again staring a coming Armageddon in the face. His story of a faraway, hidden valley where all things are possible offered hope, an escape from the harsh realities of the Western world. And Hilton, it has to be said, had done his homework. In his novel he mentions by title some of the books found by Conway in the monastery's library: 'the *Novo Descubrimento de Grao Catayo ou Dos Regos de Tibet*, by Antonio de Andrade (Lisbon, 1626); Athanasius Kircher's *China* (Antwerp, 1667); Thevenot's *Voyage à la Chine de Pères Grueber et d'Orville*; and Belgatti's *Relazione Inedita di un Viaggio al Tibet*'.

This esoteric list of the pioneering journeys of the early Christian missionaries sent into Tibet from India and China shows that Hilton possessed a great knowledge of the exploration of Tibet by Westerners – hardly surprising, since he is known to have spent weeks researching the subject of Tibet in the Reading Room of the British Museum. And if he knew so much about the early Jesuit and Capuchin travellers, he would have been equally familiar with more recent explorations of western Tibet carried out by Dr Sven Hedin and of the dramatic discoveries of lost cities buried under sand and walled-up caves stuffed with ancient manuscripts and paintings on silk scrolls made between 1900 and 1908 by Sir Aurel Stein, along the Silk Road through inner Asia. We can assume, too, that he would have been aware of the journeys of the Americans Stanford and Rock in Tibet, Mongolia and China which were extensively illustrated in *Life* magazine and the *National Geographic*. And in the same year in which he sat down to write *Lost Horizon* James Hilton would surely have read in the press of the exciting finds being reported by the Italian Tibetologist Dottore Giuseppe Tucci. In *Indo-Tibetica* (1932), later published in English as *Secrets of Tibet*, Tucci provided the first detailed account of the long-abandoned Buddhist monasteries and temples of the kingdom of Gu-ge in the gorge of the upper Sutlej in far western Tibet – the same kingdom which the Portuguese Jesuit Antonio de Andrade had visited and written about in his *New Discoveries of Grand Cathay or Two Kingdoms of Tibet* three hundred years earlier. And, of course, Hilton had not forgotten that curious stunt, the RAF's air raid on Kabul, which had taken place when he was an eighteen-year-old.

The name James Hilton chose to give his hidden paradise – 'Shangri-La' or 'Snowy Mountain Pass' – was entirely his own but the idea behind it was not. His inspiration came from Tibetan legend, from accounts of a kingdom hidden beyond the Himalayas known as the land of Shambhala.

The legend of Shambhala had been introduced to the West by the famous nineteenth-century Tibetologist Alexander Cosma de Koros. His writings had been taken up and widely disseminated by the Russian mystic and charlatan Madame Blavatsky, founder of the Theosophical Movement, who claimed in her book *Secret Doctrine* (1888) to have been initiated in Tibet into an esoteric brotherhood of mystics. Her theosophical philosophy was taken up with enthusiasm by Mrs Annie Besant (*Ancient Wisdom*, 1897) who helped to create a popular image of Tibet as a land of all-knowing, venerable lamas and ascetics tucked away in remote mountain lamaseries. Rather more recently (1915), the Third Panchen Lama's treatise *The Way to Shambhala* had been translated from the Tibetan into German, and then in the late 1920s the White Russian Buddhist Nicholas Roerich had popularised the subject further through his writings (such as his essay 'Shambhala the Resplendent', 1928, an excerpt from which introduces this chapter) and mystical paintings. James Hilton could have drawn on any one or all of these sources.

The legend states that the hidden land of Shambhala lies within eight snow-capped mountain ranges which resemble the eight-fold petals of a lotus. At its heart is a vast mountain shaped like a four-sided pyramid so as to resemble a three-dimensional mandala. On the east side of the mountain is the 'near lake' and on the west side are two 'white lotus lakes', all filled with various jewels and each 12 yojanas (the distance it would take a bullock-cart to cover in twelve days, so roughly 120 miles) in width. On the south side is a park and a great palace in which reside the kings of Shambhala, known as the Holders of the Castes.

This palace of the kings is square in shape, with four entrances to north, south, east and west, and is nine storeys high. According to the *Great Commentary on the Kalacakra* written by the nineteenth-century Tibetan scholar Mipham, its surfaces are richly decorated with every sort of precious jewel and metal: 'Along a coral edge on the outer wall are dancing goddesses. At the top of the outer walls are hanging pendants of silver and protruding lintels of turquoise. Its windows are of lapis lazuli. The doors and lintels are of emeralds and sapphires. It has gold awnings and banners, and a roof of jewels and heat-producing crystals, while its floor is of cold-producing crystals. Its pillars and beams are of zebra-stones, corals, pearls and so forth.'

Each of the kings of Shambhala rules for a century. The

people they govern enjoy wealth and happiness and are free from sickness. Their harvests are good and they pass their time prac- tising Dharma, the religious 'Law' of Buddhism: 'There is not even a sign of non-virtue or evil in these lands. Even the words "war" and "enmity" are unknown.'

Indeed, so very advanced has this society become in its progress towards ultimate enlightenment that it has vanished from human sight and has moved on to a parallel spiritual plane. Although hidden openings to Shambhala are said to exist, only the pure of heart can find them and so enter this hidden paradise. Even so, Shambhala remains a goal always to be sought, because it is a gateway to the celestial kingdom. And because it is still linked to the world axis, Shambhala also provides a means for the celestial forces above to directly influence the lower plane of existence on which we mortals live. Thus the kings of Shambhala continue to watch over human affairs and will inter- vene to save humanity from self-destruction. Indeed, the legend states that as the end of the present temporal cycle of the dark age, the kali yuga, draws to a close there will be increased suf- fering as mankind becomes increasingly materialistic. The forces of evil will seek to invade Shambhala and the last of its kings will be forced to intervene to defend his kingdom. He will then take on the enemies of enlightenment in one ultimate apocalyptic battle.

Not only does the Shambhala legend identify these enemies of enlightenment; it also gives — rather too precisely for comfort — the exact time and place for the coming apocalypse:

At the time of the Wood-Monkey Year of the Nyi-drol-je age [i.e. 625 CE] in the land of Me-ka [Mecca] a teacher named Dar- dan organised a new religion and propagated the La-lo teachings [Islam]. Many non-Buddhists adopted the La-lo reli- gion and destroyed many Buddhist monasteries. It has been explained that the La-lo religion will last for 1,800 years. In the future there will be many nationalities of La-lo who will join forces. After the Fire-Monkey Year of the Dong-ngag cycle [2327 CE] the La-lo king, who is considered a manifestation of the anti-gods, will gather his forces west of India in a place called Tri-li. He will come to rule the central part of India south of the Sita river [Tsangpo-Brahmaputra] and all of Tibet and half the world. While he proudly and madly rules like a wild elephant, the La-lo ministers will come to feel that there is no one more powerful in the world than this king. Thus they will begin to lead their military forces to Shambhala.

Then in India on the banks of the Sita river there will be a great war with the La-los. The twenty-fifth Holder of the Castes, Dragpo Korlo-chan, will ascend the golden lion-supported throne of Shambhala. He will stab the king of the La-los and the anti-god forces of the La-los will likewise be defeated by the forces of the twelve gods. Then, starting from India and going in a clockwise direction, the other lands will be ruled by the Holder of the Castes. The teachings of the Buddha will flourish greatly. The human life-span will gradually increase to 1,800 years and the perfect age will dawn anew.

The exact nature of Shambhala has been a subject of debate within Tibet for centuries. Although the story comes to us from Tibet, the origins of the legend can be traced to a quasi-magical religious teaching known as the Kalacakra Tantra, the 'Wheel of Time Thread'. The Kalacakra tantra belongs to the highest level of Mahayana teaching. In brief, it offers a crash course of mystical meditational practices which enables those who follow it to achieve enlightenment in a matter of years rather than lifetimes.

Tibetan sources state that the Kalachakra tantra was introduced into Tibet sixty years after its first appearance in India and that it was brought to India by a young man named Tsi-lu-pa. In the year 966 this Tsi-lu-pa arrives unannounced and unknown at the gates of the great Buddhist monastic centre of Nalanda in Bihar and draws the micro-macrocosmic mystical seal of

Kalacakra over the portal of the main entrance. He claims to come from a kingdom far to the north of India called Shambhala. The abbot of Nalanda is the great scholar Naropa. He disputes the teachings of the Kalachakra tantra with Tsi-lu-pa, loses the debate and accepts the new teaching, which he passes on to his disciples, one of whom introduces the Kalacakra tantra to Tibet in the year 1026. Its title, 'Wheel of Time', refers to the animal cycle of twelve years – the years of the hare, dragon, snake, horse, sheep, monkey, hen, dog, pig, mouse, ox and tiger – which formed the first dating cycles used in Tibet. Naropa is said to have added the five elements of earth, air, fire, water and wood, so as to create a sixty-year time cycle, which he passed on to his disciple Atisha, who in turn introduced it to Tibet.

It is from these several disciples of Naropa that the Kalacakra teachings have been passed down from guru to disciple in an unbroken line to the present day. In the fourteenth century these several transmissions of the teachings were synthesised into one text which was then developed by the great Lama Tsong Khapa, founder of Ganden monastery and teacher of both the first Dalai and Panchen Lamas, to become the core teaching of the Gelugpa sect which, by accumulating both temporal power and property under the two reincarnate lamas, became the central church of Tibetan Buddhism and the keepers of orthodoxy.

Tsi-lu-pa remains a mystery figure. We don't know who he was or where he came from. It has been argued that he was a Shaivite (follower of Shiva) yogi from the Garhwal Himalayas since the word 'Shambhala' means 'held by the source of happiness' and the term 'source of happiness' is a common Hindu synonym for Shiva, the tantric god of yogis.

Another school of thought links Shambhala to the popular Tibetan belief in hidden refuges in the Himalayas called beyul. There are said to be twenty-one of these 'hidden lands', all of which have been rendered invisible by the tantric master Padmasambhava (better known in Tibet as Guru Rinpoche) many centuries ago in order to provide hidden retreats for the faithful in times of danger. Each beyul is to be used only when a specific crisis occurs and is supposed to remain hidden and closed until that time, only allowing access when certain conditions have been met.

That such beyul really exist is beyond dispute. In recent years at least half a dozen have actually been located and explored through the use of guides written in Tibetan – one in Bhutan, one in Sikhim and no less than four in Nepal. These guides are part of an extensive body of so-called 'recovered' literature which goes by the name of terma or 'concealed treasure' – sacred objects and texts which are hidden away to await rediscovery at the appropriate time by persons known as terton or 'treasure seekers' who have special powers to divine or sniff it out.

Each of these beyul terma sets out in painstaking detail exactly where the beyul is to be found, how to locate its entrances, when it may be entered and what rituals have to be carried out before entry can be made. For example, in the terma relating to one such beyul, *Bas-yul mkhan-pa lung-gis lam-yig sa-dpyad dang-bcas-pa bzhug-so* (*Guide to the Hidden Land of the Valley of Artemisia*, translated by Giacomella Orofino, 1997) the Guru Padmasambhava sets out the following conditions:

> When the happiness of the people is almost at an end and the time for invasion from neighbouring countries has come for Tibet, the Tibetans must escape to a hidden land towards the south on the border of the Mon [Mongolian and non-Tibetan people, possibly the land of the Monpa bordering Assam] territory. The people of Tibet will have to renounce their native land, their fields, their wealth, their servants and everything, as one does with a stone that has crumbled to pieces. He who makes a serious effort to reach this place will succeed.
>
> These are the signs to open the door: when the great and the small mountain of Ti-se [Kangri Rinpoche – Mount Kailas] are destroyed, that will be the sign to open the door. When the

temple of Samye is destroyed, when offerings are no longer made to the three divinities, the moment to open it will already have come. The moment to open it will have really come when the conflict becomes enflamed in the Shri territory; the moment to open it will have really come when the laws in the province of Tsang [Tsangpo river valley region in central Tibet] are destroyed and the administration of the province falls. When the descendants of the kings of Mang-yul [south central Tibet] are killed, the moment to open it will have come. If there are conflicts on the border of Brin mtshams [Chumbi valley], the moment to open it will have come. If a fortress is built on Mount Bri and Bri Chung, the moment to open it will have come. These are the external signs indicating the moment to open it.

During the last 500 years of the spread of the Doctrine, when the teeth of all those who have passed the age of fifty fall out, the moment to open it will have come. In Tibet the king will be no more and his dependants will struggle among themselves, in the country the monks will not keep their vows, the practitioners of tantra will not keep their samaya [vows] but wander like wild dogs, the people will eat flesh and blood without shame, the women who have no children will couple promiscuously, the people will be careless of their lives and struggle to acquire food and wealth with their minds filled with vanity and falsity, and so there will no longer be happiness in Tibet. For the virtuous this will be the sign to journey to one of the hidden lands.

The guide then directs the reader to the entrance to the hidden valley – located some miles east of Mount Everest and north of Makalu – where two weeks must be spent in meditation and the performance of complex rites which include blood sacrifices:

They should perform the mdos rituals [thread rituals to trap spirits] to balance the action of the sde-brgyad [class of demonic spirit]. They should offer food to the sman-tshun [feminine deities of place], construct seventeen red rgyan-bu [wooden tablets inscribed with images of deities], offer seven black birds, as a naga [serpent spirit] lives in that cave, make a gtor-ma [sacrificial cake] for the naga and an offering of water, make an offering of brang-rgyas [ritual offering of food] and a support of a black sheep and recite this prayer: 'Do not create obstacles to the yogin in search of the hidden land.' Let a libation be offered, then invoking Padmasambhava, they should follow the current of the stream.

Only after completing this obstacle course of complex rituals designed to weed out the spiritually unworthy does the refugee finally gain access to the hidden land.

Teachings on the subject make clear that a beyul exists on three levels: at the lowest plane it may be seen through ordinary sensory experience as a peaceful, fertile valley without any spiritual associations but where it is still possible to experience positive thoughts and well-being; on a higher plane, the beyul may be enjoyed by yogin as visions of the 'real' secret places; and, on the highest plane, it is revealed to those who have reached a high degree of spiritual awakening as a place of ultimate reality where intense mystic ecstasy is achieved, together with eternal youth, beauty and wisdom.

Much the same thinking has been applied to Shambhala, even though Shambhala is not a beyul but an earthly paradise that once was and will come again. Thus the Third Panchen Lama in his *Way to Shambhala* suggests that it, too, exists on three levels: as a yogic symbol of the state of Kalacakra attainment; as a pure land to be attained by the enlightened; and as an actual physical entity on this earth.

Ever since Shambhala appeared on the Tibetan scene in the eleventh century its religious teachers have argued over the nature of its existence. To some it represents a metaphysical paradise similar to Dewachan, the heavenly kingdom of the Buddha of the Western Paradise, Amitabha. But others see it as taking actual geophysical form: Tibetan historical texts from the twelfth century onwards list it as one of the six 'essential countries' of this world, which are: Tibet, India, China, Phrom (Khotan), Brusha (Gilgit) – and Shambhala.

As to where this earthly Shambhala is situated, all who accept Shambhala in geophysical terms agree that it lies north of the Indian sub-continent and west of Tibet. Some pundits, like the eighteenth-century Tibetan scholar Londol Lama, are prepared to be more specific. In his commentary on the history of the Kalacakra, Londol Lama states that Shambhala lies to the north of the Himalayan ranges near the western end of the Kangri Ti-se mountain range. Hindu religious commentators take the same view.

If it has any earthly location, Shambhala – the hidden kingdom which James Hilton simplified into 'Shangri-La' – is to be found in what is now far western Tibet.

But why? Why place this earthly paradise in the most isolated, frigid, barren corner of the Tibetan plateau?

2 *In the Beginning*

> The present is the key to the past.
>
> Charles Erasmus Darwin

LATE MAY 1998

The moment we cross the Himalayan watershed we are in utterly alien terrain. Every variation of the colour green is absent with the one exception of aquamarine, which lurks in cracks in the ice. Two weeks ago the route was impassable, now the sun is high and hot enough to have burned up all the snow below 15,000 feet except in the steepest gullies. These are like vertical bowling alleys, with many millions of rock fragments gradually defrosting high above us, so the temptation to take each one at a gallop is strong. The widest forms part of a bowl so vast that you can see the trail ahead of you cutting across the rock and ice like a horizontal crack until it is opposite but with several thousand feet of intervening empty space.

Thereafter the trail drops in an extended dusty slide and scramble which takes us right down the Karnali river again – but now the Mapchhu Khambab, the Peacock-Mouth River, or, to be precise about it, the River Formed from the Mouth of a Peacock.

The Himalayan chain is behind us. In front, on the top of a rise about 600 feet above the river and standing out against the ochrous flank of Gurla Mandhata, flutters a square of red. Through binoculars I can see five gold stars and, below the flag, figures in olive green uniforms.

As dusk fades we're joined briefly in our camp below the Chinese border post by an impassive frontiersman shouldering a musket with a long, smooth-bore barrel that looks at least a century old. He has eyes only for the heights of the ridge we've just descended. My binoculars pick out a herd of about a dozen blue sheep grazing some 2,000 feet above us in the last rays of the sun. The hunter zigzags up the scree at remarkable speed and in what seems like minutes has worked his way round until he is above the sheep. Soon afterwards we see a puff of blue smoke, followed by a bang that echoes across the valley. The sheep scatter and the hunter bounds after them. Both disappear from view but the hunt continues because we hear a second gunshot about ten minutes later. It's dark by the time the hunter passes through our camp again. He grunts that he has wounded a female and will return in the morning to follow her tracks.

A fair contest and no logical reason to wish the blue sheep had all escaped unscathed. But the snow leopard and the musk deer have already been hunted to extinction in Humla. The bhurel will be the next to go.

A little bridge marks the frontier. No signposts. We climb up to the guard post where half a dozen Chinese soldiers feign indifference to the arrival of a party of gweilo. But they behave perfectly decently and make only a perfunctory check of our baggage. Squatting on their hunkers and staring out over the valley as they drag on their ciggies, they look a long way from home.

We receive a warmer welcome from a Tibetan I shall here rename Sonam, who is to be both our guide and our official liaison officer in Tibet. Sonam manages to be both ingratiating and patronising at the same time, and within thirty seconds we have all arrived independently at the same conclusion: Sonam is a prick. This is unfortunate because he is to be our main link with Tibet.

Waiting for the lorry to arrive to take us on to the regional capital at Purang, we watch a tiny figure coming down a side trail which leads to Limi, the most northerly valley in Humla and still closed to foreigners. She's dressed like a Nepalese and her looks could pass for local but what gives her away is a heavy Western-style backpack. She turns out to be a young Chilean woman named Sandra, a bona fide Buddhist on a pilgrimage to Kailas but without any of the right papers: no permit to trek through Humla; no Chinese visa to visit Tibet; no dollars.

Sandra gracefully accepts our tea and biscuits. While the Chinese shake their heads and try to sort out what to do with her, she tells her story. She has been living in a Tibetan monastery in India and has set her heart on reaching Kailas. Her last dollars bought her a plane ticket from Kathmandu to Simikot and from there, overlooked by the local officials, she began walking north. She travelled alone for eight days and crossed three high snow passes, sleeping in a tiny tent and living mostly on mizu soup. She's very lucky to have survived the journey but she puts this down to the protection of the Buddha. When the Chinese officials tell her that she has to go back the way she came, Sandra smiles and says no. She will die, she says.

Sandra has a calm beauty that charms us all, Chinese, Nepalese and English. Her smile dazzles. She has bewitching brown eyes. She sits cross-legged on the ground chanting her prayers and telling her beads, waiting for fate to lend a hand. We all fall in love with her. It is agreed that Sandra will come with us to Purang.

We are not yet on the roof of the world, but we are now working our way along the guttering after emerging from the drainpipe. This is a new dimension. The sunlight is so bright that it hurts the eyes. It bounces off a vast canvas of white alluvial terraces and carved-out ravines, of sepia-, ochre- and russet-coloured hills, of dark cliffs like huge cracked slates and jagged snow peaks set sharp against azure cloudless heavens. This sky presses down on a horizon which stretches into infinity without ever going out of focus. Dick sets his camera down in despair, saying that the scale is too vast. I would agree with him but for the fact that my left eye has seized up: despite sunglasses it's gone snowblind after catching too much reflected light on the way down from the Nara Lagna. The slightest chink of light hits the eyeball like a red-hot poker.

We camp in a meadow beside the monastery of Khorzhak, one of a number of villages set among neat, cultivated fields on both sides of the valley. Money is being spent here on 'rural uplift': new irrigation channels are being laid; nurseries of young willow trees are being planted; and telegraph poles without wires herald the arrival of electricity and the telephone.

The monastery has also been completely restored. Every roof is flat and topped with what looks like thatch but is actually a wall of juniper brush stored away for kindling. Small windows with black frames are set deep into the whitewashed walls, each topped by a lintel of trimmed juniper twigs which make fine nests for the local sparrows.

Khorzhak Gompa was formerly one of the most important monasteries in far western Tibet. It belonged to the Kagyupa sect and had ancient links with Bhutan, which is why it escaped being totally razed by the Red Guards. Sonam takes us into the main building. We disturb three surly, card-playing monks who demand dollars of us. Propped up on the altar of the central temple is a large colour photo of a young boy whom we are informed is the new Panchen Lama. I look to Sonam for confirmation and although he avoids my eye he gives the very faintest shake of the head. We are being shown a portrait of the Chinese pretender. I warm to him.

Do these three dodgy characters know anything about

Khorzhak's famous silver statue, the Avalokiteshvara? Black and white photographs suggest it was modelled in the Pala style of Indian Buddhist art and dated from the eighth or ninth centuries. It could well have been brought to far western Tibet from the great Buddhist school of learning of Nalanda on the Indian plains, perhaps by the great teacher Atisha himself. The statue is said to have been sawn into pieces and carted away in 1967. I should like to know its fate, but my lingering antipathy towards Sonam makes it impossible for me to ask him to interpret for me. Pride leaves me ignorant.

Purang is the regional headquarters of Ngari province. We are required to present our papers here before we can travel any further. The town can be summed up as a single sandy street about 500 yards long lined by a dozen large concrete structures which house Chinese soldiers and officials. Bored Chinese conscripts hang around in twos and threes or mooch about with hands in pockets, peaked caps pushed well back, jackets unbuttoned at the collar, cigarettes hanging from their lips. Downtown Purang is three storerooms stocked with Chinese goods and surly Chinese shopkeepers. It is left to three tarts to wave the Tibetan flag. They teeter up and down the dusty highway in an absurd parody of Western allure, all high heels, lipstick and rouge.

There is an officers' guest house and a tourist guest house. We are required to spend one night in the former, even though there isn't any room for us and the tourist guest house appears to be totally empty. A pair of military officers are ejected and their rooms given over to us. Two rosy-cheeked Tibetan women concierges look after the place but their duties appear to be limited to knitting and filling jumbo-sized thermos flasks with hot water. Anything more falls outside their job description and all requests are met with looks of incomprehension or amazement. The charitable explanation is that they are engaged in some subtle form of passive disobedience and not just plain stupid.

Binod and his lads take everything in their stride. Sangay, who is our chef, and Mohun, his assistant, hunker down in one of the two rooms to rustle up our supper. Somewhere along the way they have collected Thupden Lama, a villager from Humla, who acts as pani-wallah. He fetches water, washes up and serves as general dogsbody. He also turns out to be extremely valuable as the only one in our party who speaks both Nepali and Tibetan.

Much of the next morning is spent hanging around outside the gates of the PLA headquarters while Sonam gets our papers cleared. Among the many large signs over the gate is one in English. It reads:

> WELCOME A-
> LL FRIENDS
> OF THE WORL-
> D TO PURANG
> FOR BUSINES-
> S, PILGRIM,
> OR ENTERPRISE-
> S

Our problem is Sandra. Sonam regards her as a major nuisance and wants to dump her. We don't. I override Sonam and talk with the most senior Chinese officer, a tall, fair-skinned captain with strong northern Chinese features who turns out to be extremely sympatico. He listens when I put her case and when Sonam starts to interpret he waves him to be silent and speaks to me in almost flawless English. He accepts that Sandra is a bona fide pilgrim and he will allow her to proceed so long as she stays with us. But she must surrender her passport. This Sandra refuses to do. Impasse, with Sandra in tears. The Chinese captain cracks and it is agreed that Binod will hold Sandra's passport instead. Sandra rewards him with a radiant smile and a blessing. Sonam sulks.

We are free to proceed. As our lorry grinds its way out of the

Peacock-Mouth River gorge and on to the Tibetan plateau – climbing out of the guttering and on to the roof – we can now see that there is a Chinese Purang and an indigenous Purang further to the west, centred on cave dwellings set into the side of a cliff in a series of terraces. A temple here reached by ladders now belongs to the Gelugpa sect but its name, Tsegu Gompa, or Nine-Storey Monastery, points to a much older origin as a pre-Buddhist temple of Bon – nine being the most auspicious number in the Bon religion (after the Nine Ways of Bon. In Tibetan Buddhism the key number is four, representing the four Noble Truths, four Paths, four Awakenings of Mindfulness and the four Dwellings of Buddha relating to the cardinal points). What is certain is that cave-dwellers lived here and further along the cliff face in the area known as the Nepali Bazaar for at least a thousand years before the arrival of Buddhism in western Tibet.

But the real glory and the power of Purang lay in the buildings on the top of the ridge immediately above the cave dwellings. For centuries a fortified castle stood here from which the lords of Purang governed the area, and beside it a large monastery, Simbiling, inhabited by several hundred monks. Everything was flattened by Chinese artillery in 1967.

Our lorry chugs northwards until we emerge on to open rolling hills of barren, brown earth. Gurla Mandhata rears like a huge beached whale to our right with great shoulders and fins of snow high above us. A lone black wolf watches us warily from a hilltop until we are safely past, then turns and trots out of sight. A pile of rocks and prayer flags marking the crest of the Gurla pass appears ahead of us and as we sweep towards it a shout goes up. Hands point and there peeping up over the far horizon is a white mountain with a sharp outline like a sphinx or a Trafalgar Square lion: Kailas! Kangri Rinpoche – the Blessed Snow Mountain! Yungdrung Gutseg – the Nine Stacked Swastikas Mountain of Bon! Even from a distance of some forty miles its appearance is so clear and so utterly perfect that it is impossible not to be filled with delight and awe.

We have brought with us a roll of prayer flags – yellow, green, white, red and blue. This is unfurled and tied to the roof ridge behind the cabin of the lorry. From here the lorry races downhill towards the lakes of Langak Tso and Mapham Tso while our flags flap and its passengers sing and whoop with delight. Behind us a great plume of brown dust billows into the sky.

Within half an hour we stand beside the sparkling dark blue waters of Langak Tso, the Lake of Five Islands, known to Hindus as Rakas Tal, the Demon Lake where the demon king Ravanna has his palace, and similarly demonised in some Tibetan texts as the Black Lake of Poisoned Ripples. Whichever way you look at it, the lake has drawn the short straw when compared with all the positive qualities conferred on its sister lake half a mile to the west. But that is the way things have to be to achieve cosmic harmony: virtue has to be balanced by wickedness in equal measure.

For all its negative associations Langak Tso thrills us with its powerful beauty. Winds blowing in from the west send waves piling against its eastern shore where thin crusts of ice have been squeezed by wind and waves and then packed and piled into neat ripples and walls. A group of terns bob on the waves, looking strangely out of place. Kangri Rinpoche floats a little closer.

A short backtrack and ten minutes grind in low gear takes us up and over the spine of the narrow isthmus of high ground which now separates the Demon Lake from its more elevated sister. Mapham Tso, the Lake Unrivalled, is revealed to us in all its perfection: a perfect bowl of clear blue water. We are at an altitude of 14,950 feet. The air is so clear that the complete circuit undertaken by pilgrims is easily visible. We can make out the roof of Trugulho Gompa which seems close at hand but is still six or seven miles distant. Down we plunge towards the lakeside, startling a single grazing kiang, the wild ass of Tibet. It gallops easily in parallel, more gracefully than one would expect of an ass, with flowing mane.

A water course stops us about half a mile short of Trugulho Gompa and here we set up camp for the night. It is mid-afternoon and we have found what must be one of the most starkly beautiful sites in the world. At our backs the northern ramparts of Gurla Mandhata; lapping at our feet the waters of the Lake Incomparable, formed, so the Hindu puranas say, in the mind of God; on the skyline the Kangri Ti-se mountain range set like the pediment of a Greek temple with the white throne of Kangri Rinpoche at its centre. For some minutes after sunset its summit holds the sunlight and is bathed in a soft shade of pink.

Everything would be perfect but for the wind, which cuts through thermal underwear like an ice-pick. It starts soon after midday and grows in intensity and coldness throughout the afternoon until sunset, when it suddenly ceases as if turned off by a switch. It is a classic case of convection. The sun heats up the Chang Tang plateau and causes air to rise, which in turn draws in colder air to fill the vacuum. In our case, this air is being sucked off the Himalayan snow ranges and is ice cold.

We have made camp on top of a warren of pika or mouse hares, known to the Tibetans as chipi. These delightful creatures are about the size and shape of guinea pigs, tailless and with neat rounded ears. In the last of the twilight I squat for a few minutes outside my tent and within less than a minute several chipi have popped out of their burrows to feed in the short scrub grass. Their young have no inhibitions and are soon scampering within two or three feet. But the cold quickly gets through to me. I rise stiffly and in a flash the creatures are gone.

Sandra has pitched her tent a little apart. She is with us, but not one of us. She asks for nothing but accepts gratefully and gracefully the food and medicine that she so clearly needs. I fall asleep to the murmur of Sandra chanting her mantras, like the drone of bees in a hive.

Outside my tent I know that the Nine Stacked Swastikas Mountain is glowing in the light of a gibbous moon.

In the beginning was the void. Then a wind which grew in
power and concentration to form a double thunderbolt. From
the thunderbolt came thick clouds, from the clouds, raindrops
as wide as cartwheels to create the primeval ocean. The wind
churned the ocean, causing a foam to gather which coagu-
lated into solid matter. From its centre rose the cosmic
mountain Rirab Lhunpo, rising eight times ten thousand
leagues above the great ocean and sinking as deep below;
Rirab Lhunpo with its four faces: the north face of shining
gold, the south of malachite, the east of crystal and the west
of silver.

From the highest point of Rirab Lhunpo grew a tree whose
trunk extended down through the mountain like a spine. Its
branches burst with flowers, fruits and vitality, and soon the
whole summit was crowded with trees, flowers, meadows,
rivers, hills and valleys; a pastoral paradise of such delight that
the gods made it their home.

So begins the story of creation as told in the Tibetan *Jigten
Chagtsul*, a cosmography which has its roots in the ancient
world's most enduring creation myth, with a pedigree that can
be traced back through Persia to Mesopotamia and ancient
Sumer. Its richest forms are found in the Hindu puranas, its most
distant echoes in Taoist and Biblical cosmography. Its central
feature is the cosmic mountain, best known as Sumeru or Meru,
the axis of the universe. The ever-fruitful tree at its summit
extends from the Chinese Kien-mou to the Persian Haoma, from
the Muslim Lote to the Nordic Yggdrasil.

A lake encircles the base of the cosmic mountain and surrounding the lake is a ring of mountains, which is itself
surrounded by another lesser lake and a ring of lesser mountains,

and beyond them more lakes and more mountains; in all, seven lakes and seven mountain ranges. Surrounding the last and lowest mountain ring is the outer ocean. Four worlds float on the outer ocean, each with its own shape: the world to the north is square; the world to the south is triangular; the world to the east is crescent-shaped; and the world to the west is circular. Our world is the triangular world, known to Tibetans as Dzambu Lying.

The four-sided mountain surrounded by a lake forms one of the most basic of archetypes: the square within the circle. The square is the prime symbol, symbolising the earth and the stability of the earth; it provides the square base upon which Buddhist reliquary mounds — in Sanskrit stupa, in Tibet, chorten — are built, just as earth supports heaven. The circle is the symbol of wholeness, of understanding and of water. In three-dimensional

form it becomes a hemisphere, the breastlike mound of the stupa. Next in growing complexity comes the concept of four sides, adding a third dimension to the square, which extends into four quarters or four directions, each of which can take on different qualities and forms, whether as cardinal points, gods, colours, jewels, animals or other symbols.

The stupa is nothing less than earthly representation of Mount Sumeru or Rirab Lhunpo. It also forms a primal diagram whose five parts symbolise the five elements of earth, water, fire, air and spirit in ascending order: a square plinth; a rounded dome; an oblong harmika; a tiered angular spire; and, at the top, bindu-shaped finial. At the heart of each is a wooden pillar or tree trunk representing both the primal tree and the cosmic axis.

The first such stupa/chorten were built to contain relics of the Buddha Gautama Shakyamuni, and were raised in the eight kingdoms of the sub-continent which followed his teachings. They later became repositories of offerings and were built at significant sites to symbolise the Buddha-mind. Emperor Ashok is said to have had 84,000 such stupas built throughout his Indian empire. In Tibet most chorten are reliquaries, with the bones or ashes of a revered person interred in their base, while others may enclose the spirit of a local demon. An isolated chorten near Purang is said to encapsulate the warlike qualities of a Dogra general named Zarowar Singh, who in the early 1840s had been foolish enough to invade this region with a small army from Kashmir. A combination of Tibetan cavalry and the Tibetan winter did for him and his troops. Fragments of his flesh were handed out as talismans and his bones were buried in this chorten to make it a power-place.

The primal diagram of the square encircled or the circle squared serves as a cryptogram of the unconscious, a meditational mandala that mimics the creation of the universe in microcosm. Every mandala has its central focal point through which runs an imaginary central column. By mentally aligning one's backbone with this central column during meditation or an act of ritual you become at one with the universe, placing yourself at the very core of the cosmos, in alignment with the axis mundi, the lightning rod that draws down power from the heavens.

According to the *Jigten Chagtsul*, our world was lifeless until some of the gods descended from the cosmic mountain and made it their home. All was well at first because the gods were self-sufficient. But they were tempted to eat a curd found on the surface of the earth and with each taste their powers began to dwindle. They lost their immortality, together with the gifts of meditation and the ability to generate light. They became humans and lived in darkness until the sun, moon and stars were created.

Still they lived in innocence, each person feeding off a plant which every day bore just one fruit, until the day when one human took another's fruit, so setting off a chain reaction of greed and hunger. Selfishness, lust and violence became part of the human condition, now subject to the cycle of life, suffering and death.

The great Tibetan plateau itself lay under water until raised through the intervention of the gods. In Tibetan Buddhist cosmography this is attributed to the protector of Tibet, Chenresig, Lord of Mercy. At first, the land was tenanted only by spirits of place, mimayin, who lodged in every feature of the landscape — in rocks, in water and in vegetation. Later a whole series of fearsome non-humans in various forms inhabited the plateau. The tenth and last of these were apelike creatures called gongpo, 'enchanters', who were clever but savage and misused their gifts. Then Chenresig and his consort Dolma sent their incarnations to Tibet in the form of a monkey and a rock demoness. They mated and had six children, one for each of the six realms of being, so that each had its own character and attributes. They lived in caves on a mountain above the Yarlung valley in south central Tibet and when they had multiplied to 400 they went their different ways. After many generations these ape people evolved into humans, spreading out across the plateau to found the four clans of Tibet.

In strictly geological terms Tibet's history begins about 100 million years ago when the area of the earth's crust which now occupies the Tibetan plateau lay under the Tethys sea. The land south of what is now the course of the 'great one' – the Tsangpo river – as it drains west to east across southern Tibet formed part of a quite separate land mass. It was the leading edge of an Indian tectonic plate that was sliding inexorably north towards the Asian land mass. As the two plates approached, the former began to slide under the latter, forcing it to rise. This crust buck-led along the line of impact to create the Kangri Ti-se Shan and Nyanchenthang Shan, mountain ranges which run east–west like loose belts across the Tibetan plateau. The ocean began to drain away and by about 50 million years ago the Precious Snow Mountain had taken shape as the highest point in a long chain of islands.

The great collision between the land masses of Asia and India began about 45 million years ago. The trapped 'Tibetan' crust began to rise in huge folds as well as sinking and sliding south under the Indian land mass along the line of the Tsangpo and upper Indus valleys. By about 20 million years ago the Himalayan ranges had started to take shape, but then about 2 million years ago a fresh period of rapid uplift – the most dra-matic in the geological history of the world – caused further massive movement. As India's northward thrust continued, huge fractures opened, contracting the Tibetan plateau and raising it higher still, particularly in its western corner. Instead of empty-ing off the plateau westwards through one massive Indo-Gangetic channel, the waters of Tibet now began to flow in diverse directions, flowing west along the Tsangpo valley rather than east and at several points along the Himalayas cutting south through the mountain ranges as they rose.

The great rise continued. A million years ago the Tibetan plateau stood at an average height of about 9,000 feet above sea level and the central Himalayan range at about 12,000–15,000 feet. But by 10,000 BCE another 4,000–5,000 feet had been added to both the plateau and the Himalayas. The most recent calculations indicate that this rapid but uneven rise continues at a rate of between 1 and 5 inches a year, or somewhere between 8 and 40 feet every century. This suggests that within the last 2,000 years the rise has been sufficient to add as much as 800 feet to the Himalayan wall, with profound consequences to the climate and landscape of the Tibetan plateau.

For many millions of years after the first upheavals the plateau was a terrain of hot tropical forests and swamps, giving way to temperate grasslands and open steppes over which grazed a wide range of herbivores. This in turn gave way to a period of extreme climatic harshness culminating in the last ice age, which reached its most hostile conditions about 18,000 years ago. Of the ruminants only the hardiest remained. The largest of these were two members of the bison family, the main meat-providers of early central Asian and north American man: the drong, or wild yak, burly forebear of the present semi-domesticated Tibetan yak (the delightfully but inappropriately named *Bos grunniens* or 'grumbling ox'), now only found in the most remote corners of the Chang Tang; and the musk ox (*Ovibos moschatus*), long ago hunted to extinction on the plateau but still found in the southeast corner of Tibet and in neighbouring Bhutan. Another large ungulate that proved to be of great service to man was the Bactrian camel, domesticated at about the same time as the yak about 5,000 years ago to become the cargo-bearer of the central Asian trade routes. The wild horse (*Equus caballus przewalski*), lives on in the genes of the stocky ponies of Mongolia and Tibet, while its second cousin, the wild ass, known to Tibetans as the kiang, standing at about thirteen hands, still happily roams the Chang Tang in small herds. According to Tibetan lore, it thinks of itself as the fastest of all creatures, which explains the bizarre behaviour of this creature when it sees a vehicle approaching. Instead of turning away and making for safety, kiangs seem to enjoy galloping on a parallel track with the vehicle for some distance and then swerving to run in front of it, which probably explains why they made such easy targets for the troops of the PLA in the aftermath of its liberation of Tibet.

Of the lesser ungulates, several species of goat made themselves at home in the mountain ranges: the nyan (great Tibetan sheep) and the Marco Polo sheep, whose great downward-curving horns would become the most sought-after of all hunting trophies; the nawa (blue sheep), which the Nepalese call bhural, and its cousin the urial; the long-horned Himalayan ibex; the black-faced tahr; and the markhor, domesticated as the Tibetan goat called the changra. Several forms of deer roamed the more open plains, including the small white-rumped gowa (Tibetan gazelle); the long-horned chiru (Tibetan antelope) and the shawa (Tibetan deer), whose antlers are valued for their medical properties. In the uplands Tibetan hares are still aplenty, as are the chiwa, large marmots who live among boulders and scree, and the delightful chipi, a form of gerbil which inhabits large warrens in the open grasslands and is now so plentiful that it is said to be threatening the grazing of the yak, sheep and goats that live off the land.

All these herbivores were preyed upon by several species of large carnivore, including lions and tigers. Of these only the zig or snow leopard remains. It is on the brink of extinction and rarely seen even in its last certain habitats in Nepal's western Himalayas, although a number of smaller wild cats such as the yi (bobcat) are still found in Tibet. Other hunters of the Chang Tang include the plateau dog, chang-gu (wolf), and the wah (fox). Also worthy of mention are the two species of large bear still found in Tibet: the red bear (*Ursus arctos isabellinus*) and the rather larger Tibetan blue bear(*Ursus arctos pruinosus*). This last comes closest to matching the dzu-teh or 'man thing', one of a number of fabulous or still unidentified beasts listed in the Tibetan bestiary, while leaving unexplained the smaller apelike creatures classified as thel-ma, mi-teh and mi-gu.

The last ice age ended about 10,000 years ago and was followed by a dramatic warming of the Tibetan plateau which left it far wetter and more vegetated than it is today. The glaciers retreated, leaving numerous lakes in scoured-out valleys, together with all the classic detritus of moraines and boulders. Among the largest of these lakes was a saucepan-shaped expanse of water immediately to the south of the Kangri Ti-se range in far western Tibet. It was probably about 20 miles wide from north to south, with a handle that extended northwest to give it a length of some 50 miles. At the midpoint its waters lapped up against the southern flank of the highest mountain in that range, a snow peak that can be seen from far off as a white pyramid of snow.

By now the Himalayas had grown to a 16,000–20,000-foot high wall that extended right the way along the southern edge of the Tibetan plateau, presenting an all but impassable barrier to the rain-bearing clouds that blew across from the Bay of Bengal from late June to early September. The result was ever-increasing desiccation, particularly in far western Tibet and the upper reaches of the Tsangpo. Here the deep valleys, filled with soft, sandy clay and pebbles scoured off the surrounding mountains, dried out into flat pasturelands dotted with small lakes. The great lake south of the snow pyramid shrank to half its size to become two large lakes, separated by a narrow isthmus of high ground but still linked by a twisting flood channel which carried the overflow from the higher eastern lake down to the western lake as the snows melted in early summer. Only in very recent times has this annual overflow ceased to occur, a phenomenon which local Tibetans attribute to Tibet's current ill fortune.

At just under 15,000 feet above sea level, the larger of the two lakes is said to be one of the highest bodies of fresh water on earth, its waters among the purest. It is well stocked with several species of fish and even, so it is unreliably reported, fresh water dolphin. In the late spring and early autumn enormous numbers of geese, ducks and cranes rest here as they migrate between the Indian sub-continent and Siberia.

Over the last two to three millennia these two lakes, together with the snow peak just to the north, have accumulated an extraordinary number of names and attributes. The Precious Snow Mountain has been known to the outside world as Kailas since the first Hindu puranas were written but it has many more ancient appellations. As a Bon text declares:

The gods call it Dad-do Ri-rang (High Mountain of the Gods).

In Tajik it is called Gyer-rbang Hri-do (High Mountain of Bon) and Ge-kod Nan-lun.

In Shang-shung it is called Ri-bo Gans-can.

In India it is called Ma-nam Sarba (Mountain of Sea Water).

In China it is called Ta-la Ha-spu (Snow Mountain which Cannot Be Melted by the Sun).

In Nepal and the Mon region it is called Sarba Bhi-na (Snow Mountain).

In Kashmir it is called Sin-ha Ra-ya (Water's Flower).

In Uddiyana [modern Swat] it is called Ka-sar Ma-na (Water's Fruit Mountain).

In Na-yab it is called Lan-kar Sag-pa (Mountain which Subdues the Demons).

In Gru-gu it is called Ma-sangs Nan-po (Demons' Palace).

In Jang it is called Ka-la Yu-gsog (Great Snowy Mountain).

The Nan-Deities called it Gangs-gnan Ti-se and the Water Spirits call it Ba-gam Tag-rtse (White Abode).

The two most popular titles are missing from this list: among the Bonpo the mountain is known as Yungdrung Gutseg, the Nine Stacked Swastikas Mountain. To the far larger majority who are Buddhists it is simply Kangri Rinpoche, the Precious Snow Mountain.

The larger of the two lakes, roughly circular and about twelve miles in diameter, is best known to the outside world by its Sanskrit name, Manasarovar, the Lake Conceived in the Mind of

God. However, every Tibetan knows it as Mapham Tso, the Lake Unrivalled, or even simply Yu Tso, the Turquoise Lake. It is said to resemble a mandala in shape and it takes five days to circumambulate.

The smaller lake beside it is Rakas Tal, Demon Lake, to Hindus, who ascribe to it every sort of negative quality. Tibetans call it Langak Tso, Lake of Five Islands, and regard it as the natural partner and other half of Mapham Tso. Its irregular shape has been likened to the four continents of Tibetan geography drawn together or, equally imaginatively, to 'a hide made from human skin'.

Two other lakes lie within half a day's walk to the northeast. The smaller is described in old Bon manuscripts as being similar in shape to 'a silver mirror laid flat on the ground'. It was known as Gur-gyal Lha-mo, Gods' Lake, and lay at the foot of Mount Posri. Today it is divided into three shallow lakelets which are really no more than appendages to the big lake, Mapham Tso. A few miles away and another 200–400 feet higher is Gunko Ngulmo, which is said to resemble 'a large piece of blue silk stretched on the ground'. This also drains into Mapham Tso.

About 3,000 years ago a mini ice age helped to set the stage for western Tibet's present harsh, dry environment. Forests gave way to open prairie, prairies to desert steppes. A short – but highly significant, in terms of human settlement – interlude of warmer winters and wetter summers between about 800 BCE and 400 CE was followed by a return to more hostile conditions.

The far west is now the driest corner of Tibet. It also experiences the lowest temperatures, with an annual precipitation of less than 100 millimetres and a mean temperature lower than minus 10 degrees Celsius for much of the winter. Most days are bright and sunny but, with fewer molecules in the rarefied air to conduct the sun's heat, atmospheric temperatures remain low. The ground receives heavy doses of solar radiation which causes hot air to rise and in turn draws cold air off the Himalayas and other mountain ranges. The result is the fearful ice-pick afternoon wind of the

Chang Tang, often accompanied by dust storms and whirlwinds. As well as chilling bodies, this dust-laden wind acts like sandpaper on the landscape, rubbing away at every inch of exposed ground, sculpting stone into weird shapes, grinding down every built object, be it a chorten or a mane wall, to a point where it is hard to tell what is man-made and what is natural rock.

Together, low temperature and high wind stunt all vegetation. To minimise exposure most plants extend only a few inches above the ground. Yet appearances are deceptive. When the snows melt the prairie land between the Himalayas and the Kangri Ti-se range provides grazing for vast herds of yak, sheep and goats in the form of herbaceous perennials, alpine meadow grasses that are stunted but still rich in nutrients. Sheltered dips in mountainsides and steppes burst into colour as aconites, anemones, saxifrages, buttercups, primroses and other flowers blossom. On the marshy ground around lakes and pools and alongside springs grow sage and other hardier grasses that can withstand the winter frosts and so provide fodder all the year round.

Even the higher alpine meadows grow clover, sedge, dandelion, foxtail and wildflowers, as well as low shrubs such as honeysuckle, barburry and juniper. But nothing grows tall. Only in the lower valleys – in the canyons of the upper Sutlej and the Karnali – is there such a thing as a tree. And even here the dwarf willows and poplar which thrive elsewhere in the lower and warmer valleys of eastern Tibet are only found in carefully tended copses near human settlements. It is the same with crops. Highland barley can be cultivated up to 14,000 feet and is grown extensively in eastern Tibet, but in the far west of the country it is found only in those same sheltered river valleys that drain the plateau.

By a quirk of geotectonics that has given rise to much philosophising, the headwaters of all four of the great rivers which together water northern India lie within forty-five miles of the shores of Mapham Tso: the Ganges, Indus, Brahmaputra and Sutlej. Of these only the last has direct relevance to my story (see *A Mountain in Tibet* for a fuller account of the other three). The infant Sutlej has its traditional source in a little brook that drains into Mapham Tso, although today its highest sources are the streams which flow down through the valleys east and west of Kangri Rinpoche. Seeping rather than flowing out from Langak Tso, it meanders as a stream across the open plain for some forty miles in a northwesterly direction before being brought up short by a jumble of hills which form the eastern limits of the Zanskar range. Here the river turns west and digs itself deeper and deeper into the soft grey clay to form a stupendous gorge. It then twists its way through the Himalayan ranges and foothills to emerge on to the plains of the Punjab.

Within Tibet the river is known as Langchen Khambab, the River that Emerges from the Mouth of a Bull Elephant, so named because a mountain at the northern end of the gorge is shaped like a standing bull elephant. For this reason a local proverb has it that 'the oxen of Gu-ge are stronger than others because the Langchen Khambab flows through the heart of the country of Gu-ge'. Gu-ge, the local name for this region, is said to mean 'cave country', which accurately describes one of the most remarkable features of an extraordinary landscape.

Just over the hills to the east of Mapham Tso is the source of the Tamchok Khambab, the Horse-Mouth River which flows east through Tibet as the Tsangpo and then turns south to fall into Assam as the Brahmaputra. Over the hills to the south of the lake are the headwaters of the Mapchhu Khambab, the Peacock-Mouth River, which flows south as the Karnali, the northernmost tributary of the Ganges. The snow that melts off the northern slopes of Kangri Rinpoche forms the headwaters of the Senge Khambab, the Lion-Mouth River, which runs due north and then northwest before dropping off the Tibetan tableland into Ladakh as the Indus. The Senge Khambab's upper course drains a high country known historically as Rudok. The valley floors border on 16,000 feet but, being wide and flat, provide good grazing in the summer months. In 1985 members of

A woodblock print from a Tibetan pilgrimage guide, showing the disposition of the two lakes Mapham Tso (Manasarovar) and Langak Tso (Rakas Tal) south of Kangri Rinpoche (Kailas), with the Senge Khambab (Lion-Mouth: Indus) to the north, the Tamchok Khambab (Horse-Mouth: Tsangpo) to the east, the Mapchhu Khambab (Peacock-Mouth: Karnali) to the south and the Langchen Khambab (Bull Elephant Mouth: Sutlej) to the west.

an expedition from the Cultural Relics Institute in Lhasa, drawn to this area by reports of carvings, made a series of remarkable discoveries. At a number of sites where cliffs started at valley floor level hundreds of images have been hammered, scraped or tapped on to the rock face.

These carvings depict a wide range of animals from yak and sheep to antelope and wolves, drawn simply, but often capturing the movement and the essence of each animal. Other subjects include symbols associated with nature-worship and shamanism: the sun and moon, trees, fire, eagle-like birds, swastikas (both clockwise and counter-clockwise, but mostly the latter) and ovals representing the cosmic egg. Human figures are also present, dressed in the same robes that you see nomads wearing today. In some scenes they wear masks, in others they are engaged in acts of hunting, herding, journeying, dancing and offering sacrifices.

These petroglyphs have still to be dated but the absence of Buddhist imagery or inscriptions suggest that they were completed at least before the seventh century CE, probably far earlier. Recent research by Chinese paleobotanists indicates that the plateau, previously considered to be either totally or only marginally inhabitable, was well vegetated and sustained neolithic and perhaps even palaeolithic settlement.

A quick glance at any physical map of Tibet and central Asia will tell you why Tibet's isolation has been so long maintained. To the south and west you have the Himalayan barrier; to the north the Kunlun Shan wall and beyond it the Taklamakan desert; to the east, the comparatively open but vast Chang Tang, the 'north land' which runs on for a thousand miles before it descends in the gentler country bordering China. Only at one point is there a breach in these natural defences: the narrow corridor between the Karakoram range and the western end of the Kunlun Shan.

Early Chinese records speak of wild tribes of hunters, the Qiang, wandering across the Tibetan plateau with their herds of sheep, goats, yak and horses and raiding Chinese settlements as early as 1400 BCE. Later records speak of people called the Tufan, made up of numerous tribes. It is generally assumed that these first Tibetans came out of the same proto-Mongol stock pool of inner and east Asia which fanned out across the steppes and tundra into Siberia, the Kamchatka peninsula, Alaska and beyond on the trail of big game, everything from mammoth and woolly rhinoceroses to reindeer and wild horse.

In Tibet large-scale nomadic pastoralism became possible once the drong had become semi-domesticated and cross-bred with the cow to produce the yak and the dri; not for nothing is a herd of yak called nor, meaning 'wealth'. A cycle of trans-humance evolved to take full advantage of the short summer. The seven winter months were passed in the shelter of the lower valleys below an elevation of 12,000–13,000 feet, then in mid-May, as the snows began to melt, all the livestock were driven to the higher pastures. Sheep and goats took possession of the lower alp, while yak were taken as high as 18,000 feet, since their multiple stomachs can cope with the rough sedge grasses which goats and sheep cannot digest, until mid-August, when they were brought back down to the best grasslands which had been left ungrazed so that they could build up the fat reserves to see them through winter.

The yak's pelt carries three levels of fur, each of which is put to different use: the coarse outer coat primarily for tent-making, the middle for ropes, and the soft undercoat for blankets and cloaks. Sheep and goats have also adapted to survive the Chang Tang. Like their masters, they have developed greater lung capacity and carry more haemoglobin in their blood. The milk they provide in the summer months is boiled and converted into yoghurt, then churned into butter and stored. Yaks provide milk all the year round but it is too rich for drinking and is converted into a hard, dry cheese.

The bulk of Tibet's five million non-Chinese are still nomadic herders, inheritors not only of their ancestors' lifestyles but also their strength of character, their ability and preference for living off the land in the most hostile conditions, their natural affinity with the great open spaces and their religious disposi-tions. The arrival of tea from China in the seventh century, together with brightly coloured thermos flasks, plimsolls and flat caps in the twentieth, are probably among the most signifi-cant of the few material changes that have affected the lifestyles of these pastoralists in the last few thousand years.

Early Tibetan genealogical texts found among the great heap of early manuscripts and scrolls recovered by Sir Aurel Stein and others in the walled-up cave at Tun-Huang speak of four main Tibetan tribes – the Dong, Tong, Se and Mu – gradually wresting control of Tibet from the spirits, demons and monkeys of earlier ages. Each tribe had its own language and culture, just as each was associated with particular elements and totems which represented that tribe's particular bla or spirit: the Dong are linked with earth and the Tibetan antelope; the Tong with water and the yak; the Se with iron and the Tibetan wild ass; and the Mu with wood and sheep.

Tibetan tradition maintains that each tribe established itself in its own corner of Tibet: the Dong along the eastern border-lands of China; the Tong in the south central plains country; the Se in the northeast round Koko Nor; and the Mu in the land of Shang-shung in the far west.

The four tribes divided into twelve, then twenty-five and finally forty kingdoms, each ruled over by petty kings whose names, together with those of their realms and capitals, were committed to memory by tribal bards and genealogists and built up over many centuries until finally set down as chronological tables after Tibetan was established as a written language in the seventh century. These genealogical tables chart the rise and fall of dynasties as each little kingdom struggled with its neighbours for local supremacy. Among the earliest and most constant of these kingdoms was Shang-shung, the country of the Mu in the far west.

A kingdom really only comes into its own with a settled pop-ulation and good defences. In far western Tibet the landscape provided a ring of breastworks that no military engineer could ever improve upon, but landscape and altitude combined to restrict settlement to just two areas. Of the four great rivers, the broad upper valleys of the Indus and Tsangpo are too high and too exposed to favour permanent settlement. However, in the cases of the upper Sutlej and upper Karnali both rivers have worn deep gorges through the soft alluvial clay and shingle: within a span of some 70 miles the main water course drops from 14,000 to 12,000 feet, a difference of 10 degrees in average temperature.

This was where the first settlers to the plateau's far west sat out the winter months, digging out rock shelters for themselves and for some of their livestock in overhangs along the lower levels of the cliffs overlooking the river and, at the lower end, planting crops on the river terraces. With the thaw in early summer they moved out of the valley to graze their yak, sheep and goats on the grasslands above. From rock shelters they progressed to caves, both man-made and wind-blasted, which in time expanded into troglodite complexes made up of hundreds and even thousands of caves interlinked by wooden stairways and platforms.

The standard history books say that Tibetan civilisation started in south central Tibet; specifically, in the Yarlung valley in about the second century BCE. These histories may well be wrong. Evidence is growing that it was here in Tibet's far west, in cave communities in the valleys south and west of the mountain Kangri Rinpoche and the lake Mapham Tso, that Tibet's first civilisation came into being – and with it the old religion known as Bon.

3 *The Religion of Humans*

> In the oldest religion, everything was alive, not supernaturally but naturally alive . . . For the whole life-effort of man was to get his life into contact with the elemental life in the cosmos, mountain-life, cloud-life, thunder-life, air-life, earth-life, sunlife. To come into immediate felt contact, and so derive energy, power, and a dark sort of joy. This effort into sheer naked contact, without an intermediary or mediator, is the root meaning of religion.
>
> D. H. Lawrence

EARLY JUNE 1998

The white dome of Kangri Rinpoche is the first to catch the sunrise. The surface of the turquoise lake, which has gleamed all night like a steel mirror, grows dark and then its far side suddenly blazes with fire as sunlight pours over the saddle of the Maryam La sixty miles to the east.

The Tibetans endow the Lake Unrivalled with eight properties: purity, clarity, cleanliness, mildness, coolness, unspoiled, delicious to drink and harmless to the stomach. It looks clean and cold. By chance, we have camped at one of the four points round the lake where pilgrims stop to pray and to immerse themselves. All through the day – and even the night – groups of Tibetans circumambulating east to west pause here at the lake's edge to scoop up handfuls of water and splash their faces. Just the one handful. Unlike Hindus, they interpret the injunction to immerse themselves in its healing waters in symbolic rather than literal terms. Not unreasonable, given that even now in late May a thin crust of ice still lines the water's edge.

But it doesn't seem quite right to come all this way and not take a dip in the lake. I wander down to the lakeside, check that no one in camp is watching, do a quick strip and plunge in. I reckon that I can complete the whole exercise in under ten seconds. What I have failed to take into account is the shallowness of the water here. Ten seconds and it's barely up to my calves. The only thing to do is to break into a run and then – when the water reaches my thighs – dive. The shock is electric, and so physically traumatic that even before I have surfaced I feel sure my heart must have stopped beating. For a few seconds I stagger about like a punch-drunk: gasping, heaving, totally spaced out. Then I totter back to dry land and fall on to my clothes, blowing and panting like a landed trout. I think no one has observed me but soon I see other members of our party stealing off to the lake's edge one by one, making their own submissions, each in their own style.

At breakfast we are joined by the abbot of Trugulho Gompa and four of his monks. They want to hitch a ride to the Saga Dawa festival which takes place on the morning of the full moon, the day after tomorrow. We roll out the blue tarpaulin for our guests and line up to present kadaks and be blessed. Indeed, with the abbot in camp, no wind to chill us to the bone and the sun shimmering on a turquoise millpond, we do feel singularly blessed. For the first time since leaving Nepalganj a sense of well-being returns to me. I am surrounded by beauty on an epic scale and I am extraordinarily fortunate to be here.

The abbot rides shotgun in the seat of honour beside the driver in the lorry when our little convoy climbs out of the Mapham Tso bowl and heads north along the strip of high ground separating the two lakes. We stop at the Ganga Chhu, the channel which once linked them but is now as dry as a desert wadi, except at the point immediately below the upper lake, where a hot spring feeds a bubbling, brackish, scummy-looking pool. Sonam suggests we might like to wash here. No takers. Hard to see how Moorcroft and Hearsey (described in *A Mountain in Tibet*) could possibly have missed the channel when they camped here in 1812. Local lore contradicts itself: one view is that no one can remember when Mapham Tso last overflowed along the Ganga Chhu, another that it filled up in the early 1980s when the Chinese eased up on religious persecution. What everyone does agree on is that the two lakes are still inextricably linked.

Perched on an outcrop of red rock at the head of the channel overlooking Mapham Tso is Chiu Gompa, the Sparrow Monastery. This is where every circumambulation of the holy lake should start and end. Only in the winter, when the lake is covered in great sheets of ice, is it possible to walk along the lakeside all the way round. At other times of the year long detours have to be made around reed beds, bogs and mouths of streams, adding another day's walk to the circuit.

By mid-morning the cursed wind has sprung up again. I should be up there exploring the gompa. After all, the great Guru Rinpoche is reputed to have spent the last week of his life meditating in a cave here. Instead I hide in the Landcruiser, the only place of refuge from the sun's glare and that awful wind. Even thinking is an effort; it's as if my mind has more or less shut down, the body having decided that in its present convalescent state intellectual enquiry has no place in its hierarchy of needs.

In the early afternoon we cross the Barkha plain that covers the ground between the lakes and the Kangri Ti-se range. This is a landscape from hell, an emptiness of sand and gravel over which the wind rages, whipping up storms of sand and numerous whirling sand-devils. Except that it isn't empty. A straggle of dots in the distance reveal themselves to be groups of Tibetan men and women, nearly all of them past middle age – or looking as if they're past middle age – who are trudging towards the Precious Snow Mountain. Further on, a peppering of black and white spots on brown enlarges into vast herds of yak, sheep and goats stretching far into the distance. At first sight there's nothing here for them to graze upon. You have to look hard to see that the first shoots of summer grass are breaking through what a week or two ago must have been frozen ground.

Scattered here and there among the livestock are the black tents of nomads. We divert to the closest and stop for a few minutes of cross-cultural confusion. Three drogpa women come out to stare at us while we stare at them. They wear brightly coloured aprons, silver necklaces and bracelets, turquoise earrings and brooches. Their faces are swathed in scarves and shawls, just as ours are hidden behind ski goggles, dark glasses, bike masks and — for those whose noses are small enough — Chinese surgical-type masks which hook over the ears. Sweets are offered and we are invited into the tent. The wraps come off to reveal three over-awed young women: never seen a foreigner before and now six all at once. Imagine the situation reversed: you're hanging out the washing in your semi in Pinner when six Tibetans turn up out of the blue, dark hair done up in pigtails, black chubas, embroidered boots tied up at the knees, daggers dangling from waists, terrible teeth, huge smiles.

The women go through the motions that good manners demand — putting dried yak dung on the fire, making fresh tea, churning up butter and salt in a cylindrical churn that looks like a brass-bound bazooka — but their hearts really aren't in it. The relief is mutual when Sonam conveys our regrets that we have to move on.

All day the Nine Stacked Swastikas Mountain has been drawing closer but it suddenly looms huge in the sidelight of late afternoon. Unlike any other mountain of comparable height that I have ever seen, it rears up out of the plain without benefit of foothills or surrounding base. It stands clear, an impression heightened by the two deep V-shaped clefts on either side cutting into the Kangri Ti-se range almost to the level of the plain, so that the mountain really does appear to stand alone. This separateness is further reinforced by the snow which, in the summer months, covers Kangri Rinpoche's summit, shoulders and flanks and nowhere else. The rest of the high ground on the range is black or brown or ochre. Add to that the arresting striations on the Precious Snow Mountain's south face – a deep vertical scar cut across a series of horizontal strata lines, one of which stands out above the rest so as to form a cross – and you have a mountain that cries out for attention, that demands sanctification. With a half-closing of the eyes and a little imagination the striations on the south face become the Nine Stacked Swastikas of the Bon faith – or the scratch marks that mark the final defeat of the gods of Bon by the more powerful forces of Buddhism.

This last, epic struggle for control of the Bon holy land is said to have taken place during the lifetime of Tibet's great poet Jetsun Milarepa, the 'cotton-clad' yogi, also known as the Great Sorcerer. Recent research has shown that the bulk of Milarepa's famous songs, as well as the autobiography dictated by Milarepa to his disciple Rechung, are the work of a sixteenth-century scholar. In other words, they were written several centuries after Milarepa's death in 1135 and should be seen as representing sixteenth-century Buddhist ideals – in particular, the ideals of the Kagyupa school of Buddhism of which Milarepa was a very influential member – rather than the true story of Milarepa's life and the actual verses which he himself uttered. Even so, the contest between Milarepa and the Bon priest Naro Bon Chung expresses an important truth in the form of allegory. It shows the Kagyupa sect wresting control of the holy lake and the holy mountain from the last of the Bonpo and establishing their own monasteries in their place.

The celebrated story of how Jetsun Milarepa subdued Naro Bon Chung is set out at length in *The Hundred Thousand Songs of Milarepa*. Their struggle began when they met by the shores of Mapham Tso. The Bon priest challenges Milarepa and, when he hears that he has come to the holy mountain to meditate, demands that the Buddhist yogi follow the Bon teachings. 'On the contrary,' replies Milarepa, 'if you want to stay here in future you must follow the teachings of *my* religion.'

The Bonpo suggests they settle the issue by having a contest: 'Let us see whose miraculous powers are superior. Whoever wins can remain here and be regarded as the rightful owner of this place, and the one who loses must leave.'

He then opens the first round of the contest by straddling Mapham Tso with a leg on each side of the water.

For a reply, Milarepa seats himself above the lake and, without his body appearing to grow any bigger or the lake any smaller, entirely covers the lake. He then sings a song which begins:

The famous Ti-se Mountain covered with snow
Symbolises the pure, white Buddhist doctrine.
The waters flowing into the famous turquoise lake of
   Ma Pham
Symbolise deliverance to the Realm of the Absolute.
Ti-Se, where dwell the heavenly Devas with worldly bodies,
Is the king of all snow mountains on this world.
This place belongs to the followers of Chos,
To the followers of Milarepa.
If you heretical Bon priests will practise the dharma
You will also be able to benefit mankind.
If not, you should leave and go elsewhere.
My powers are far greater than yours –
Watch me and see what I do!

The yogi then picks up the entire lake with all its waters and places it on the tip of one finger. Naro Bon Chung admits defeat but demands another round, so they move north to continue their struggle at the Precious Snow Mountain.

The little settlement of Darchen sits on a rise at the base of the mountain, an ugly jumble of modern shacks dominated by a guest house built in the 1980s for Indian pilgrims. Like all Tibetan guest houses, this is built on the lines of a caravanserai: a large Chinese flag flies over the gateway, leading into a square courtyard which has rooms on three sides and a high wall on the fourth. You park your lorry as close to the door of your room as you can, partly for reasons of security but also to give the diesel engine the benefit of any heat that might help to stop its fuel from separating. The gate is locked at night and the courtyard is patrolled usually by two or three mastiffs who pass the time fighting over leftovers, barking at each other and howling at the moon. The one recent innovation has been the addition of a latrine. This has not been a success, since the idea of building a cesspit or some sort of drain to go with it seems to be regarded as an unnecessary extra. The result is entirely predictable. The latrine soon fills up and that's that. So the traveller is then faced with a choice: either to add to the dunghill or to go elsewhere. Since most latrines in Tibetan guest houses are multi-occupancy without intervening partitions, you soon learn to pick your time and place.

Running the guest house – or rather, doing anything but running the guest house – are two young soul sisters to the pair we encountered in Purang. They too confine their duties to providing huge thermos flasks of hot water and knitting. They too have honed the technique of the open-mouthed, incredulous stare down to a fine art. But Darchen guest house has the edge on Purang in two respects. Firstly, it has a tourist shop, a little storeroom stocked with Coca-Cola and Chinese champagne, both of which explode into cascades of froth when opened and have an identical taste, and car stickers featuring Kangri Rinpoche. Secondly, it has a cinema in the corner of the courtyard, consisting of a tarpaulin suspended from two walls and held up by a number of wicker panels lashed together. Its dominant feature is a sound system which, when we first arrive, fills the courtyard with amplified screams, shouts, gunfire and explosions. Barney pokes his head in and discovers Sylvester Stallone grunting Mandarin.

We are not the only foreign visitors. Soon after we've made ourselves comfortable in two of the guest rooms a convoy of

Landcruisers arrives with a party of twenty-one Indian pilgrims. They're wrapped up like dressed turkeys but their faces are grey and pinched; every one of them looks frozen and miserable. We soon learn why. They have flown from Bombay to Kathmandu and have then been driven across Tibet more or less non-stop for four days. They have had no time to acclimatise, with fatal consequences. One of their number has died the previous day from acute mountain sickness in the form of pulmonary oedema, and a second, a middle-aged dentist, is seriously ill with the same condition. We offer Diamox but this is a preventative and not a cure. There is only one effective treatment for AMS and that is descent. Even a drop of a thousand feet could be enough. Binod and Mel urge the Indians to act now before the patient gets any worse, but they seem to be in a state of mass shock. They prefer to meditate and pray.

We have our own problems, because Sandra is in trouble again.

The most important man in Darchen is the chief of the district police, known in Tibet as the Chide Lekhung or Public Security Bureau. The PSB has far more clout than the PLA and is the real political power in the land. Binod and Sonam have held long discussions with the PSB chief about Sandra. He is demanding that Sandra should pay a hefty fine for not having an entry permit. Sandra has no money so this isn't possible. Perhaps a spot of British diplomacy will do the trick, so that evening I tidy myself up and call on the PSB chief with a bottle of Scotch and 200 cigarettes tucked under my jacket.

The PSB office is a small shack with a notice saying 'SHOP' painted in English over the door. Sonam leads the way in and introduces me with much deference to the PSB chief, who is lying sprawled on a bed along with two members of his staff. He presents a figure sinister to the point of caricature. His features are Tibetan but his manner is Chinese in that he greets us with a long, expressionless stare. He says nothing but allows Sonam to ramble on. When Sonam pauses he still says nothing. His only action is to draw on a cigarette, which he smokes through a long cigarette holder in the manner of Talullah Bankhead. He and his colleagues wear olive green uniforms but his is covered by a long, fawn-coloured gaberdine trenchcoat, double-breasted with belt, worn draped over the shoulders and unfastened. On his head he sports a trilby. He even has a thin spiv's moustache. It is pure Raymond Chandler but marred somewhat by a shock of long black hair that springs out from under the trilby in all directions. This gives the PSB chief a saturnine Harpo Marx touch that makes him even more creepy.

Sonam translates my speech: I extend greetings from the British people to the friendship-loving people of the Tibet Autonomous Region of the People's Republic of China and as a token of that friendship I offer this gift of a bottle of Johnny Walker Black Label and 200 Benson & Hedges. Sonam doesn't know about the whisky and cigarettes and his voice cracks when I pull them out from under my jacket and lay them on the table. The PSB chief sits up and stares at them and then at me. 'Mistake,' mutters Sonam and groans, 'oh-ho-hoh.'

The PSB chief replies in Tibetan but looks directly at me as he speaks. His voice is dispassionate: to offer such gifts to Chinese officials is illegal and insulting. Frosty silence, broken by Sonam's unhelpful moaning, 'Oh-ho-hoh, big mistake.'

I do my best to apologise. I explain that my concern is for Sandra only. She is a genuine pilgrim who has endured extraordinary hardships to get here and has no means to pay the fine. We will guarantee to look after her and take her back across the border when we have completed our circuit of the mountain.

Although he says not a word of English it is plain that the PSB chief understands me. He speaks without waiting for interpretation: Sandra must pay the fine, or she goes to jail.

But she has no money.

Then *you* must pay the fine.

A compromise is finally reached: Sandra is spared the fine and can stay in Darchen overnight, but tomorrow morning she has to be taken to the border. She must leave Tibet by the same way she entered it. I return to the others with a heavy heart, and take Sandra to one side and break the news to her. Tears roll down her cheeks but she accepts the decision without further fuss. 'The karma has changed,' she tells me. 'I'm ready to go back now.'

We are all down at heart. Sandra has become our good-luck charm and no one wants to see her go. We vent our anger on Sonam who has demanded that I pay him an extortionate amount to drive Sandra back to Purang and the Nepalese border. After much arguing Mel takes Sonam in hand and reminds him how much petrol and driving our late arrival in Tibet has saved him. He crumples and Mel becomes the hero of the hour.

Darchen is at 14,500 feet and at this altitude none of us sleep too well – except Mel, who sleeps loglike and has one of those snores that rises to a crescendo every few minutes. My stomach tends to react badly to rows and tension and at five in the morning I have to make a rush for the john. It is a hard, clear, bitter cold night. I am all set to squat in the multi-occupancy latrine when I am joined by another early riser. Horrors! No trilby, but the wild hair and the gaberdine over the shoulders are a dead giveaway. The PSB chief ignores me but there is no way I can ignore him. I hoist up my salopettes and scuttle away to find myself another hole.

Sandra leaves after breakfast. We have loaded her rucksack with as much food as it can hold, as well as a few dollars. She hugs us each in turn and just before she climbs into the Landcruiser she hands me her prayer beads. I am to leave these in the snow as her offering when we cross the shoulder of the Precious Snow Mountain at the Dolma La. Sandra kept herself apart but was always a presence among us. We will miss her.

This little tragedy is accompanied by a far more serious one. The condition of the Indian dentist with the pulmonary oedema has deteriorated in the night. Binod and Mel have done all they can but their advice has fallen on deaf ears. If he is to survive he has to be taken lower without any further delay. The only place where he stands a chance is Purang, where the valley floor is about 1,500 feet lower than Darchen. He could go in the car with Sandra but his colleagues decline the offer. They are too busy praying.

Not long after Sandra's departure Binod reports that the dentist is now in a coma. His fellow pilgrims are frantically trying to revive him with injections of adrenalin. Finally and at long last they decide to listen to Binod's pleas to move him to a lower altitude and at this point the PSB chief steps in to say that their permits are not valid for Purang. They may take their Landcruiser only as far as Mapham Tso. This is useless because the lake is hardly lower in altitude than Darchen. Mel tries to get this across to the leader of the Indian party. Finally he starts shouting, 'Listen to me! You've *got* to get him to Purang. Get that into your head! Bribe the driver or take over the Landcruiser if you have to, but don't let him stop at Lake Manasarovar. You *must* go on to Purang!'

The Indians nod their heads and it seems that the message has at last sunk in. The pilgrim is carried into the Landcruiser and driven away. When we return to Darchen some days later we learn that they stopped at the lake and he died there, by the shores of holy Manasarovar. Indeed, the Indian pilgrim party never made their parikarama of Shiva's mountain; after this second death they packed their bags and drove back to Kathmandu. I hope they sue their travel agent for criminal negligence in selling a tour whose itinerary virtually guaranteed acute mountain sickness.

After the departures of Sandra and the dying dentist we turn our minds to the coming festival of Saga Dawa, the most important festival of the Tibetan calendar. It marks three major events in the life of the Buddha of our age, Gautama Shakyamuni: on this day he entered his mother's womb through her rib-cage in the form of a six-tusked white elephant; on this day at the age of thirty-five he achieved full enlightenment at Bodgaya; and on this day at the age of eighty-one he passed into the state of parinirvana.

Having completed the teaching of his dharma, Gautama Shakyamuni summoned his disciples and instructed them to study the scriptures and to respect and care for each other. He appointed his successor and then uttered his last words:

· All composite things are impermanent.
All contaminated things are misery.
All things are empty and lack intrinsic identity.
Nirvana is peace.

He then lay down on his side 'like a lion in repose' and passed away. His head was turned to the north, to signify that his teachings would one day take root there.

Saga Dawa is marked throughout Tibet as an unofficial public holiday. In the past the Dalai Lamas would go in procession from the Potala to make offerings and pray at the Jokhang and Ramoche temples before proceeding to the Norbu Linka, the summer palace of the Gelugpa tulku lamas. Here they would picnic and go boating on the lake. But no special ceremonies are performed to mark Saga Dawa in the way that, for example, festivals such as Monlam (Great Prayer) or Mane Rimdu (Driving Out of Evil) are celebrated – except here at the foot of the Precious Snow Mountain.

I have a special interest in witnessing the Saga Dawa ceremonies at Tarboche. It is my belief that Saga Dawa, like the Tibetan New Year festival known as Losar, has very little to do with Buddhism. It goes back to much earlier days and relates to far more fundamental beliefs.

Before there was Bon there was what Tibetans call mi-chos, the 'religion of humans'. Mi-chos is the animism shared by all the early nomadic peoples of central Asia, and it lingers on among peoples such as the Inuits and the Tungus, who preserved their independent way of life as hunters or stockherders long after others from the same gene pools had gone through a process of cultural transformation. The Finno-Ugric racial groups, now scattered widely across the northern Asian landmass from the Ugrian tribes of western Siberia to the Sami Lapps of Scandinavia, share a common ancestry and language, and a religion which manifested itself in spells, incantations, sacrifices, spirit possessions and magic drumming, and revolved around individuals who mediated between man and the forces of nature through their links with divine or demonic beings. Almost identical beliefs and practices can still be found among the minority communities of the foothills and higher valleys of the Himalayan ranges, the hundreds of hill tribes who occupy the cultural no man's land between Hindu India and Moslem Pakistan to the south and Buddhist Tibet to the north, ranging from the Kaffirs of Kafiristan to the Duflas of Assam.

Whatever they chose to call it, theirs is the religion of humans, the mindset which governed the behaviour of the first nomadic pastoralist hunters who made the Siberian tundra, the Kirgiz steppes, the Turkestan and Mongolian tablelands and the Chang Tang plateau their home. They lived in the open air by day and slept under the stars by night, so that the sky dominated their lives quite as much as the land they walked over. They looked to the heavens for signs of changes in the weather and the coming of rain, navigated over the steppes by the stars, measured time by the moon, drew warmth from the sun by day and fire by night, feared the wind.

Their universe rotated around the constant feature of the Pole Star, the axis of the world of which they were the centre. It found expression in two symbols which are among the earliest that can be found scratched or daubed on all sorts of surfaces throughout inner Asia and beyond. One is the cross, with man at the centre of the four cardinal points. The second is an extension of the same symbol, but with a limb projecting at an angle from the end of each arm. It is an image of rotation about a still centre, of a cycle that represents movement and renewal. The four bent arms symbolise the rays of the sun as it makes its progress across the sky but it may also be seen as a churning or whirling motion.

In China this symbol is called lei-wun ('thunder rolling') and denotes eternity or the infinite. In India it is known as the swastika, from the Sanskrit *swasti* ('well-being') and is used as an auspicious symbol of good fortune linked to the sun. To the Swiss shaman-cum-psychophilosopher Carl Jung the swastika was an archetypal symbol, a rotating mandala that signified a 'projection of an unconscious collective attempt at the formation of a compensatory unified personality'. A conscious attempt by the National Socialist Party to use the swastika to form the 'compensatory unified personality' of Germany in the 1920s has made this a hateful symbol in many eyes. But that in no way lessens the significance of the crux gammatica in Asian religion or its talismanic power.

In Tibet this most ancient of symbols is called yungdrung and has two distinct, quite separate meanings. In its oldest form, the four arms of the swastika extend towards the left or counter-clockwise (卍), representing the wind deflecting the sun's rays as it spins across the sky from left to right (in the northern hemisphere, at least). It is no accident that the majority of swastikas found on Tibetan petroglyphs are of this counter-clockwise model. In this form the swastika symbolises permanence, a weapon that carries the force of indestructible reality. In its later form, in which the arms extend to the right in the clockwise direction (卐), the swastika has come to represent good fortune. To those who accept this as the orthodox model, it represents natural, right-handed movement which follows the 'white' path and leads to good fortune, whereas the counter-clockwise swastika represents unnatural, left-handed movement which follows the 'black' path, leading to ill fortune. All over India the orthodox swastika can be seen drawn on the lintels of the doorways leading into village houses and their courtyards; in Tibet both orthodox and counter-clockwise swastikas appear in equal number, often side by side, not only on buildings but also on the decorated fronts of lorries.

The religion of humans interprets the forces of nature as essentially hostile, but by seeking to live in harmony with one's biosphere life can be made easier. Everything in nature has spirit or energy, so it follows that the earth is sacred and there can be no divide between the spiritual and the earthly.

The earth is not only sacred but feminine. As well as being the source of all creation and growth it harbours the mysteries of nature's elemental forces. Every time the nomad pitches his tent he secures it into often hard ground with ropes and pegs, an act of forceful, conscious penetration establishing the security of his home and his family, while also binding them to the earth. It gives the nomad a degree of control over the mother earth and helps to make the earth spirits more manageable by pinning them down. It is also an act of fertilisation and regeneration. No accident, then, that the ritual dagger of inner Asia – the four-sided instrument which in Tibet is called the phorbu – is shaped like a tent peg or a spike. No wonder, either, that in time the fearsome Tibetan tantric deity Dorje Phorbu or Indestructible Dagger comes to wield his magic weapon as an instrument to bind and destroy demons, because this is the power-tool of the shaman.

The nomad's tent has to be a simple structure, as easily erected as struck. In its basic form it is square and secured by four long guy ropes at its four corners. A central pole supports its roof while four poles planted several feet beyond the corners raise the guy ropes at mid-point like cantilevers. The pole at the centre is all important because, like the surrounding tent pegs, it too drives down into the soil, linking earth and sky. It is the earth–sky conducting rod, the spine known in Tibet as the darchen or darboche. Every monastery has such a darchen at the middle of its square courtyard.

Likewise, the arrival of Buddhism in Tibet in the middle of the seventh century CE was accompanied by a spectacular act intended to bring the entire landscape of Tibet under control. The Tibetan landscape is so intrinsically hostile to man, in its chaos of heaped mountains, piles of sharp rocks and sandy soil, that it must be the work of some malignant force that has heaped spells upon the land. In Tibetan lore this malignancy is attributed to a hostile ogress lying face up over the country. The notion of taming this supine demoness by geomancy – the art of controlling the earth through magic – is credited to the Chinese princess Weng Chen. It was part of the Buddhist dowry brought to Tibet when she married Songtsen Gampo, the Yarlung king who first unified Tibet. Princess Weng Chen's magic took the form of an ambitious programme to read the landscape and tie down the ogress in much the same manner as that employed by the inhabitants of Lilliput when they captured the sleeping giant in *Gulliver's Travels*. The ogress was pinned down to the earth at certain key points of Tibet corresponding to vital points of her body. The first 'peg' took the form of the newly built Jokhang temple in Lhasa which, by happy chance, lay exactly over the ogress's heart. More temples were constructed at eleven other key locations in central Tibet to cover and pin down the ogress's shoulders and hips, elbows and knees, hands and feet. Together, these twelve temples are still regarded as the first Buddhist structures to be raised in Tibet, an immensely successful coup for the new but foreign faith which led to the construction of a further 108 temples, all said to have been built in the first 'diffusion of the Dharma' (the Buddhist doctrine) that took place in Tibet in the late seventh century.

The religion of humans accepts that the earth's powers are distributed unequally. Certain features of the landscape affected the lives of the early wanderers more directly than others: danger or bonus points in their travels such as the crossing points of rivers and mountains; sites that offered shelter or succour such as springs or caves or good grazing, places of good or ill fortune. These were ruled by their own life-forces, and were the dwelling places of intangible elementals – spirits, demons, or ghosts of the dead – which might harm or help the travellers in their daily lives.

The Tibetan word for such life-forces is bla, and the space which it fills is called gnas, which can be a physical place but equally a bodily form, an area of space or even totally abstract non-space. Vital interaction takes place between bla and gnas in the form of a mutually determinate relationship: gnas filled with bla becomes a power-place, be it a blade of grass, a lake, a person or a deity. The one gives life and expression to the other.

The Tibetans call such power-places rten, defined as 'abode of a deity', which come in all shapes and sizes, from a cave associated with a person of great spirit-power in the past to a juniper bush. Indeed, the juniper is a much favoured abode of spirits, which is why a juniper branch is often used as a kind of wand in many sacrificial rituals or is waved to purify a place or a person. The juniper's berries are also chewed or smoked to induce trances and out-of-body experiences.

All rten absorb the life-force of the associated spirit: they become at one with it as gnas becomes a manifestation of bla. This is why the terms Tibetans most often use to describe a pilgrimage are gnas-mjal, which translates as 'to encounter/meet a gnas' and gnas-skor, 'to go round a gnas'. The pilgrimage is a meeting with a spirit of a particular place or the god in residence in the form of a circular journey round it. By making an act of encirclement the pilgrim focuses on, taps into and draws upon the spiritual energy of the gnas, and also adds to the power of the rten, building up a sort of spiritual charge by the repetition of rituals.

This double action is the basis of all pilgrimage in Tibet, both Buddhist and pre-Buddhist. It is a virtuous act which allows pilgrims to express their devotion through physical action but it is also a give-and-take, a projection on to the central power-field of organised mental actions and an absorbtion of that power so as to build up a charge of spiritual merit. It is a direct sensory relationship between a person and a place in which physical contact through every one of the senses is all-important. The pilgrim·sees, using both eyes and mind; vocalises through prayers; listens, for messages external and internal; centres the body, aligning it so as to be at one with the bla; touches with hands, forehead or body; tastes by accepting blessed food and water or by eating some part of the ground; collects, by taking some small part of the place; and exchanges, leaving some article of clothing or bodily part behind.

Such complex actions are often visualised rather than actually performed, so they can easily be overlooked or misunderstood by the casual observer, but they are fundamental to the pilgrim's desire to open a direct metaphysical channel with the bla-gnas. Such mental construction, the calling up of a spirit or deity by visualising it, lies at the heart of all ritual practice in Tibet.

Direct physical contact with the bla-gnas leads to spiritual empowerment. This lies behind the apparently bizarre behaviour of the men and women who can be seen prostrating themselves full-length on the stone flags in front of the Jokhang temple in Lhasa and who proceed round mountains like caterpillars, stretching themselves full-length so that their foreheads make contact with the ground with every 'step'. Unlike the acts of self-mortification found among *penitenti* in Catholicism and some sects of Islam, it is all about empowerment.

All objects at power-places, however humble, carry the empowerment associated with the spirit of that place. Places such as hot springs, with their self-evident direct links with the underworld, have certain kinds of earth prized above others as 'sacred flesh'. Pilgrims dig into the ground in search of small mud balls regarded as medicine pills, eaten both to cure bodily ills and to banish demons. The same holds true of power-words and incantations associated with a particular power-person.

Every Tibetan carries on his or her person a power-point in the form of a silver amulet containing written texts worn close to the vital organs of the heart and stomach. They protect their wearers by warding off evil spirits but they also empower them by providing spiritual energy.

The most visible form of the personal amulet in Tibet is the prayer wheel. The outside of the wheel is made of thin silver usually embossed with the six-syllable mantra of the bodhisattva of compassion, Avalokiteshvara (in Tibetan, Chenresig), *Om Mane Padme Hom*, while inside are strips of rolled-up paper carrying printed sutras, sacred texts or invocations which are said to both absorb and radiate Buddha-energy. A small ball and chain attached to the cylinder helps it to be spun by a flick of the wrist and to continue spinning as the holder walks along. Every revolution of the prayer wheel carries and so 'speaks' the messages contained therein, building up the spiritual charge of its owner.

Power-places, power-people and power-objects still lie at the heart of Tibetan religion, just as they did in the days of the religion of humans when the world was governed by spirits rather than gods. But where you have belief in one the other almost inevitably follows.

The bla-gnas concept evolves quite naturally into a hierarchy of spirit powers. Certain life-essences together with the spaces they inhabit are judged more potent than others, and the most dynamic have their own higher agendas far above the affairs or the reach of humans. Their bla is the sky and they come to be thought of as divinities or gods, lha in Tibetan. Others are less removed; they belong to the realm of earth and water and take the forms of dre (demons), lu (serpent spirits, more widely known by the Sanskrit term naga) and other lesser elementals.

Among the more terrible of the dre are the nyen who live in the mountain peaks. The larger the mountain, the more powerful its denizen nyen. All are without exception gods of fire and brimstone, quick to anger, pitiless in their wrath, jealous and capricious in mood. They poison travellers with their foul air and their all-enveloping mists, they discharge thunderbolts and avalanches, rain down rocks, hailstorms, blizzards, torrential rain and high winds as the mood suits them. Every valley is at the mercy of whichever mountain god overlooks it. But the same mountain god also protects its own. Those who acknowledge its suzerainty and who make the right submissions will usually – but not always, because mountain gods are notoriously fickle in granting their favours – receive protection.

Every mountain pass in Tibet is marked by cairns of stones, known as labtse, built up by passing travellers as offerings to the guardian of the mountain. Even if the weather conditions are perfect the wise traveller seeks to insure himself by carrying a small stone up to the saddle of the pass and adding it to the existing pile of stones. As well as pleasing the local nyen, this act of piety helps to keep cairns in a state of repair so that they can perform a secondary duty as route markers when the weather closes. On the more significant passes travellers add darchok, strings of prayer-flags also known popularly as lung-ta ('windhorses') because they carry prayers in the wind. Their colours represent the five elements, starting with yellow at the base (symbolising earth), then green (water), red (fire), white (air) and at the top blue (space or ether).

As they pass each labtse travellers shout out '*Lha-gyel-lo so so*' ('May the gods be victorious') because each marks the subduing of the resident genius loci and its conversion by Guru Rinpoche, Tibet's first apostle of tantric Buddhism whose omniscience is popularly extended to every power-point in Tibet.

The mountain gods are of the sky rather than the earth and as such are usually masculine, just as those spirits drawn from earth and water are most often feminine. These latter take the form of black serpents and are most often found in lakes, rivers and streams, whose purity they protect. But they are also guardians of the earth, all that grows upon it and all the mineral wealth it contains. They guard most jealously what is theirs, so that whatever is mined, hewn or harvested from the earth has to be paid for by propitiation or offerings. It is said that some years ago an enormous nugget of gold the size and shape of a Tibetan mastiff was dug out of the ground somewhere along the strip of high ground that separates the two lakes at the base of the Precious Snow Mountain. Its discovery so appalled the local governor, that he ordered it to be reburied immediately before its theft could bring down the wrath of the nagas of the lakes, whose powers are said to be unlimited.

The world space of the Tibetan nomad is filled with every sort of spirit-force from bla and lha to nyen and lu. They are all-pervasive and affect every aspect of his daily life. In his daily routine he has to take full account of a number of domestic gods whose powers are limited to their specific roles: some are protectors of the person, others are guardians of specific areas of the home. Within the nomad's tent the three most important domestic deities are the guardians of the central tent pole,

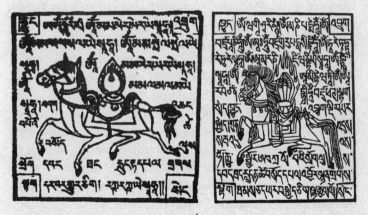

The lung-ta or 'wind-horse' woodblock print appears on prayer-flags throughout Tibet as well as on scraps of paper which are thrown into the air. The prayers are activated by being blown by the elemental forces of the wind.

the hearth and the food store. Without are the protectors of livestock, horses and the fields. All require oblations, offerings of food – particularly such staples as tsampa and butter – and the burning of incense.

Interaction with these gods and spirits governs life. Some are bad spirits who, if they cannot be avoided, have to be appeased; others are benevolent spirits whose goodwill the nomad seeks to win through prayers and offerings. These spirits are also in constant opposition with each other and their struggles for supremacy over the great spaces above the open steppes draw man in. So human history becomes a battle between the opposing forces of good and evil, and man begins to grope his way towards the notion of dualism in his religious thoughts.

Midway between the gods of the sky and the spirits of the earth is the surface world upon which we humans live. This middle ground between upper and nether worlds is also populated by ghosts. Some are spirits of the departed who have died without the proper ceremonies to enable them to find their way to the afterlife or who have been unable to tear themselves away from this world's attachments. Others are more sinister; ghouls and flesh-devourers condemned by the sins of past incarnations to shadow lives beyond the pale of human existence.

Benevolent or malevolent, it is to everyone's advantage to find ways to placate the gods, spirits, demons and ghosts and turn their powers to good use. Various permutations of offerings, sacrifices, gestures and incantations are tried and tested, and some are found to be more effective than others, particularly when accompanied by drumming, rattling and the ringing of bells. In time these become established recipes or rites for dealing with the spirits, to be handed down by word of mouth from one generation to the next.

This oral transmission of arcane, often secret knowledge has played a central role in Tibetan culture from the earliest times. Tibetan histories refer to pre-Buddhist storytellers and singing bards as protectors of the kingdom who upheld the order of the world. The correct recitation of legends of origin was as much a religious act as any recitation of sutras. Even after the invention of the Tibetan script in the mid-seventh century CE and the development of woodblock printing soon after, oral transmission remained of paramount importance. Even to this day monks of all the many Tibetan religious schools continue to receive direct oral transference of scriptures, liturgies and teachings from a qualified teacher in a master–disciple relationship. The bulk of their religious training is given over to thousands of hours of chanting and committing to memory huge tracts of scriptures, prayers and other sacred texts, while those with special aptitudes for memorisation will go on to learn the entire contents of monastic libraries – even, so it is said, the entire Buddhist canon, the Triptaka, consisting of many thousands of volumes. They become, as it were, walking libraries of learning.

This tradition of learning by rote and handing on knowledge has enabled the people of Tibet to keep their heritage alive to a degree and on a scale with few parallels elsewhere. But it is double-edged. Because so much weight is placed on the correct transmission of spoken texts, their authenticity is placed beyond question. And because such high value is given to these texts as authentic transmissions, they are also open to abuse as extremely potent instruments of revisionism.

Now from the song to the singer: just as some rituals are more effective than others, so certain individuals are better ritualists than others.

In every tribal community emerge individuals marked out from the rest, part of the community yet set apart from it by some trait which they turn to their advantage. This disability often shows itself in behaviour that Western man would classify as neurotic or even schizoid: introversion, trance states, fits, hysteria, hallucination, even outbursts of aggression and mania. These are the universal hallmarks of the shaman. The word 'shaman' was introduced into ethnography from the Tungus people of Siberia where it has the specific meaning of 'Buddhist monk', but it almost certainly has much older roots. It may well be derived from the Sanskrit sramana, a practitioner of austerities; or from the Chinese sha-men, an inspired person who communes with the celestial beings; or even from the Tibetan shen, a word first used to describe Bon priests who specialised in blood sacrifices. This last word has affinities with Sino-Turkic notions of the soul: shen in Chinese means both the spirit element of the soul and the heavenly spirits.

One of the first written accounts of inner Asian shamans at work comes from the Venetian traveller Marco Polo. In describing the Chinese provinces bordering on eastern Tibet – an area that continues to this day to have strong associations with the Bon tradition – he has some unfriendly words to say about local medical practices:

> When someone falls ill, he sends for the magicians – that is, the conjurers of devils and guardians of idols. When these magicians have arrived and the patient has told them of his symptoms, they begin forthwith to play on their instruments and leap and dance until one of their number falls prostrate on the earth or the paved floor and froths at the mouth and lies like one dead. This is because the devil has entered his body. And in this state he remains. When his fellow magicians, who are present in force, see that one of their company has collapsed in the way I have described, they begin to speak to him and ask with what malady the patient is afflicted. To which the reply comes: 'Such and such a spirit has touched him, because he has incurred his displeasure.' When they have uttered many words and many prayers, the spirit who has entered into the prostrate magician makes answer.

To effect a cure, a blood sacrifice is made:

They slaughter the sheep and sprinkle the blood in the places prescribed, as a sacrifice in honour of the spirit named . . . They have wood of aloes and incense, with which they go to and fro censing the place, and they make a great show of lights . . . Finally the spirit answers: 'Since the sacrifice and all else that is required has been performed, he is forgiven and will recover soon.' When this answer has been received, after the libations have been duly poured and the lights lit and the incense burned, they say that the spirit is now fully propitiated . . . The same practice is observed throughout Cathay [China] and Manzi [Southern China] and by almost all the idolaters, owing to their lack of physicians.

Here we have a textbook description of the shaman as a specialist in achieving trancelike states during which his soul is believed to leave his body, either to ascend into the sky or descend into the underworld.

Few parts of the world provide richer hunting grounds for budding '-ologists' in search of shamans than the Himalayan ranges. Many a young anthropologist and ethnographer from the School of Oriental and African Studies in London has crouched by the hearth of some obscure village hut in the foothills of Nepal and watched spellbound as the local jaddu-wallah (magic man), lha-pa (person belonging to a god), jankri or dammu goes through his business. The student soon learns that there is no shortage of spirit mediums, particularly among those communities with cultural and racial links with Tibet. He or she also discovers very quickly that spirit possession, more often than not, runs in the family and that shamans-to-be nearly always receive their 'call from the gods' in their early teens. And then, just when he has observed enough cases of spirit possession and taken enough notes to make up what he feels will amount to an extremely impressive doctoral thesis, he makes a shattering, but all-important discovery: the Himalayan shaman, when he puts on his white robes, his harness of bells and his feathered, crowned headdress, is following a well-ordered, stereotypical routine shared with thousands – if not hundreds of thousands – of other shamans.

The young anthropologist/ethnographer hurries back to London with his notes, tape-recordings and photographs. He rushes into SOAS and there, as his eye sweeps along the library shelves, his worst suspicions are confirmed – scores of neatly bound doctoral theses all saying more or less the same thing with only minor variations. Together they demonstrate the quite extraordinary consistency and universality of the shaman's experience.

In sum, this research shows that the shaman has certain characteristics: a set belief in the form of myths and legends; a set ritual for entering a state of ecstatic trance; a set spirit or spirits which he invokes at the beginning of a ceremony and which acts as his guide; and a set costume and trappings which include a mirror to observe the spirits, a narrow-sided drum to tap, bells worn as anklets, bracelets or a necklace (or attached to his drum as a tambourine) to shake, a horn of some kind to blow and some form of rod or spear – which can be as simple as the branch of a tree or as complex as a trident – to hold as a wand.

The shaman takes care in selecting and marking his sacred space, knowing it to be a meeting place between two worlds. He may draw a circle on the ground to create such an area, using his stick or a sword or by marking it out with flour or seed, by banners and cords or even by laying a circle of blood.

Before ritual comes purification, the banishing of all that is unclean. The air is cleared of all malignant forces with smoke and incense using juniper brush, cedar bark, resins, herbs and butter-oil lamps. Fire is always present or represented by such ritual objects as the dorje, the double-headed thunderbolt which symbolises the power of lightning – fire from heaven – and banishes evil. (The action of cracking the fingers of the right hand into the palm of the left used to make a point in Tibetan religious debates is known as the 'lightning bolt' and represents the strike of fire on earth.) Cleansing the body is equally important, although for Tibetan shamans the gesture of pouring water into the mouth from a silver water carrier and swilling it out is quite sufficient.

Drumming and chanting are central to the ritual: sound pulses set up vibrations which can affect reality in many different ways. Even words have power and can set up powerful reverberations on psychic as well as physical levels. The actual act of spirit-possession, sometimes described as a séance, follows an equally circumscribed pattern. A model example is described in a paper presented by Per-Arne Berglie at the Tibetan Studies Seminar for Young Tibetologists in Zurich in 1997 under the title *On the Question of Tibetan Shamanism*:

> The drumming and singing became faster and faster and the body started to rock to and fro. Suddenly the dpa-bo [shaman] leapt on to the floor and began to dance. The god had now entered the body . . . When the excited spirit-medium had calmed down, the possessing god introduced himself, usually with rather mocking words, and asked what he was supposed to do now . . . When the help had been given, the god was duly thanked and all the gods started to leave. Then, in the case of the dpa-bos, the final part of the séance started . . . During this part the dpa-bo used to swing and shake his head and body violently. The singing now had a general content and was full of good advice, sometimes of an almost proverbial nature. All the séances ended with the spirit-medium leaning backwards in a sitting position, the head usually falling forward as the rigs-lnga [crown] slid off his head.

The harnessing of spirits carries risks but brings its own rewards. As a traveller between the sacred, earthly and profane worlds the shaman has special access to a defined cosmos and can act as an intermediary, a channel between the world of men and the spirit world. He can control spirit entities, which communicate through his medium, giving him the ability to prophesy, heal and divine. He can also control and so exorcise spirits which have taken possession of other people or have established residence in a particular place. The natural law applies, in which every cause has effect. The greater the energy raised by the offering, sacrifice or ritual, the greater the response. This energy (so it is claimed) can be used to attract the spirits to produce fertility, good hunting, or good weather for the crops, or to repel them to appease or destroy ghosts, or divert disaster.

By contending with the spirits on behalf of others, a shaman can perform all manner of services to his community, anything from drawing out an evil spirit that had taken refuge in a child's head to predicting the harvest by the interpretation of cracks in the shoulder blade of a sheep. He is a healer, diviner, soothsayer and magician. A shaman who can demonstrate such powers becomes an important figure in the community. His powers can be used for good or for evil, so that he is as much feared as respected.

But the shaman is not a priest, although plenty of priests and monks within Tibetan religion are clearly shamans. He has acquired his calling through direct and personal communication with the supernatural and acts by intuition rather than by institution. He works alone yet often lives within his community, taking a wife and family, whereas the priest or monk belongs to an order which sets itself apart from the mainstream of society. The shaman is primarily a product of hunting and pastoral communities, the priest of settled, crop-producing societies.

The figure of the shaman dances, rattles, shakes and speaks in strange ancestral voices right across the ancient world of inner Asia and beyond to the Americas. He and his kind share the same archetypal myths and legends, the same world-view of a three-tiered universe which exists so that man can rise or fall, with a heavenly world above, a hellish world below and a 'world tree' or *axis mundi* which holds all together. In Tibet, along the

Himalayas and elsewhere over much of inner Asia and beyond this shamanistic cosmography is expressed as the three realms: the realm without form, the highest form of consciousness which is itself neither conscious nor unconsciousness, both intellectually and spatially infinite; the realm of form, which includes the realms of the gods; and the realm of desire, which contains all the earthly gods, humans, ghosts, animals and the damned.

Axial symbolism – the concept of the pole or world axis which links heaven, earth and hell as different planes joined by the central spine around which everything turns – is fundamental to the shamanistic tradition. It is the fulcrum of all creation, providing the core stimulus for human existence: the spiritual ascent of the world axis. It is the cosmic tree, the ladder by which the pure mind ascends from the lowest to the highest sphere – the same cosmic tree that crops up all over Eurasia in mythologies in forms that range from the ridiculous to the sublime; from the Germanic fir tree associated with the gift-bearing yuletide Santa to the pine trees in the yurts of the Altai Tatar which their shamans climb in symbolic journeys to the heavens.

From the dehar of the Kailash Kafirs to the medicine men of the Eglulik, the shamans of inner Asia and the Paleo-Arctic share beliefs and modi operandi to an astonishing degree. What does this suggest?

One explanation is that powerful cultural ties have been maintained and reinforced over several millennia between peoples who today live huge distances part. This is unlikely when one considers the stormy history of inner Asia from the Huns onwards.

A second is that these tribes developed similar religious ideas because they experienced similar environments and lifestyles, a respectable theory favoured by most ethnographers in this field.

A third possibility, which is gaining new champions in ethnographical circles as the supporting evidence grows, is that there existed a centre of origin, a cradle of shamanism from which the cult spread to the four corners of inner Asia. If it existed it would have had to have been located somewhere within inner Asia, close enough to the settled cultures of Mesopotamia to be influenced by Babylonian myths – in particular, the complex cosmography of the cosmic mountain Sumeru/Meru/Dzambu Lying, but also close enough to the ancient overland trails linking China and northern India. This strongly suggests the open steppes south and west of the Aral Sea and both banks of the Amur Darya (the Greek Oxus), peopled during the first millennium BCE by nomadic tribes whom the Persians lumped together as the Sakas and the Greeks at the time of Herodotus the Massagetae (writing in the mid-fifth century BCE, Herodotus describes the latter as sun-worshippers and horse-sacrificers). After the invasion of Alexander the Great in 331 BCE, this 'cradle' became better known as Margiana (south of the Oxus), Sogdiana and Ferghana (north of the Oxus) and Bactria (the upper Oxus). Today these four areas comprise parts of Turkmenistan, Uzbekistan, Khirgizstan and Tajikistan.

In nearly every shamanistic culture in inner Asia, Siberia and the Arctic Circle the shaman either has his origins or finds his powers in a mystical land that is of this world yet apart from it. Hidden among mountains far away – or at the source of a long river – it can be visited only in dreams or in the highest state of ecstatic trance. It is both the birthplace of shamanism and its ultimate homeland. In Tibet it is celebrated as the land of Shambhala.

4 *The Kingdom of Tibet*

This is the path. Whoever walks on this path travels to the end of his sorrow. I showed this path to the world when I found the roots of sorrow.

From the Dhammapada

EARLY JUNE 1996

For several days pilgrims have been gathering under the Precious Snow Mountain. A tented camp has sprung up a mile or so west of Darchen on the meadows where the Lha Chhu, the River of the Gods, emerges on to the plain. Thirty or forty Dong Feng lorries are parked on a rise above the river, the prayer flags on their struts giving them the appearance of a dressed fleet of sailing ships. On the camping ground itself are several hundred close-packed tents, mostly square cotton marquees of the sort you'd expect to see at a medieval tournament or a classy Italian lido. They are white with black borders, many decorated with the eight auspicious symbols. The most popular is the eternal knot, balpe, often seen on the door curtains of Tibetan houses.

Every tent is packed with families or groups of friends who have gone to great lengths to come here and who are evidently going to make the most of it now that they have arrived. Men and women have dug deep into their dowry chests for their best and brightest outfits: blouses and costumes of exquisite silks; heavy turquoise- and amber-encrusted silver jewellery draped over the hair and worn as earrings, pendants, necklaces, amulets, bangles, waistbelts, tinder pouches and purses; headgear of every shape and description from silver fox fur hats trimmed with gold filigree to imported Homburgs.

Our blue and orange beehive tents look horribly out of place but no one seems to mind — except the PSB chief. No sooner have we pitched camp than he shows up in a Landcruiser and fines us 15 dollars a head. We're not quite sure why; something to do with camping in the wrong place. Sonam makes himself scarce.

Mel makes a big hit here at Tarboche. He is sitting outside his tent when an elderly Tibetan woman limps up and points to her knee. She wants medicine. Since we don't have a doctor with us our policy is to avoid giving out any sort of drug and to treat only superficial injuries. Many years ago in Nepal I was asked to help an old lady who was obviously on her deathbed. She wanted medicine to ease her pain, so I gave her half a dozen aspirins. A few days later I heard that she had died, poisoned by a Westerner.

But Mel, as a specialist in the treatment of sports injuries, is on safer ground. He examines the knee and diagnoses a swollen patella. Out comes his sleeping mat and blow-up mattress and twenty minutes later the old lady is glowing with satisfaction and tiger balm. Even before Mel has finished a queue starts to form. Word sweeps through the camp and despite Mel's increasingly impassioned cries of 'Muscuskeletal injuries only!' he sees every sort of complaint. Some he has to turn away but a great many bad knees and backs are treated and by nightfall his prestige is riding high. A Buddhist monk brings him a gift of a plate of brightly coloured cakes which have been blessed by the abbot of Trugulho Gompa.

On the night of the full moon of the fourth month of the

Tibetan calendar, the Nine Stacked Swastikas Mountain gleams like a stalagmite in a cloudless sky. Despite the numbers in camp, by nine o'clock every tent is silent. There is a sense of anticipation, of contained excitement of the kind that makes me think of Christmas Eves long past.

The sunlight strikes our tents at exactly 7 a.m. but everyone in camp seems to have been up and about since dawn. The smoke of several hundred campfires rises up in little plumes that merge into a wispy bank of fog over the river. Today is Saga Dawa.

After breakfast we follow the crowds heading towards a natural amphitheatre about a quarter of a mile from and several hundred feet above the river. Here a most extraordinary sight greets us: 2000–3000 Tibetans have gathered, some standing or squatting on the surrounding slopes, but many more walking in a wide circle round a central point and in such numbers to create the impression of a enormous revolving multi-coloured wheel. In the open ground at the hub of the wheel lies a great wooden prayer pole made up of the trunks of several pine trees tied end to end like the mast of a sailing ship. Completely festooned with bright new prayer flags, at its midpoint four ropes of about two hundred feet long have been attached, and they too are entirely covered in flags. The darchen has been aligned to face due north and lies with its base adjacent to a hole at the centre of a mound of stones.

On these stones stands the master of ceremonies dressed in a magnificent yellow silk robe and a red belt. His head and much of his face are hidden by a red hat with a wide brim from which hang long tassels. He becomes known to us as The Man in the Lampshade. He is aided by a number of less magnificently clad deputies who dash here and there like the director's assistants on a film set. Their main job is to lead the crews whose job it is to raise the pole into the air. These are divided into pullers who man the ropes, and pushers who operate a number of V-shaped lifting levers, each made up of two poles lashed together at one end.

The lifting ceremony proceeds by stages. A band performs in the shape of a dozen or so red-hatted monks from the nearby Kagyu monastery at Gayangdrak, blowing giant alpine horns and conches, clashing cymbals and banging drums. We have a choir in the form of a posse of nine shaven-headed Buddhist nuns who chant prayers and perform ritual hand gestures in perfect, exquisite unison. The smoke of surrounding incense fires fills the air and the circumambulators swirl round and round spinning their hand-held prayer wheels in a cloud of dust. Then The Man in the Lampshade raises his hands and a great shout goes up. The pullers pull and the pushers push with their crossed poles. The ropes go taut, the lifting levers are jostled into place and the great pole jerks into life. Its tip rises by perhaps a foot or so.

With every heave the surrounding spectators cry 'Lha-so-so! Lha-so-so!' and throw little squares of prayer papers up into the air. As the great tree rises, longer braces are positioned to support it between pulls. The numbers in the pulling crews grow until we have as many as a hundred men on each of the four ropes. There's a scramble among the men to grab sections of the rope and the two or three policemen present have to intervene to hold them back.

As the pole climbs towards the vertical so the tension mounts.

A point comes when the braces no longer serve any purpose and everything rests on the four ropes and those who are pulling them. The Man in the Lampshade and his assistants gesticulate and rush from one team to another, making minute but critical adjustments to the direction and strength of the pulls. It is vital that they get this last stage right so that the prayer tree can sink into its foundation at exactly the right angle. It *must* be vertical. If the darchen tilts to the slightest degree disasters and ill fortune will follow for Tibet for the next twelve months.

To ensure that no such catastrophe takes place two lorries provide more pulling power. The ends of the two most important ropes are tied round their front bumpers and when the time comes to heave they play their part by inching back in reverse. Finally, a last shout and a tug and the darchen drops into place with a shudder. It is absolutely, perfectly vertical. Once this is seen to be so the entire amphitheatre erupts with cries of 'Lhaso!' and clouds of prayer papers. Led by the monks with their braying horns, the spectators swarm down to join in the circumambulation and the whole arena becomes one massive swirling whirlpool of dust, colour and excitement.

The main ceremony is over by half past ten. At the base of the darchen people queue to prostrate themselves. They throw handfuls of tsampa flour into the air as offerings to the gods and wrap ceremonial scarves around the trunk or on one of the four supporting guy ropes. Many place their heads briefly against the trunk itself to make direct contact with the life-force with which it is now imbued. This has nothing to do with Buddhism, and everything to do with Bon and mi-chos, the 'religion of humans'. The maypole they have erected is the primal tree, the cosmic axis, the earth-sky conducting rod linking heaven and earth and the underworld.

The mood lightens. The great moving swirl begins to fragment and break up. Some people join hands and start to dance. Others start singing. Many more begin to wander back to their tents, laughing and shouting cheerfully at each other. This is a rare opportunity for young men and women from isolated communities to see new faces and find marriage partners, so there's a lot of preening and strutting, showing off and eyeing up. There's also a great feeling of shared community. Again, it makes me think of Christmas, when you come out of church full of bonhomie and good intentions, your spirits lifted by an hour of singing favourite carols and hymns and the way cleared for a long afternoon of eating, drinking and present-opening.

But not everyone spends the rest of the day enjoying themselves. Overlooking the Tarboche arena is a flat shelf of rock rather like the deck of a giant aircraft carrier which juts out over the valley. This is the Cemetery of the Eighty-Four Mahasiddhas or Great Enlightened Ones, and is one of the most auspicious sky burial sites on the whole of Tibet.

The practice of sky burial – in Tibetan durtros – was probably introduced to this area by the Kagyupa sect which became dominant here in the twelfth century. But this rock platform and the surrounding caves and rock shelters had already been a favourite meditation centre for yogis and teachers, Bon and

Buddhist, for many centuries. The double association of meditation site and cemetery makes this is a major power-point and a must for pilgrims, who leave personal items such as teeth, hair or items of clothing as offerings. It has particularly strong associations for the yogis who follow the path of Demchog, the Buddha deity most closely linked with the Hindu Shiva. They come here to set their minds on death as the means to rebirth, perhaps even to perform the chodpa ritual by evoking the lords of darkness and all their attendant spirits, the undead, the hungry ghosts and the flesh-eating ghouls.

The cemetery is deemed to be at its most auspicious during Saga Dawa, which is why so many pilgrims head up there as soon as the darchen ceremony is over. I don't feel strong enough to make the climb and return to camp but Chris decides to follow them.

The Tibetan custom of not simply exposing their dead but also stripping off the flesh and smashing up the bones horrifies those of us who are used to hiding them away in sanitised boxes. But however much it equates with the Buddhist ethos of the destruction of the ego and the impermanence of all earthly things, the fact is that Tibetans still find the dismembering of their loves ones extremely harrowing. Only the closest members of the family accompany the deceased on this last journey. While undertakers divest the corpse and go about their grim business they lie on the ground weeping. The process of dismemberment takes about an hour and, quite understandably, the mourners don't take kindly to foreigners coming up and recording their distress. In recent years there have been several well-publicised incidents where foreigners who have tried to photograph jagor ('feeding the birds') have been stoned or beaten up by enraged mourners.

But Chris doesn't know any of this. He doesn't know this is a sky burial site and he doesn't realise that what he is witnessing is a sky burial. He takes some photographs and leaves. Nobody challenges or threatens him.

'I did wonder about the smell,' he admits later.

'Feeding the birds' may be a misnomer. Tibetan mastiffs are to be avoided; their job is to protect the livestock and the tents of their owners and they are trained to attack strangers on sight. They are always hungry and hang around campsites, wary and ever alert, waiting for scraps. Yet here at Tarboche the mastiffs are fat, sluggish and unusually docile. They turn up their noses at our leftovers. Can it be that they dine at night up on the rock platform of the Cemetery of the Eighty-four Mahasiddhas?

I'm still not strong enough to want to do more than lie in my tent and read. This is difficult because we have visitors throughout the day. Quite apart from Mel's afternoon surgery, all sorts of people want to satisfy their curiosity about us, the Inchi (British) in their bright round tents. These visits are conducted so politely and with such good humour that it's impossible to take offence. A smiling face – or two or three – appears at the door of your tent and then its owner hunkers down to check out what you are and what you've got. Two minutes usually does it and then, with another big smile, the owner moves on.

The universal request is for portraits of the Dalai Lama, the possession of which has just been made a criminal offence in Tibet. We have already made a deliberate decision not to bring any such images in with us, not for our sakes but to avoid putting others at risk. The wisdom of this decision seems to be confirmed when a monk in maroon robes more or less pushes his way into my tent and tells me in broken English that just a week ago the Chinese authorities attempted to search the monastery at Ganden for pictures of the Dalai Lama. This former stronghold of the Dalai Lama's Gelugpa sect was flattened during the Cultural Revolution but has been painstakingly reconstructed and now 300 or 400 monks are in residence. My informant tells me that the monks put up a fight and two were killed. Four days later I am given an update: after encountering initial resistance, the authorities surrounded the monastery with soldiers and stormed the building, killing another thirteen monks. This is later confirmed by reports received in Kathmandu.

The most interesting of my visitors is a Bonpo with a weal of ingrained dust on his forehead. Communication is a slow business. Sonam is out of camp and the only other member of our party who speaks Tibetan is the cook's mate, Thupden Lama, who speaks Nepali but not English, so Binod Rai also has to be involved to translate my English into Nepali for Thupden.

The Bonpo is thirty-three, has a wife and three small children and lives several days' walk away to the east. He came here on foot and has just completed his third circuit of Kangri Rinpoche, each made by prostration, lying full length on the ground so that his forehead touches the earth with each forward stride. Each circuit has taken him thirteen days rather than the usual three if he did it on his feet. His ambition is to complete another ten. As well as absolving him of all his sins in this and each previous lifetime, that will also qualify him to make the quasi-mystical inner kora of Kangri Rinpoche, which only adepts are allowed to undertake. The entrance to this inner circuit is a narrow ravine just north of Darchen which leads to Gyangdrak monastery. This, the Bonpo tells me, is where Shenrab Miboche, who is to the Bon religion what Gautama Shakyamuni is to Buddhism, lived and taught when he first came to Tibet from the mystical land of Olmo-lungring to the west.

Towards the end of the afternoon a bizarre incident puts the cap on an extraordinary day. Some heavy drinking has been going on all round us in the surrounding tents and a fight breaks out. We emerge from our tents to see two wild-looking Tibetan men engaged in the rolling-in-the-dust sort of fight that you see in old-fashioned westerns. This continues for quite some time and a crowd gathers to cheer the combatants on. But then it suddenly turns nasty. One of the men draws the short sword that many Tibetan males habitually carry at their waists and starts hacking at his opponent. He draws blood but, fortunately, his sword seems to be pretty blunt. Then having got his adversary down on the ground he picks up a large stone and attempts to dash out his brains. At this point members of the crowd step in to stop the fight.

Just when everything seems to have calmed down the man with the rock gives his opponent a final mighty whack on the head and flattens him. At exactly that moment we hear a police siren and over the hill races the PSB Landcruiser. The man with the rock drops his weapon and starts to run. He splashes through the river and makes off across the meadow on the far side.

Our old friend the PSB chief is accompanied by four policemen in green uniforms. He gives his orders and the three youngest set off in pursuit. They call on the fugitive to stop but he goes on running till he comes to an enormous pile of black scree at the foot of a dark cliff, which itself must be several thousand feet high. One policeman has now gone to the left and one to the right so there is nowhere to go but up. He slowly starts climbing up the cliff with the third policeman on his heels.

The PSB chief, meanwhile, has had the Landcruiser driven across the stream and when it pulls up he emerges with a rifle in his hand. We see him hand it to the fourth policeman and then gesture at the fugitive, now just a tiny white figure set against the cliff, like a scratch of chalk on a blackboard. Scores of people are now gathered along the river watching this chase and I've no doubt every one of them has that same awful sinking sensation of knowing that something terrible is about to happen but feeling powerless to stop it.

We hear the crash of the rifle shot and then a murmur of relief passes through the spectators as we see the fugitive climbing even faster. Half a minute passes and then a second shot is fired. This stops the man in his tracks. He doesn't move a muscle until the policeman climbs up to him. Then he turns and holds out his arms to be handcuffed. It takes ten minutes to bring him back to the car. When he arrives the PSB chief gives him a loud smack across the face and bundles him into the back seat. The

Landcruiser roars away to Darchen with its siren howling. We all go back to our tents.

In all the excitement no one has paid much attention to the man who lost the fight. After dark Mel slips over to his tent and looks inside. He is conscious and has a nasty headache but with no signs of concussion. Nor have the sword cuts inflicted any serious damage. He is going to have a hangover in the morning. Mel decides that this is one of those instances where the no-doctoring rule can be safely broken and he gives him a couple of Panadols.

We speculate on the fate of the assailant. But early next morning he is spotted cleaning the PSB chief's Landcruiser and later that same morning he turns up in camp. He has been sentenced to take care of the man he tried to kill until he recovers. Now the full story comes out: the two men are brothers who were given a sum of money by another man to undertake the kora of Kangri Rinpoche on his behalf, but before they could start the circuit the younger brother spent all the money on drink, which so incensed the older brother that he tried to kill him.

They do things differently here.

This little outbreak of violence seems very much in keeping with the Tibetan character. In the West we have taken up a view of the Tibetan people that matches our sentimentality towards Tibetan Buddhism, extracting the bits that appeal to us and pretending that the rest doesn't exist. Far from being calm, contemplative souls, most Tibetans that I have met have been passionate, emotional and thoroughly earthy types. Though charged by their religion to be non-violent and compassionate, they are not in their nature a peace-loving or compassionate people – as their history bears out.

So central is Tibet to the West's image of Buddhism that it is sometimes difficult to remember that the tantric Buddhism of Tibet is about as far removed from mainstream Buddhism as is possible, as well as being a form of Buddhism which only took shape a millennium and more after the death of its founder, Siddhartha Gautama Shakyamuni. This prince of the Shakya clan was born in about 540 BCE as the son of the ruler of a small kingdom in what is now southern Nepal. As a child he remained sheltered from knowledge of the outside world and at sixteen he married a princess who bore him a son. It was not until he was twenty-nine that he became aware of the sufferings of the world. He then decided to become an ascetic and spent six years practising the most severe austerities without finding the true nature of existence. Enlightenment finally came to him as he sat meditating beneath a pipal tree on the Indian plains at the place now known as Bodh Gaya.

· Acknowledged thereafter by his disciples as the Buddha or 'Awakened One' of our times, he spent the remaining years of his life preaching the Dharma (in Tibetan, Chos), the doctrine of the Middle Way as a path to spiritual liberation; of salvation achieved through meditation, contemplation and the renunciation of desires, leading eventually to the bliss nirvana, the end of existence and suffering. He died in about 440 BCE. His remains were cremated and his ashes were divided into eight reliquaries that, along with his few personal possessions, were distributed among his chief disciples.

During his lifetime Gautama Shakyamuni founded a number of monastic centres where his followers could withdraw from the world. After his death a series of councils were held to draw together his teachings and to develop the rules of discipline for the monastic life, the Sangha, which, together with the Buddha and the Dharma, came to form the three core elements of Buddhism known as the Three Precious Jewels.

In these early years the Dharma was largely confined to ascetics drawn from the Brahmins, or priestly caste, within the

Indian sub-continent. It was not until Ashok, the Mauryan emperor of India, converted to Buddhism two centuries later in about 260 BCE that this new teaching became popularly accessible. Under the enthusiastic patronage of the first ruler to bring the sub-continent under one government, Buddhism was promulgated in all corners of India and a number of state-funded Buddhist centres of learning came into being.

At about the same time – give or take half a century either way – as Emperor Ashok was consolidating his Indian empire, a warrior named Nyatri Tsenpo made his own bid for power in Tibet. His achievement was the conquest of the Yarlung valley, a southern tributary of the Tsangpo in central southern Tibet, where he laid the foundations of a dynasty popularly known as the Seven Heavenly Kings.

King Nyatri Tsenpo's origins are unknown but the popular Buddhist account of his ancestry states that he descended from the gods on a sky-rope 'like rain falling from heaven to nourish the earth'. He married a queen who bore him a son and when the boy was old enough to ride a horse Nyatri Tsenpo returned to the heavens on his sky-rope. For seven generations each king followed this pattern of ascent to heaven after handing over the reigns of government to his successor.

However, the eighth king, Drigum Tsanpo, proved to be mortal. Buddhist texts state that he fell under the spell of a powerful court magus named Azha, a shen or priest specialising in animal sacrifices, from a country of magicians far away to the west. Azha possessed exceptional powers of divination and warned the king that he would die by the sword. This came to pass when the king challenged the master of his horse, Longam, to a duel. Longam fooled the king into thinking that he could win the contest only if he tied a mirror to his forehead, carried the body of a dog slung over one shoulder and the body of a fox over the other, and whirled his sword above his head as he attacked. By following these outlandish instructions the king made himself an easy target: his sword severed the sky-rope linking him to the heavens and the animal corpses on his shoulders drove away his protecting spirits. Using the flashing mirror as a target, Longam shot his master dead with an arrow.

Drigum Tsanpo (*c.* 50 BCE) thus became the first Tibetan king to require burial in the earth. This, so the story goes, provoked a crisis at the Yarlung court because nobody knew how to perform the death rites appropriate to a king. Eventually, three powerful magi were summoned from the far western countries of Kha-che (Kashmir), Bru-sha (Gilgit) and Shang-shung. One of them was a diviner who could foretell the future using strings, the shoulder blades of animals and his own oracular powers. The second specialised in conducting the funerary rites of those killed in blood and used his magic knife to carry out the rites known as the 'Taming of the Dead', which prevented the spirits of the dead from returning to haunt and hurt the living. The third of the three magicians was the most powerful. Wearing a tiger skin and carrying a turquoise swastika in one hand and a sword in the other, he could fly through the sky mounted astride his tambourine-drum and slice through iron or stone with a feather. His special skills included the subduing of demons who pursued the dead and the worship of the gods by offering blood sacrifices and fermented barley. These talents so impressed King Drigum Tsanpo's successor that he was made the court bla-chod, the priest presiding over the death ritual of kings.

Together, the three shens performed all the necessary rituals to ensure the dead king's safe passage to the afterlife. His body was anointed with gold dust, packed about with gold, silver, turquoise and other treasures, surmounted by a golden image and buried within nine walls.

The funeral of King Drigum Tsanpo marks the start of a royal cult of the dead in south central Tibet which revolved around the complex rites of Bon. It is in this select role – as priest-magicians at the court of the Tibetan kings – that the Bonpo, or followers of Bon, first make their appearance in mainstream Tibetan history. The word 'Bon' means 'priests who invoke', and those initiated into its mysteries acquired the ability to use ritual to invoke and control the most powerful of the spirit forces. They were, in a word, shamans – but not your ordinary common-or-garden shamans drawn from the area round Yarlung. These were super-shamans, non-Tibetans imported from a homeland of shamans far away to the west. They could protect the living from the spirits of the dead and secure the safe passage of the dying from this world to the next. But foremost among their powers was the ability to raise the spirits of the dead through the ritual known as chod.

This ritual is often described as a tantric rite but is practised among shamans as far afield as the Arctic Circle and America. It is a ritualised self-sacrifice in which the shaman offers his flesh to demons in order to acquire greater spirit power. This sacrifice is visualised by the ritualist, whose death is mentally realised. It usually takes place in a site associated with death and demons such as a cemetery: the shaman draws all the evil present into himself and then allows the demon spirit to disembowel him, draw out his entrails and scatter his blood in the air. He then uses his magic knife, the phorbu, to kill the demon. It is said that only the most powerful magician can perform this most danger-ous of rites without destroying himself in the process.

The Lazarist priest Abbé Huc came across just such a ritual while travelling from Peking to Lhasa in 1845–6. On the south-ern border of Mongolia he met some pilgrims hurrying to a monastery to witness a shaman known as Bokte Rinpoche 'man-ifest his power, kill himself, yet not die'. Although Abbé Huc did not witness the ceremony in person he set down in great detail what was reported to him:

> The Bokte . . . advances gravely, amid the acclamation of the
> crowd, seats himself upon the altar and takes from his girdle
> a large knife which he places upon his knees. At his feet
> numerous lamas, arranged in a circle, commence the terrible
> invocations of this frightful ceremony. As the recitation of the

prayers proceeds, the Bokte trembles in every limb, gradually working himself up into frenetic convulsions. The lamas themselves become excited; their voices are raised, their song observes no order and, at last, becomes a mere confusion of yelling and outcry. Then the Bokte suddenly throws aside the scarf which envelops him, unfastens his girdle, and, seizing the sacred knife, slits open his stomach in one long cut.

While the blood flows in every direction, the multitude prostrate themselves before the terrible spectacle, and the enthusiast is interrogated abut all sorts of hidden things, as to future events, as to the destiny of certain personages. The replies of the Bokte to all these questions are regarded by everybody as oracles.

When the devout curiosity of the numerous pilgrims is satisfied, the lamas resume the recitation of their prayers, but now calmly and gravely. The Bokte takes in his right hand blood from his wound, raises it to his mouth, breathes thrice upon it, and then throws it into the air with loud cries. He next passes his hand rapidly over his wound, closes it, and everything after a while resumes its pristine condition, no trace remaining of the diabolical operation except extreme prostration. The Bokte once more rolls his scarf round him, recites a short prayer in a low voice, and then all is over.

Huc reported that these 'horrible ceremonies' were a frequent occurence in the 'lamaseries of Tartary and Thibet'. He ascribed them to Buddhists but it is significant that he was in Bon country when he came across the chod ritual, in an area of Mongolia where the old ways had been little affected by Buddhism.

Long after the Dharma had prevailed within the borders of Tibet in the local form of Buddhism known as Chos, Bon magic continued to be practised on the periphery, as Marco Polo witnessed in Mongolia in the thirteenth century. The Venetian traveller never crossed the borders of Tibet but he knew of the existence among the Tibetans of some remarkable magi: 'Here are to be found the most skilful enchanters and the best astrologers according to their usage that exist in any of the regions hereabouts. Among other wonders they bring on tempests and thunderstorms when they wish and stop them at any time. They perform the most potent enchantments and the greatest marvels to hear and to behold by diabolic arts.' Some of these marvels he witnessed at first hand.

At Kublai Khan's newly built palace at Shang-tu – Coleridge's stately pleasure dome at Xanadu – Marco Polo met Tibetans whom he called 'wise astrologers and enchanters who by their skill and their enchantments would dispel all the clouds and bad weather from above the palace so that, while bad weather continued all round, the weather above the palace was fine.' These were known to the Mongolians as Bakhshi, enchanters who 'do what they do by the arts of the Devil; but they make others believe that they do it by great holiness and by the work of God. For this reason they go about filthy and begrimed, with no regard for their own decency or for the persons who behold them; they keep the dirt on their faces, never wash or comb, but always remain in a state of squalor.'

The presence of these Tibetan shaman-magicians at the court of the Great Khan can be traced back to the conquest of Tibet by Genghis Khan, since when Tibet had provided the Mongols with spiritual leadership. The first of Kublai Khan's Tibetan spiritual advisers was Drogon Chogyel Phakpa of the Sakya monastic school of Tibetan Buddhism. He was based in Beijing as the Great Khan's imperial preceptor from 1260 to about 1280, so Kublai Khan's courts would probably have been well stocked with Sakya monks during the time that Marco Polo was in Mongolia. But Marco Polo makes it clear that there were two sorts of Tibetans at Kublai Khan's court: the Bakhshi and 'another order of devotees' called the Sien-seng. While the Bakhshi were 'entitled according to their order to take wives. And so they do, and rear children in plenty', the Sien-seng were, by contrast, 'men of extreme abstinence according to their own observance, [who] lead a life of great austerity . . . They also have their heads and chins shaven. They wear black and blue robes of sackcloth; if they should happen to wear silk it is still of the same colours. They sleep on mats of wickerwork. Altogether they lead the most austere lives of any men in the world.' He observed a fierce rivalry between these two orders, each regarding the other as heretics.

If these Sakya monks were the Sien-seng, who then were the Bakhshi? All the evidence points to their being Bonpo.

The Tibetan histories imply that the Bonpo adopted the role of court magi at Yarlung at some point during the later years of the Seven Heavenly Kings, approximately the second and first centuries BCE. They were regarded as outsiders, living in seclusion among the royal tombs. As magicians and conjurers of spirits they preserved their mystique with terrifying displays of their powers and so came to exercise a powerful and supposedly malign influence over the kings of central southern Tibet. Their supremacy at court and their support among aristocratic circles lasted for some eight centuries and ended only with the arrival of Buddhism in the seventh century CE – or so we are told.

The problem that every student of Tibetan history has to face is that this history comes almost in its entirety from Tibet's monastic institutions. Virtually every surviving document from Tibet's past has religious overtones to a greater or lesser degree. And why not, since virtually every one is written by theocrats for theocrats and with theocracy as its main subject? Not just any theocracy, of course, but theocracy as understood and practised in mainstream Tibetan Buddhism, Chos. Small wonder, then, that Tibetan history presents itself in the starkest terms of white and black; as the triumph of Chos over the forces of darkness. Prominent among those forces of darkness is Bon, the first and greatest enemy of Chos.

However, the triumph was not complete. Orthodoxy did not prevail throughout Tibet. Pockets of non-orthodoxy, Bonpo and Buddhist, held out and survived the passage of the centuries.

These non-orthodox communities also had their own scholar-monks intent on preserving their versions of theocracy, and they, too, set out versions of Tibetan history, long concealed, long neglected, long overshadowed, long dismissed as fabrications. Only now, in the new climate of tolerance and access to scholarship encouraged by the Dalai Lama, is it possible to lay out the writings of the minority beside the texts of the majority and so arrive at a more accurate understanding of Tibet's early history.

Here, for example, is the Bon view of the important role at the royal court of Yarlung played by the Bonpo shen at the time of the first mortal king, Drigum Tsanpo, as given in the Bonpo text known as the *Nyi-sĝron*: 'During the period of the Seven Religious Kings each king had a shen bodyguard, so the shen had great influence. At that time Ga-cu, Ya-gong, Phen-si and Lde-brus [founded] large religious centres and temples and shrines.' These religious institutions were maintained by forty-nine Bonpo shen, made up of ascetics, preachers, drummers, scholars and magicians. There were nine such magicians, each with one special power, ranging from the ability to make aromatic herbs gather themselves, to floating an ocean on a piece of coal. Ten of the shen are said to have acted as the king's ministers at his councils of state.

But things began to go wrong for the Bonpo when King Drigum Tsanpo – 'born to be an enemy of Bon' – reached the age of twenty-seven. What seems to have started out as differences among various Bon factions over religious doctrines ended in the expulsion of all Bonpos from the king's territories, along with their teachings: 'He [the king] abolished it all. Not even an echo of it was heard. Priests were banished beyond the borders [but] retribution for abolishing Bon fell upon the king . . . He was murdered by his subject Longam who wrung his neck.'

A decade of civil war followed this act of regicide, after which the royal line was re-established and the Bonpo shen were once more restored to their previous positions of power at court. Over the next six centuries they retained their influence, always with the support of the clan leaders of south central Tibet, the aristocracy which provided the king with his ministers. 'The sun of everlasting Bon shone,' state the Bon histories. 'The darkness of the mind of converts was removed as [the country] was flooded with the rays of learned teachers, the so-called "Six Ornaments of the World of Learning".' These six Bon sages – proficient in exoteric knowledge, esoteric knowledge, cosmogony, medicine, languages and general knowledge – were said to come from the six most important countries of the age. Three came from India, China and Tibet, and three came from countries beyond Tibet's western borders named as Phrom, Shang-shung and Tajik.

The first manifestations of a rival religion appeared during the extended reign of King Lhatotori Nyentsen, who is said to have ruled for 120 years spanning the fourth and fifth centuries CE. Both Bon and Buddhist texts record the arrival of various Buddhist sacred objects that are said to have landed on the roof of the king's palace. Although not understood, these objects were venerated as 'awesome secrets' because of their spiritual power. This may represent the arrival at the Yarlung court of Buddhist traders, probably from Khotan and the Tarim Basin, bringing texts and religious objects incomprehensible to an illiterate people.

A century and a half later the Yarlung ruler known as the first of the Nine Religious Kings came to the throne. On his accession in about 617 CE at the age of thirteen he took the name Songtsen Gampo, 'the one who is powerful, just and profound', and then set about living up to his title. Songtsen has two claims to fame: as the king who first united Tibet under a central authority, and as the patron who first opened Tibet's doors to Buddhism. He is now revered as a bodhisattva and a reincarnation of Tibet's protective deity, Chenresig.

The process of uniting the twelve ancient petty kingdoms of Tibet under one central authority had already begun when Songtsen Gampo took up the reins of power. The young king finished the business, transferring his capital from the Yarlung valley to Lhasa, where he built himself a stronghold on the Marpori hill which later became the thirteen-storey Potala Palace. Like his royal predecessors, Songtsen was a follower of Bon and acknowledged the spiritual paramountcy of the Bonpo shen at court. However, his conquests brought him into diplomatic contact with powerful neighbours – China, Nepal and Khotan – whose rulers were all Buddhist. In the case of Nepal the contact may have been more personal since the exiled king of the Kathmandu valley was given shelter in Tibet for some years before returning to Nepal to reclaim his throne, probably with the assistance of Songtsen Gampo. His reward may very well have been the hand of the Nepalese king's fiery-tempered daughter, Princess Bhrikuti Devi, a marriage that had far-reaching consequences for Tibet.

Wonderfully fantastical accounts are given in the annals of the settlement arrived at between the two kings and of Princess Bhrikuti's coming to Tibet. But strip away the hyperbole and a clear storyline emerges: the Newar king of the Kathmandu valley is a devout Buddhist, unwilling to marry off his daughter to a non-Buddhist barbarian, so he sets him a series of tests in the manner of the labours of Hercules. Songtsen Gampo wins his bride but as part of the marriage settlement is required to 'establish all the people of Tibet in the ten golden precepts (of Mahayana Buddhism)' and to 'erect 108 temples whose doors faced the country of Nepal'. Princess Bhrikuti, for her part, is extremely reluctant to go to a 'place of darkness and ignorance' and as the price of her compliance demands three of her father's most prized objects of worship: two statues cast in precious metal of the Buddha Gautama Shakyamuni and the Maitreya Buddha-to-come, and a statue carved in sandalwood of the goddess Tara. These are transported in great style to Lhasa, where a simple shrine, built in the Newari style by imported craftsmen from the Kathmandu valley, is built to house them.

Having secured an alliance with Nepal, Songtsen Gampo sent

armies against his neighbours to the west, north and east. After eight years of war against the Chinese emperor Tang Tai-tsung, a peace treaty was signed. Its settlement included the marriage between the Tibetan king and the Chinese emperor's daughter, Princess Weng Chen. This brought a second wave of Buddhist influence equal, if not greater, to the first.

The Chinese princess brought a Buddhist statue, known today as the Jobo Rinpoche, which portrayed the Buddha Gautama Shakyamuni at the age of twelve. It is the most revered Buddhist image in Tibet. One of the best known tales of Tibet tells how the cart carrying the Jobo became stuck in the mud as it approached Lhasa. The Chinese princess consulted her divination tables and so learned about the giant ogress whose supine body covered so much of Tibet. The lake which then covered much of the Lhasa plain was filled with the ogress's heart-blood, nourishing a host of hostile demons, serpent spirits and other elemental sprites united in their opposition to Buddhism. These evil forces had to be overcome. To destroy their power, the lake was drained and filled in with earth. Foundations were then sunk, upon which was raised a lhakang or 'god-house' to house both the Nepalese and Chinese statues. This came to be known as the Jokhang, the 'house of wisdom'.

The Jokhang is the first acknowledged Buddhist place of worship in Tibet and is thus regarded as the spiritual centre of the country. As you join the throng of visitors circling the inner ambulatorium you can put an ear to a hole in a pillar and listen to the sound of lapping water underground, which is said to be the blood-lake of the still supine but tamed ogress.

The Bonpo version of these events is, of course, rather different. This introduces a third foreign princess whom the Tibetan Buddhist annals ignore: the daughter of the king of Shang-shung.

Until recently the kingdom of Shang-shung was regarded as more legendary than real, but its existence is now beyond dispute. Its territories waxed and waned over the centuries but its heartland remained the same: the high country in the far west of the Tibetan plateau which has the Precious Snow Mountain, Kangri Rinpoche, at its centre. For perhaps as long as a thousand years Shang-shung had been known to the people of south central Tibet as a powerful kingdom – and as the stronghold of the Bon religion.

The Chinese annals record that a Shang-shung army attacked Chinese territory in 637–8 CE, which suggests that Shang-shung was powerful enough to present a serious threat to King Songtsen Gampo's ambitions. There may have been a period of tension between these two kingdoms which the two rulers sought to resolve by a double marriage: the Tibetan king marrying the daughter of the king of Shang-shung, and the latter marrying Songsten Gampo's sister, Princess Sad-mar-kar.

Whether the first of these two marriages was a success is not known, but the second certainly was not. It was not consummated and when King Songtsen Gampo sent a message ordering his sister to fulfil her duty she replied with a series of messages in the form of four songs. These were delivered to her brother the king – presumably through the mouth of a bard – together with a sealed parcel containing turquoise stones wrapped up in a woman's dress.

Found among other early Tibetan documents from the eighth and ninth centures preserved in the Tun-huang caves, the four songs are among the earliest surviving examples of the Tibetan verse tradition. In one Princess Sad-mar-kar sings of the isolation of her husband's palace, the Silver Castle of Kyunglung, set deep in the heart of the Valley of the Garuda in the far-off land of Shang-shung. In the first two verses she laments the ill fortune which has taken her so far from her home and all its comforts:

The land that has fallen to my lot
is the Silver Castle of Khyunglung.
All around people say:
'Seen from without, it is a rocky cliff.

Seen from within it is all gold and treasure.'
But as for me and my opinion,
I wonder, 'Is this a fit place to live?'
How sad and lonely I am.

In a second song, the Tibetan princess uses coded language to urge her brother to come to her rescue, telling him to 'hunt for wild yak' and to 'go fishing with spears'. Combined with the jewels and the woman's garments, her verses had the desired effect. The king heard the songs and opened the sealed package, and got the message: that if he failed to rescue her he was no stronger than a woman but that if he came to rescue·her the jewels would be his reward.

Whether egged on by his sister or not, King Songtsen Gampo did indeed invade Shang-shung and Princess Sad-mar-kar's unfortunate husband was killed. However, Shang-shung's independence was maintained for a little while longer by the Tibetan king's early death at the age of thirty-six. This was followed by a brief period of insurrection, possibly a Bonpo-inspired reaction against Songtsen Gampo's Buddhist innovations.

Songtsen Gampo's successors in Lhasa continued his expansionist policies with considerable success. In the 670s what was now the tributary kingdom of Shang-shung was used as the springboard for a series of raids on the Chinese garrisons north and south of the Taklamakan desert which eventually won Tibet control of the central corridor of the Silk Road. A second phase of Tibetan expansion in the west began in the 720s when Tibetan armies, acting in alliance with the Turks far to the northwest of the Tibetan plateau, invaded the valleys of the Karakoram west of Shang-shung, conquering the three kingdoms of Ladwag (Ladakh), Balti (Skardu) and Bru-Sha (Gilgit).

In 730 the fifth of the Nine Religious Kings, Tride Me-Agtsom, followed his illustrious forebear's example by marrying a Chinese princess who was no less of a devoted Buddhist than her predecessor. In fact, she was meant for his son, but the unfortunate youth had died shortly before her arrival so the old king did the decent thing and married her himself. Under his young wife's guidance, King Tride Me-Agtsom offered shelter to Buddhists from countries as far to the west as Khotan, Gilgit and Turkestan and allowed them to build a small temple in the Yarlung valley. It may also have been the Chinese queen who persuaded the king to invite to Lhasa two Buddhist monks from Gandhara who had established themselves in a cave on the slopes of Kangri Rinpoche. Although they refused to make the arduous fifty-five-day journey to Lhasa, they sent a package of sutras to join the growing pile of 'awesome secrets' in the Jokhang temple.

As in earlier centuries, these pro-Buddhist activities did not go down well with the king's Bonpo ministers. When in 741 the Chinese queen caught smallpox and died it was seen as a sign of the disapproval of the old gods. So much pressure was put on the king that he was finally forced to expel all Buddhist monks from the kingdom and pass a law forbidding the practice of Buddhism within his territories.

Without teachers, disciples and schools to spread the word, Buddhism remained no more than a court cult. Bon was still the faith that mattered.

But it was now only a matter of time before the first Buddhist teachers appeared in Lhasa, which happened in the year 778. As the Bon chronicles put it: 'In the Year of the Earth-Ox the perverse prayer of a demon and he who acted like a monk but was filled with the five poisons brought about the appearance of pernicious Buddhist monks, a demon having entered the heart of the king and the merit of the realm of Tibet being low. The time came when the sun of the Doctrine [of Bon] was made to set.'

The king who caused the sun of Bon to set was Tride Me-Agtsom's son, Trisong Detsen, ruler of Tibet from 755 to 797. He greatly enlarged its borders, sending his armies so deep into China that they briefly occupied the imperial capital of Xian, and extending Tibetan influence as far south as the Bay of

Bengal. He also pushed westwards through neighbouring Shang-shung to overcome Phrom (the Tarim Basin kingdoms of the Silk Road bordering the Taklamakan desert) and Tajik (properly, the upper basin of the Amur Darya and beyond, but in this context more probably the Karakoram and Pamir country bordering Phrom).

As a result of these western conquests Tibet secured control of the Silk Road, which it held on to for the best part of two centuries.

According to Bon history, the final overthrow of Shang-shung came about because the Tibetan king feared the military threat posed by the vast army of his neighbour, King Ligmigya, who possessed 990,000 troops compared to Tibet's modest 42,000. Unable to overpower the Shang-shung army in battle, King Trison Detsen resorted to subversion: he offered the eighteen-year-old youngest queen of the king of Shang-shung a wild yak's horn full of gold dust, together with a promise of two-thirds of the kingdom and promotion to the role of his first wife, if she would betray her husband.

The young queen took the bait and suggested a place where her husband could be ambushed as he travelled over a high pass on the border between Tibet and Shang-shung: 'Since the king of Shang-shung has an army which could cover the earth, and the Tibetan king has an army which could not even fill the middle part of a cow's skin, the Tibetan king could not subdue him by direct attack. But if you would use deceit and craft to subdue him then, next month with his attendants, he is travelling to an assembly in Sum-pa from Shang-shung. So wait for him and kill him.'

The queen then left a coded signal at the pass which told the king of Tibet exactly when the king of Shang-shung was coming and where his army should prepare the ambush. The message consisted of a bowl full of water and filled with a lump of gold, a piece of shell and a poisoned arrow head, which the king had no difficulty in decoding: 'The king said, "The bowl full of water means they are coming at the full moon of the next month. The piece of gold and shell means that Gold Cave and Conch Cave of Dang-ra should be garrisoned in readiness, and the poisoned arrow head means that [the king of Shang-shung] is to be cruelly murdered."'

Armed with this vital intelligence, King Trisong Detsen hid his troops in the two caves and attacked King Ligmigya's convoy as it came through the pass. The Shang-shung king was killed, his mighty army scattered and the power of Shang-shung finally broken.

Whether King Trisong Detsen kept his promise and made King Ligmigya's youngest queen his first wife is not known. What we do know is that the chief wife of the late king was determined to avenge her husband's death by striking back at the Tibetan king – and that to do so she summoned to her aid the greatest Bon master of the age. 'The king who protects Bon is dead,' she declaimed. 'The silken knot of Bon morality is smashed. The golden yoke of government is smashed. The land is going to pieces while the doctrines of eternal Bon are in decline. Since times like these have come upon us, I beg you to perform an evil act.'

The person she turned to was the magician and medicine-man Gyerpung Drenpa Namkha, also known as Lachen ('Great Lama'). Gyerpung (a Shang-shung word meaning 'teacher of Bon', thus the Bon equivalent of the Tibetan word 'lama' and the Sanskrit 'guru'). Drenpa Namkha ('Sky Recollection') is the first Bonpo personage in Tibetan history who can be positively identified as a real rather than mythological figure. He is Bon's main champion in the first round in the Bon–Buddhist struggle, the Bonpo opposite number to Guru Rinpoche, the champion of Chos. He occupies an honoured place in the lower tiers of the Bon pantheon among the lesser deities known as drubtob shen ('priests who have obtained spiritual perfection'), tuwoche ('great magicians'), and the fairy spirits known as khadroma ('skywalkers'). He is usually portrayed holding a swastika staff in his right hand and a skull-cup in his left, but may also be shown in the posture of meditation, his right hand pointing to the earth to signify enlightenment.

According to Bon tradition, Gyerpung Drenpa Namkha was the most powerful of the shens who attended the courts of the Seven Heavenly Kings of Tibet some 800–1,200 years before the reign of King Trisong Detsen. By becoming a master practitioner of Bon ritual he had acquired the power to extend his lifespan over many centuries and so was on hand to become the chief defender of Bon during the bitter struggle between the rival faiths that came to a head in the last decades of the eighth century.

Gyerpung Drenpa Namkha told the widowed queen of Shang-shung that he had the power to raise three kinds of spells: the most powerful could sweep away the whole of Tibet, the less powerful could destroy the king of Tibet and all his court, and the least powerful could kill the king alone. The queen chose the weakest of the three and the magician then set about casting it:

The mystical hidden kingdom of Shambhala, from a
nineteenth-century Mongolian *thanka*. Hidden behind two
ranges of snow-capped mountains, Shambhala is ruled
over by a line of priest-kings.

The Shingardar stupa in the Swat valley on Pakistan's North-West Frontier, formerly known as Uddiyana or Orgyan, which was visited by the Chinese monk Xuanzang in 630 CE. Its distinctive shape characterises Gandharan architecture of the second century CE.

Part of a third-century stucco relief from the base of one of many stupas at the Buddhist complex of Takht-i-Bhai, on Pakistan's North-West Frontier. The supporting figures thought to represent Atlas may well be images of Mithras.

The Tibetan wild ass or *kiang* still roams the Chang Tang or
northern plain in small herds of ten to twenty animals, which
group together when threatened.

For many Tibetan nomads the domesticated ox known as the *yak*
(male) or *dri* (female) is the main source of their wealth and
livelihood. Despite its three layers of hair, it cannot forage in
thick snow and thousands have died in recent winters.

A young *drogpa* or nomad. Most Tibetans in northern and western Tibet still follow a semi-nomadic way of life as pastoralists, grazing their sheep and yak on the steppe, wintering in the valleys and moving to higher pastures in summer.

The most popular Buddhist mantra or incantation, *Om mane padme hom*, is carved not only on *mane* or prayer-stones but also on the skulls of yak – a combination of folk religion and Buddhism characteristic of Tibetan Buddhism.

Storm over the Turquoise Lake: a raven circles a *chorten* or reliquary monument, with its strings of prayer-flags, on the northern shores of Mapham Tso, known to Hindus as Lake Manasarovar.

Tibetan pilgrims making a five-day *kora* or circumambulation around Mapham Tso pause on its southern shore to throw offerings of flour and ceremonial scarves to the elements. The summit of Kangri Rinpoche (Mount Kailas) can be seen in the far distance.

Chinese conscripts fool around in front of the Potala Palace, Lhasa,
home of the Dalai Lama reincarnates of the Gelugpa school and the
seat of Tibet's government from 1645 to 1959, when the present
(Fourteenth) Dalai Lama fled to India.

A living faith: a party of Tibetan pilgrims visiting the monastic
complex of Tashi Lunpo pose for a group photograph with *kadak*
scarves in their hands.

Tibetan visitors to the Jokhang Temple in Lhasa perform a kora around the inner temple. Although not the first Buddhist shrine in Tibet, the Jokhang is Tibet's most sacred temple.

Seventh-century capitals and beams support the ceiling of the
original Jokhang temple in Lhasa, now hidden within the present
larger temple. The earliest carvings and frescoes were the work of
Newar craftsmen from Kathmandu.

Pool table and players at Darchen, the starting-point of the pilgrimage trail around Kangri Rinpoche. How the table was transported here is a mystery.

Hedging bets: a portrait of the Great Helmsman, Chairman Mao, shares space with a drawing of the sacred mountain Kangri Rinpoche chalked on a wall at the monastery of Khoja.

Carrying food and bedding, an elderly couple make their way around the 27-mile circuit of Kangri Rinpoche. Most Tibetans complete the circuit within thirty-six hours.

Pilgrims climb up through snow-covered rocks to reach the 18,700-foot Drolma La, the Pass of the Tara Goddess of Mercy. To complete the circuit with full prostration all the way takes about thirteen days, but confers great spiritual benefits.

Pilgrims drawn from all over Tibet gather by the giant prayer-pole at Tarboche on the morning of Saga Dawa. Although nominally a celebration of Gautama Buddha's enlightenment, the raising of the pole is also connected with shamanist pre-Buddhist rites.

Participants in the Saga Dawa festivities burn incense in the form of juniper twigs under the shadow of the rock platform known as the Cemetery of the Eighty-Four Mahasiddhas, where the dead are brought for sky burial.

Beginning the descent into the Langchen Khambab gorge, where the weathering of the soft clay has transformed the land into a moonscape, making it difficult to distinguish what is man-made and what are natural rock formations.

The fountain-head of Tibetan Buddhism: the assembly hall at Tholing, built by the Great Translator Rinchen Zangpo in the tenth century at the orders of the priest-king Yeshe O of Gu-ge. It was from here that Buddhism spread throughout Tibet.

Part of a frieze in the Lhakang Marpo or Red Chapel, at the citadel of Tsaparang, depicting life in Gu-ge at the time the chapel was built in the late fifteenth century. It shows foreign dignitaries and others celebrating the consecration of the temple in the presence of the priest-king.

All is illusion: a few surviving stucco heads of bodhisattvas are all that remain of many hundreds of statues of every size that lined the walls of the five main chapels at Tsaparang until the Cultural Revolution of 1966–7.

The scarlet demon Tamdrin Dorje guards the left-hand side of the
entrance to the Lhakang Karpo, or White Chapel, at Tsaparang – the
only full-size statue to have survived the Cultural Revolution.

The cave of the eighth-century Bon master Gyerpung Drenpa Namka, built into the cliff above the rebuilt monastery of Gurugem, which guards the entrance to the Garuda Valley.

The present abbot of Gurugem Gompa, Rinpoche Tenzin Wangduk, looks out from the balcony of his cave. He maintains Bon custom as one of Tibet's foremost practitioners of traditional medicine.

The great Gyerpung set up his white tent patterned with deer on the island in the Da-rog lake [Langkak Tso]. He sat on his couch consisting of nine quilts of heavy silk and practised on a dram of gold for seven days. Then he divided up the dram into three parts and at sunset hurled one part at the lake on the side of Mount Yar-lha-sham-po. The lake dried up and the divinities in it fled, which is why it is called the 'Dry Lake of Yarlung'. Then in the middle of the night he hurled a second part which struck seven deer sleeping on Mount Sog-kha-pun-mo. Two died and the others went stiff, which is why it is called the 'Mountain of the Stiff Deer'. Finally, at dawn he hurled the last part, which struck the Tiger Peak Castle of Phying-ba, making the Tibetan king sick.

King Trisong Detsen knew at once why he was sick and who had caused it. Realising that only the great shaman could save him, he sent messengers to bargain with Gyerpung Drenpa Namkha. The magician agreed to help him on four conditions: 'Firstly, you must not suppress the 360 Bon texts of Shang-shung. Secondly, when members of the Gu-rub family [the royal family of Shang-shung] go to Yarlung Sog-kha [in exile] they must be free from religious and state taxes and you must seat them on your right-hand side. Thirdly, for the [dead king] Lord Ligmigya we want a golden shrine for his body marked with a large swastika. And fourthly, we want full restitution for his loss.'

The king's envoys readily agreed to these terms, so the magician then went to Lhasa to perform the rites which would undo his magic and restore the king's health:

He drew out from the nine apertures of the king's body threads of gold like tangled cotton threads which, when they were weighed, came to just one-third of a dram. He then extracted black blood and matter and pus and so relieved the sickness. The king was very grateful and did not suppress the Bon texts

of Shang-shung. He gave the land of Yarlung Sog-kha to the
Gu-rub family and sent the queen whatever was needed to
build the late king's shrine, as well as gifts in restitution.

However fanciful, this account (taken from David Snellgrove's *Nine Ways of Bon*) of the fall of Shang-shung and the
role played by Gyerpung Drenpa Namkha in securing conces-
sions from the Tibetan king suggests that the Bon religion
continued to be freely practised in Shang-shung even though its
royal family was ousted and the country reduced to the status of
an outlying province of Tibet. The territory was renamed Ngari
Khorsum and was divided into a number of regions: the north-
west became the districts of Ladakh and Rudok; the eastern
region, Sharyul; the southern regions, Gu-ge and Purang.

One man's hero is another's villain, and so it is with King
Trisong Detsen. In popular Tibetan history he is portrayed as a
devout Buddhist and an incarnation of Manjusri, bodhisattva of
wisdom. In Bon history he is vilified as a coward who had turned
to Buddhism because he hoped its priests could prolong his life
and only after being told by them that the Bonpo were conspir-
ing to take over his throne.

What both sides agree on is that Trisong Detsen was respon-
sible for opening the doors of Tibet to the Dharma: 'As soon as
the king came of age, he invited the Indian sage Santa Rakshita
and Pandit Padma Sambhava to fill the whole country of Tibet
with the blessings of the Buddhist religion.' The first to come
was the sage Shantirakshita of Zahor, abbot of Vikramashila
monastery in Bengal, whose arrival aroused enormous hostility
from the king's ministers. Attempts were made by the Bonpo in
Lhasa to remove the Jobo Rinpoche image from the Jokhang
temple and return it to China. This had to be abandoned, so the
Buddhist texts tell us, when 300 men were unable to lift the five-
foot statue. So they buried the image instead and for a while the
temple courtyard was turned into a slaughterhouse where livestock were brought to be killed.

This period of struggle between the two rival religions is symbolised in the Buddhist account of the building of Samye, Tibet's first Buddhist monastery. Work was started under Shantirakshita in the year 762 but made little progress because whatever was built during the day was torn down by male-volent spirits during the following night. Eventually, Shanti-rakshita had to accept that he was no match for the powerful demons of Tibet and sent for the most powerful tantric yogi of the age, Pandit Padmasambhava of Uddiyana, a grand master of the Vajrayana tantric school. Using his formidable yogic powers, the great wizard subdued and won over the evil spirits. Building recommenced and the 'glorious inconceivable temple of unchanging spontaneous presence' was completed in 775. Once again, Buddhism was proclaimed the official religion of Tibet.

Far better known in Tibet as Guru Rinpoche or Precious Teacher, Padmasambhava is revered as a great dharma or practitioner of the Law of Buddha. He is the St Patrick of Tibet, the thunderbolt-wielding chief saint of tantricism, vanquisher and converter to the faith of the enemies of Chos. His omni-science is demonstrated in the way his name is linked with power-points throughout Tibet. After completing the building of Samye, the great guru travelled to every corner of Tibet to win over the demon spirits. In this way every part of Tibet has its associations with the great shaman: tunnels and clefts which he dug to drain lakes; rocks moved or hurled by him; indenta-tions where he stamped his hands or feet; caves within which he meditated. Whether he actually visited these sites or not is immaterial; if the guru himself didn't go there then one of his emanations in the form of reincarnate tulkus certainly did.

Guru Rinpoche is credited with laying the foundations of the Sangha – the Buddhist monastic system, with its disciplined communities of monks and the systematic teaching that goes with it – which later transformed the human landscape of the country. The institution of the Sangha is what made possible

Padmasambhava, the 'lotus-born' tantric master from Uddiyana, better known to Tibetans as Guru Rinpoche, the 'blessed teacher'. In his right hand he holds the *vajra* or 'diamond thunderbolt' which in Buddhism signifies the unity which underlies duality.

the spread of the Dharma in Tibet but there is no evidence that it was laid by Guru Rinpoche or anyone else in the eighth century. What is more likely is that the guru gathered a number of disciples about him and initiated them into the esoteric secrets of the Vajrayana or Adamantine Vehicle. This became the foundation of the Nyingmapa school, the 'ancient tradition of early translations', the oldest of Tibet's many Buddhist monastic traditions. Many of its teachings would come to be regarded by the later mainstream schools of Chos as heretical, while the

Bonpo would always maintain that these same ideas were taken from the Bon canon.

At some stage in the Bon–Buddhist confrontation, Guru Rinpoche and Guru Shantirakshita took on their opponents in a face-to-face debate in front of the king, with the king's patronage as the prize. This was a disaster for the Bonpo who, even by their own account, made fools of themselves – despite the attendance of their chief guru Gyerpung Drenpa Namkha. Both sides record that at the conclusion of the debate King Trisong Detsen converted to Buddhism, and that Gyerpung Drenpa Namkha joined the king: he cut off the long hair that was the mark of the Bonpo shen and, to the disgust of the assembled Buddhist clergy, then ordained himself a Buddhist monk. He justified his action by asserting that Bon and Buddhism were different only in terms of relative truth.

It may well be that in the aftermath of the great debate the Bonpo were presented with a stark choice: conversion or exile. Also present at the débâcle was a second great Bon master, Gyerpung Lishu Taring of Samye, who had made a number of journeys to Shang-shung and Tajik to collect sacred texts and translate them into Tibetan. Unlike Gyerpung Drenpa Namkha, Lishu Taring refused to convert to Buddhism and went into exile. However, before he left Lhasa he placed a curse on King Trisong Detsen and prophesied the ruin of his dynasty:

May the king be a village beggar
And his ministers be shepherds.
May the land of Tibet break into pieces
And these Buddhist monks lose their dharma.
May these nuns bear children
And these Buddhist priests lead quarrelling gangs.
May their monasteries be filled with disputes
And their temples set on fire.
O may my curse be effective
And may these books of mine be found by someone worthy.

The last line of the curse refers to the Tibetan tradition of con-cealing terma ('hidden treasures') to be rediscovered in later centuries by terton ('treasure-finders') at some appropriate time. The Buddhists claim this practice was started by none other than Guru Rinpoche. The Bonpo say it was begun by *their* champion, Gyerpung Drenpa Namkha, which is far more likely because King Trisong Detsen's conversion was followed by determined efforts to stamp out Bon teachings and so the Bonpo had every reason to conceal their sacred literature. Large numbers of Bonpo fled from the Tibetan heartland and no doubt many more followed Gyerpung Drenpa Namkha's exam-ple and publicly embraced Buddhism in the hope of better days to come.

The Bonpo claim that the great bulk of the texts brought together in the fourteenth century to form the Bonpo *Kanjur*, the central canon of their faith, are drawn from earlier Bon texts written in the language of Shang-shung, texts which were hidden by Drenpa Namkha, Lishu Taring and others in ceme-teries and caves, and in the walls and pillars of their temples all over Tibet. The Bonpo further claim that many of the texts sup-posedly hidden as terma by Guru Rinpoche in the late eighth century and discovered in later centuries by Buddhist terton are in fact theirs.

The curse laid on Tibet by Gyerpung Lishu Taring could be said to have taken effect in the year 841when the grandson of King Trisong Detsen's grandson either slipped on the steps of a temple, died of an illness or was murdered by his ministers with the support of his brother, Lang Darma. Whatever the exact circumstances, Lang Darma gained the throne of Tibet, rein-stated Bon as the national religion and initiated a brief reign of terror against Buddhists which saw the settlement of many old scores. Leading Buddhist figures were executed and the monks forced into trades that required them to violate their oaths: 'All those who did not wish to give up the distinctive marks of monkhood, he ordered to take bows, arrows, drums and tambourines, and sent them to transact the business of hunters. Those who disobeyed were put to death.'

Within less than a year, however, Lang Darma's reign was brought to an end in a spectacular manner that mirrored the assassination of King Drigum Tsanpo many centuries earlier. This time it was a Buddhist lama – the ninth abbot of Samye monastery – who did the killing, and to this day Lhalung Pelgyi Dorje is still celebrated as a 'holy murderer', while his killing of the 'demon king' is commemorated in the Black Hat dances performed by the monks of every Buddhist monastery in Tibet, Nepal, Ladakh, Bhutan and India as part of their New Year's Day festivities.

Lang Darma's death led to civil war. The Tibetan empire fell apart as various contenders fought for power. In the northwest the Qarluk Turks moved in to take over the Tibetan-controlled Silk Road oases while in the east Uighur Turks seized control of Amdo. A dark age descended on Tibet which lasted for 146 years.

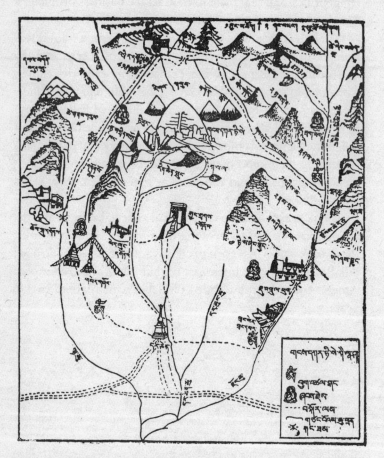

Tibetan pilgrimage map of the Kangri Rinpoche kora (Mount Kailas parikarama), with the holy mountain at the centre. The circuit starts at Darchen to the south (indicated by a chorten) then proceeds clockwise via the giant flagpole at Tarboche to Chuku Gompa on the west, then north up the Lha Chhu valley to Drira Phuk Gompa. The route then climbs over the Dolma La on the north-east shoulder of the mountain before dropping down to the Zhong Chhu and Zutrul Phuk Gompa on the east side. The central monastery of Gyang Drak marks the gateway to the inner kora, which only adepts who have completed thirteen circuits of the holy mountain may enter.

5 The Kingdom of Prester John

Where holy men dwell are places of joy. They make delightful the wild places where others cannot dwell. Because they have not that burden of desires they have that joy that others cannot find.

From the Dhammapada

EARLY JUNE 1996

One of the many remarkable natural features of the Precious Snow Mountain is that it is cut off from the rest of the Kangri Ti-se range by two deep slashes to west and east: the V-shaped valleys of the Lha Chhu and Zong Chhu. The valley of the Lha Chhu is the gateway to the Precious Snow Mountain. It must have been scoured out by a glacier during the last ice age, leaving towering black, ochre and green cliffs on either side. One hour's walk north of Tarboche is Chhuku Gompa, the first of the four monasteries that lie on the west, north, east and south sides of the mountain. It perches on the cliff face a few hundred feet above the right bank of the river, still too far for me but an easy climb for the others. The single Kagyupa monk in residence has good reason to forbid photography. Until very recently this little monastery had a magnificent collection of ancient statues which included a small white marble figure known as the Chosku Rinpoche, a representation of Amitabha said to have been brought from Lahoul in India in the eleventh century – one of those ancient statues whose true origins are shrouded in mystery and may not be quite what they seem. In 1991 the monastery was raided by a gang of thieves and sixteen statues were removed, stolen to order, so it is said, for Westerners who had come here a year earlier and photographed all the treasures in the gompa.

Dick reports back that, so far as he can judge, the Chosku Rinpoche is still there but so swathed in scarves as to be hidden from sight.

Every feature on this trail, natural or man-made, is wrapped about in religious associations requiring the dutiful pilgrim to pause and perform rituals. As might be expected, many are linked to Guru Rinpoche. On the hillside below Chhuku Gompa is the Elephant Secret Cave where Guru Rinpoche hid one of his many terma. I scour the slope through my binoculars but can see no such cave. This could be because it is too secret to be visible or because it was covered by a big rock fall that flattened the monastery a century ago.

The monastery is also the site of round two of the struggle between the Chos saint Milarepa and the Bon priest Naro Bon Chung. Milarepa began to circle the mountain in the orthodox clockwise direction but then saw his rival setting off in the Bon counter-clockwise direction. He caught him just as he was about to enter the Zong Chhu valley east of Kangri Rinpoche.

'You must follow the Bon way of circling the mountain,' cried Naro Bon Chung, seizing the yogi by the hand and dragging him up the valley behind him.

'I will not follow the wrong path,' retorted Milarepa. 'It is better that you should follow me and adopt the Buddhist way.'

He then pulled his rival in the opposite direction and, due to his superior magic, dragged him round to the western valley, Lha Chhu. Naro Bon Chung then retired to meditate in his cave at the Cemetery of the Eighty-Four Mahasiddhas, while Milarepa walked on up the valley as far as the Secret Elephant Cave. Here he stretched one leg right across the valley until his foot was in front of the Bon priest's cave and challenged him to do the same.

Naro Bon Chung could stretch his leg no further than the river and so round two also went to the Buddhist. However, the Bonpo still refused to accept defeat and resumed his counter-clockwise kora.

I want to camp on the right bank of the river upstream of the monastery for no better reason than that the great Sven Hedin camped there ninety years ago. But Sonam seems determined on the other side of the river and when we ignore his advice he goes into an almighty sulk, throwing himself down on the ground with his baseball cap over his face. He lies there while the tents are being put up and he's still lying there when everyone else is having supper. Only when it's dark and freezing does he rouse himself and pitch his tent well away from the rest of us.

Day two of the kora should be the easiest: half a day's walk up the valley. The walls of the valley here are quite astonishing in their diversity of form and colour. On our left as we walk north are a series of peaks divided by tumbling streams and waterfalls. The central three are like the flying buttresses of some gigantic cathedral and are the abodes of the three Buddhist goddesses of longevity: Drolma, Tsepame and Nyamgyalma. Opposite them, on the right side of the valley, the western flanks of Kangri Rinpoche provide an even more dramatic spectacle. The lower sections appear smooth, warm and pink-grey like the skin of an elephant and are divided into a series of spurs that also resemble the supports of monster cathedrals. At the top they drop back to form a sort of throne of the gods. Higher still, snow from the summit bubbles over like the froth on an over-filled tankard of beer.

There is no hard climbing here, merely a gentle incline, but I have to keep stopping to recover breath and strength, and I soon get left behind. During one such rest break I watch a herd of blue sheep pick its way cautiously across the lower slopes of the scree, no more than sixty yards away. Just as I'm pondering on why these shy creatures should choose to come down so low and so close to man I spot what looks like a tail sticking out from behind a small boulder. At the other end of this rock I can see the head of what must be the same animal. If I am not mistaken, what is lurking there, waiting in ambush for the blue sheep, is that rarest of all carnivores, the snow leopard! Very, very slowly I reach across my chest for my binoculars and bring them up to my eyes (or rather, my one good eye). I focus, find the boulder – and there at one end is indeed a short fluffy tail. Then pan right to the other end – and there, instead of the face of *panthera uncia*, I am confronted by the backside of a great fat marmot. What I am seeing is two marmots, both as large as badgers, going about their business of nibbling roots and shoots. Another time, perhaps.

The bird books say that the lammergeier is a scavenger and not a bird of prey. Not so, because I watch one of these magnificent birds come skimming low down the valley like a Tornado GR1 on a low-level reconnaissance run. It passes so close that I can hear its feathers buzzing, with its undercarriage down and talons outstretched ready to snatch up an unwary marmot or pika.

An hour or so further on the valley divides. The trail crosses the main stream, which has disappeared under several large patches of hardened snow, and turns to the right. The going gets a bit harder and my stops more frequent and longer. I see a figure hunched beside the path ahead of me: Terry. He has a splitting headache and nausea and doesn't think he can go any further. We sip from our thermos flasks, suck a couple of boiled sweets and think the unthinkable: perhaps we should turn back. It would be so easy now just to head back down the valley to Darchen and wait there for the others. It would be the unselfish thing to do because we wouldn't be holding them up.

This unholy debate is ended by the arrival of Mel, bouncing

like Tigger. How we hate him for being so fit. Then back comes Bagbir, too, waving a thermos flask. He pours us out two mugs of sweet tea and hands round some biscuits. When we've drunk and eaten he hoists up my pack and adds it to his own. He says nothing, only smiles. Impossible to refuse such a man.

The last hour is a daymare. I am only dimly aware of the stupendous sheet of rock and ice which has been coming into view just to our right as we slowly turn the corner of the massif: the sheer north face of the Nine Stacked Swastikas Mountain. Overpowering. Awesome. As dark as the south face is light. Breathtaking, if I had any breath left to take.

We camp tonight in the guest house below the monastery of Drira-Phuk, the Cave of the Female Yak, at an altitude of about 16,000 feet. This is the northernmost of our four staging posts round the mountain, a simple whitewashed building built over the cave which gives it its name. A Kagyupa lama named Gyalba Gotshangpa is credited with being the first to make a kora of the holy mountain in the early thirteenth century. During that pioneering first circuit he stopped here for a brew-up and collected several small stones to form supports for his kettle. To his surprise all were inscribed with mantras. Then it began to sleet and, as he looked for shelter, a dakini in the form of a female yak, a dri, appeared and led him to a cave.

We were supposed to have had our own yak for this stage of our journey, to carry our baggage. Sonam claims that none are available because so many died in the terrible snowstorms that devastated Tibet's nomadic community in the late autumn. He may well be telling the truth. In their place Sonam has managed to recruit nine young Gelugpa monks, here on pilgrimage. They are fit, strong and full of high spirits but they have only their maroon togas to keep them warm at night. While we shiver inside the guest house in our thermal underwear and down-filled sleeping bags, they lie outside, huddled up together round a small fire, taking it in turns to keep a flame going all night. It is the wind that chills, not the low temperature.

It's very plain that the three fifty-and-overs – that's myself, Terry and Dick – aren't up to completing the next stage of the kora, from here all the way to Zutrul Phuk Gompa, in one day. So we give ourselves an easy half-day instead and make camp above the moraines at the base of the final snow staircase that leads up to the 18,600-foot Drolma La. On the way we pass through an area that looks like a municipal dump. This is Siwatshal Dutro, regarded by many as the most important power-point on the circuit. Every pilgrim makes an offering here in the form of some personal item which can be as basic as some drops of blood or a hank of hair. Articles of clothing seem to be the popular choice because the entire area is strewn with ragged bits of cloth, including numerous hats. The site takes its name after a famous cremation ground near Bodh Gaya in India and the act of leaving some personal item symbolises a renunciation of all worldly goods. What takes place here is a ritual death in preparation for the rebirth which follows once the pilgrim has attained the high point of the circuit at the Drolma La. We are rather spoiling the process by camping overnight midway between these two stages, a night in a state of purgatory, as it were.

My left eye is now pain-free. For the first time since crossing into Tibet I can take full bifocal account of our surroundings. An almost unbroken stream of pilgrims passes our tent for much of the afternoon: pilgrims of all ages and from every social level, from sun-blacked shepherds in animal skins to the privileged few who sport Western trophies such as shades and parkas. A few stop to stare at our outlandish bulbous tents but for the most part they are preoccupied in their own thoughts. They trudge forward in silence or murmuring prayers, left hands working prayer beads, right hands turning prayer wheels. A mile ahead of us the trail cuts a steep diagonal across the mountainside, the pilgrims silhouetted against the snow like a line of pinpricks on white paper.

This route leading up and over the shoulder of the holy

mountain was revealed to Lama Gotshangpa by twenty-one Taras (in Tibetan, Drolma), who appeared in the form of wolves: 'He followed them and so walked to the summit of the pass where he saw them merge one into another until only one remained, which then vanished into a boulder. Ever since then the name of that pass has been famous as the Drolma La.'

At something over 17,500 feet, this camp is the highest that the three oldies of our party are ever likely to experience. I earnestly hope so. Five of us bed down early in the afternoon to keep warm but Mel and Binod scamper up the nearest peak and return full of sickening joie de vivre. Early supper at 6 p.m. and all tucked up in our sleeping bags by 7 p.m.

The first note in my diary for the following day reads: 'Night too frightful to recall.' Not so. I can vividly remember a night of fitful sleep racked by short, sharp nightmares dreamed up by a brain starved of oxygen. Double doses of Panadol do nothing to alleviate the headache. The wind tugs and bangs on the tent in sudden, irregular bursts. At midnight Dick decides that he has to have more air and unzips the opening. The temperature plummets. I am already wearing every available stitch of clothing; even so, my feet and my buttocks slowly harden into blocks of ice, as does that tiny part of my nose which is still directly exposed to the open air. Sleep is out of the question. I lie shaking, trying to think of things to think about – not easy when one's brain is only just ticking over – and listening to Dick's irregular breathing. This is alarming. His lungs attempt to draw in more air by taking deeper and quicker breaths that build up over two minutes or so into a crescendo of snorts culminating in one great gurgling gasp. At last the lungs have enough air, so they switch off and Dick stops breathing altogether. There is a medical name for this condition which I know perfectly well but I cannot for the life of me remember what it is, nor how life-threatening it is or is not. For what seems like an eternity I wait anxiously for signs of continued life. Then his lungs splutter into action again, and the cycle is renewed. Even so, there are a number of times when I have to sit up, lean over him and expose an ear to check that he really is still alive. This is not as easy as it sounds because the simple act of raising oneself on to one's elbows and twisting the upper part of the trunk leaves one panting.

By about four o'clock in the morning I've had enough. I wriggle over to the flap of the tent and very, very slowly, inch by inch, zip it up again. I defrost and fall asleep. Thirty seconds later Muhun is unzipping the tent with a cup of tea in his hand.

Up and dressed at six, stamping about in my boots to get the circulation going again. The monks are still sleeping. Again they have slept out in the open air but this time without a fire. They have piled themselves together into a heap like puppy dogs and lie completely covered by their red togas. However, it has snowed during the night so now they are half-hidden under a thin film of snow. It's hard to believe that they could survive under such conditions and, indeed, when they start to emerge, they look pretty rough. They hadn't expected this extra night on the bare mountain and their smiles are a little strained.

The blessed sun reaches us at seven and by eight we've joined the pilgrims who are already on the trail. The snow is crisp underfoot. Despite the stiff climb an overwhelming sense of happiness affects us all. Whatever our motives, every one of us climbing this staircase has had to work hard to get here. This is the culmination of days and weeks and even years. And now, for all the physical pain that we're still going through, we *know* we're going to make it. Our worries are behind us. I stop frequently to regain my breath, to ease the frantic pumping of my heart, and these moments are often shared with elderly Tibetans. We laugh at each other as we ease our loads off our backs. We mop our brows and shake our heads in shared discomfort. Then we pull on our loads, look up at the dazzling snow above us and push on. This is a shared communion, this last thousand feet.

About two-thirds of the way up the strangest thing happens. I've heard of climbers becoming aware of invisible companions at their side and now it happens to me. I have the strongest sense of someone at my left shoulder, just out of sight, walking slightly behind and above me, higher on the slope. I can even hear his boots crunching in the snow. Several times I stop and turn, expecting to see someone overhauling me on my left, but there's no one there. The conviction grows in me that it is my father. He and I had been planning a last great adventure in the mountains together shortly before his death. As a political officer in the Indian Political Service in the late 1940s and early 1950s he had spent months touring in the foothills of the eastern Himalayas as part of his job, but had never achieved his ambition of entering Tibet. Now I feel his presence at my side, silently urging me on. This is so very real that I turn and smile and lift my ice-axe in salute to him, because I want him to know that I know he's with me.

Then from far above, faintly at first, the shouts of those who have already reached the top. Now our turn approaches. The blue sky grows above the snow. A first glimpse of brightly coloured prayer flags flapping in the wind. Then more blue sky and more prayer flags, long strings of them stretching out to left and right. Another dozen steps and a big flag-covered boulder rises in front of us. The tiredness is gone. We run forward and duck under a tangled mass of flags, emerging on the other side with shouts of 'Lha-so-so! Lha-so-so!' We have left behind our old lives and are reborn. We are starting again with clean slates. Laughter fills the sky. We have come through. Our perspectives have changed: we are no longer looking up but down on the world. Hugs all round.

This is where I promised to leave Sandra's rosary, which I have carried wrapped around my ice-axe. I know now that I must leave something for my father, too, so the rosary and ice-axe stay together and are buried under a small cairn of stones. This too is a great place for leaving personal objects and all of us leave something behind here: Dick leaves a photo of his wife and another one of his recently deceased cat. It is also the custom to take something as a personal memento. I choose a string of prayer flags and leave behind some new ones, which Mel helps me erect on the highest point I can reach.

Within ten minutes of our arriving at the Drolma La the weather has changed dramatically for the worse. Clouds descend, hiding the summit and the surrounding peaks from view, and it begins to snow. The wind begins to bite.

We start the descent in a hurry, knowing we have miles to go before we sleep. We scurry past the famous frozen lake just below the pass, said to be one of the highest in the world, scarcely giving it a glance. My elation at having reached the Drolma La is replaced by an overwhelming melancholy. I know this is physically induced: the effort of keeping myself going over the last two days is taking its toll.

Warm soup, shelter from the wind and kind words are waiting for me when I reach the floor of the Lham Chhu valley. After lunch we push on again. The high spot of the afternoon is the singing of a party of young Tibetan women who overtake our party and keep pace with us for a short time. They exchange plaintive songs and occasionally join together in delightful harmony as they walk. I spoil it all with my rendering of Viktor's Farewell from the White Horse Inn. This reduces them to shocked silence and they quickly scamper ahead.

By three o'clock I'm done for again. Binod and Bagbir support me the rest of the way till we reach the rest house below Zutrul Phuk Gompa.

We have now come to the eastern 'door' of the holy mountain, although its east face cannot be seen from the monastery. Zutrul Phuk means 'Magical Powers Cave' and takes its name from a little cave over which the monastery temple is built. The most striking feature of this cave is a large capstone with dents on its underside said to have been made by Jetsun Milarepa's head and shoulders. Both sides of the valley round about are riddled with caves which for centuries have provided shelter for Bon, Buddhist and Hindu yogis, so there is every reason to suppose that

Milarepa did indeed meditate here. However, its real significance for Buddhists is that it is the scene of the penultimate stage of the magical contest between Milarepa and his Bon rival.

The two had just met on this spot when it began to rain, so they decided to build a shelter: Milarepa would lay the foundations and floor while Naro Bon Chung raised the walls and the roof. What happened next is nicely put in a guide book entitled *Ti Se Gnas Bshad* ('The Crystal Mirror'), compiled by a lama at the end of the nineteenth century:

> Bon Chung split some stones using his magical powers but the Master cut these stones through the middle using a powerful yogic stare. Bon Chung also attempted a yogic stare but was unable to perform it properly, so he was stuck with his eyes bulging out, unable to release himself. Seeing this, the Master released him and then went on to build the stone wall himself. At his command, a large flat stone positioned itself as the roof. Saying to himself, 'Too low,' he used his head to raise it higher and so left an imprint of his head on the stone. Then saying, 'Too high,' he pushed it down with his feet and so left his footprints on it.

The Bon priest now had to admit that his powers were inferior to those of Milarepa, but he still refused to relinquish his position as lord of the holy mountain. He asked for one final contest, to take place on the morning of the full moon in the next month: 'On the fifteenth day of this month we will have a race to see who can reach the summit of the Ti-se Mountain first. Whoever wins will be recognised as the landlord of the mountain.'

Very early on the morning of the full moon Naro Bon Chung was seen by Milarepa's disciples flying through the sky towards the Precious Snow Mountain. He was dressed in a green cloak, playing on a thighbone trumpet and sitting astride his shamanistic drum. Milerapa, meanwhile, was still fast asleep. His disciples woke him up but he assured them that there was no hurry. They then urged him again to take some action, so he made a sign towards the Bonpo which prevented him from rising any higher. The best that Naro Bon Chung could do was to circle round and round the mountain on his magic drum.

As soon as the sun appeared over the horizon, Milarepa snapped his fingers and in a trice was standing on top of the Precious Snow Mountain, reaching it just as the sunlight hit the summit. 'There Jetsun beheld the Gurus of the Transmission, and the tutelary deities,' says the text of *The Hundred Thousand Songs of Milarepa*:

> Buddha Demchog and his retinues all appeared, rejoicing before him . . . Meanwhile, Naro Bon Chung had reached the neck of the mountain. When he saw the Jetsun, lofty and com-passionate, sitting at ease on the summit, he was dumbfounded and fell down from the heights, his riding drum rolling down the southern slope of Ti-se. As his pride and arrogance were now utterly subdued, he humbly cried to Milarepa, 'Your power and miracle-working are indeed superior to mine! Now you are the master of Ti-se. I will leave but go to a place from where I can still see Ti-se Snow Mountain.'

So Naro Bon Chung was driven off the Nine Stacked Swastikas Mountain of Bon and it became the Buddhist Precious Snow Mountain, presided over by Korlo Demchog, the four-faced and twelve-armed wrathful manifestation of the Gautama Shakyamuni Buddha, usually portrayed in yab-yum union with his consort Vajravarahi. But by way of a consolation prize, Naro Bon Chung was allowed to take up residence on a small moun-tain peak just to the east of the Precious Snow Mountain.

Two hours walking south of Zutrul Phuk Gompa brings us out once more on to the Barkha plain. There's a delightful little meadow beside the river tucked out of the wind where we lie on the grass and enjoy a leisurely picnic lunch in the sun. Although we've dropped to about 14,500 feet the view south across the plain is still a feast to the eye. Gurla Mandhata, which the Tibetans call Memo Nanri, is due south. Even at a distance of forty miles its elongated white hump – like a great white Brahmin bull – dominates the skyline. The turquoise lake at its foot matches its epithet. The infant Sutlej draws water from the stream at our feet, as well as from the Lha Chhu and perhaps half a dozen other water courses that drain the southern slopes of the Kangri Ti-se range. It meanders out of our sight across the prairie towards the north-west.

About fifty miles away to the west we can just see the start of the mountain range that bring the Sutlej river up short just past Tirthapuri and turns it towards the west. Somewhere among those brown hills is the Valley of the Garuda.

That is where we should be going now if my illness and other delays had not lost us five precious days. But we all have families, friends, jobs and promises to keep, so we have no option but to head back to Kathmandu the way we came.

I have resolved nothing. I know I shall have to come back.

In about the middle of the third quarter of the twelfth century CE a curious round of letters arrived at the courts of Europe: epistles addressed to Pope Alexander III, the emperors of Byzantium and Rome, the kings of France and Portugal. They purported to come from a Christian ruler in the East who styled himself 'Presbyter Johannes, Lord of Lords'.

In his letter to the Emperor of Constantinople (later set down in the chronicle of Albericus Trium Fontium in 1241, who stated that it was penned in the year 1165), Prester John describes himself as enthroned in majesty in a magnificent multi-storey palace whose topmost floors can only be reached by way of a grand spiral stairway. His palace is set high on a great mountain and enclosed by a park which resembles the Garden of Eden, with a tree of paradise whose fruits satisfy hunger and thirst and provide heat for both body and soul. He himself surpasses all under heaven in virtue, riches and power:

> In the three Indies our Magnificence rules, and our land extends beyond India, where rests the body of the holy apostle Thomas. It reaches towards the sunrise over the wastes, and it trends towards deserted Babylon near the tower of Babel. Seventy-two provinces, of which few are Christian, serve us . . . Seven kings wait upon us monthly, in turn, with sixty-two dukes and 256 counts and marquises. Twelve archbishops sit at table with us on our right and twenty bishops on the left . . . When we go to war we have fourteen golden and bejewelled crosses borne before us instead of banners. Each of these crosses is followed by 10,000 horsemen and 100,000 foot soldiers fully armed . . . All riches such as are upon the world our magnificence possesses in superabundance.

Prester John's grandiloquent epistle then goes on to list some of the wondrous beasts and types of humanity to be found in his kingdom:

> Our land is the home of elephants, dromedaries, camels, crocodiles, metacollinarum, cametannus, tensevetes, wild asses, white and red lions, white bears, white merules, crickets, griffins, tigers, lamias, hyenas, wild horses, wild oxen and wild men: men with horns, one-eyed men, men with eyes before and behind, centaurs, fauns, satyrs, pygmies, forty-ell-high giants, cyclopses and similar women . . . We have some people subject to us who feed on the flesh of men and of prematurely born animals, and who never fear death . . . Gog and Magog, Anie, Agit, Azenach, Fommeperi, Befari, Conei-Samante, Agrimandri, Vintefolei, Casbei, Alanei. These and similar nations were shut in behind lofty mountains by Alexander the

Great, towards the north. We lead them at our pleasure against our foes, and neither man nor beast is left undevoured, if our Majesty gives the requisite permission.

The geography of Prester John's kingdom is just as exotic as its inhabitants:

Our land streams with honey and is overflowing with milk . . . Among the heathen, flows through a certain province the river Indus; encircling Paradise, it spreads its arms in manifold windings through the entire province. Here are to be found the emeralds, sapphires, carbuncles, topazes, chrysolites, onyxes, beryls, sardius and other costly stones . . . At the foot of Mount Olympus bubbles up a spring which changes its flavour hour by hour, night and day, and the spring is scarcely three days' journey from Paradise, out of which Adam was driven. If anyone has tasted thrice of the fountain, from that day he will feel no fatigue but will, as long as he lives, be a man of thirty years . . . In our territory is a certain waterless sea, consisting of tumbling billows of sand never at rest . . . Three days' journey from this sea are mountains from which rolls down a stony, waterless river, which opens into the sea . . . Between the sandy sea and the said mountains is a certain fountain of singular virtue, which purges Christians and would-be Christians from all transgressions.

The priest-king's epistle concludes with some heavy-handed threats that Prester John would overrun western Europe with his man-eating hordes:

These accursed fifteen nations [of Gog, Magog, etc.] will burst forth from the four quarters of the earth at the end of the world, in the times of Antichrist, and overrun all the abodes of the saints as well as the great city Rome which, by the way, we are prepared to give to our son who will be born, along with

all Italy, Germany, the two Gauls, Britain and Scotland. We
shall also give him Spain and all the land as far as the icy sea.
The nations to which I have alluded, according to the words of
the prophet, shall not stand in the judgement, on account of
their offensive practices, but will be consumed to ashes by a
fire which will fall on them from heaven.

What the crowned heads of Europe made of this extraordinary letter and its threats is not recorded, but it seems that no
reply was sent until after Emperor Manuel of Byzantium had
suffered a catastrophic defeat in battle at the hands of a Turkish
sultan in 1176. In September of the following year Pope
Alexander III sent off a letter seeking an alliance with Prester
John in order to repel the advance of Islam into Western
Europe, while making it quite plain that only the See of Rome
could claim universal dominion and that the recipient would do
well to submit himself to the Roman pontiff. This letter was
entrusted to the pope's physician, Philip, who crossed the border
of the Byzantine Empire into western Tartary – and was never
heard of again.

Nor was any further word received from Emperor Prester
John.

The identity of this bellicose Presbyter and why he wrote his
letter remain mysteries to this day. At the end of the fifteenth
century Portuguese missionaries claimed to have traced the mystery to its source – among the Christian Emperors of Abyssinia.
But this was only for want of a better candidate for, as his letter
makes clear, Prester John's hidden kingdom was located not in
Africa but in Asia.

But where in Asia?

Prester John's fantastical geography, with its references to
palaces set in orchards, trees of paradise, lifegiving springs, sin-
redeeming fountains and waterless seas, offers few clues. The
reference to Gog and Magog and other tribes shut out by
Alexander the Great can be linked to mediaeval European and

Arab beliefs that the Great Wall of China had been built by Alexander the Great to protect the civilised world from the barbarous tribes of central Asia. The references to a 'waterless sea, consisting of tumbling billows of sand never at rest' and 'a stony, waterless river, which opens into the sea' suggest knowledge of the great desert basins of inner Asia, of which the largest is the Taklamakan.

The Taklamakan, which derives its name from the Turkic and means (with some licence) 'once you enter, you never return', lies in a vast basin to the north and west of the Tibetan plateau. Its 'tumbling billows of sand' have long been the greatest natural obstacle to travellers moving along the east—west trade trails which we know as the Silk Road. Seasonal streams wash alluvial sand down from the mountains into its wastes and are themselves then swallowed by sand. This 'sandy sea' then drains by way of the Tarim river into Lop Nor, a once significant waterbed now shrunk to an archipelago of salt-crusted marshes whose waters evaporate in the summer months.

Two thousand years ago enough precipitation occured to sustain human settlements which served as caravan stops along its fringes. A prolonged wet period extending from about the second to the fourth centuries CE greatly eased the burdens of travellers and facilitated the expansion of trade links. Towns and even cities grew and flourished, tucked away in sheltered valleys, becoming repositories of religious art that reflected the different beliefs of the travellers who passed through. Then from about the fifth century onwards a dry phase began which more or less coincided with a period of political upheavals. Trade dwindled and the caravanserai became isolated. Many were abandoned to the advancing sands.

Among the many travellers who passed through the staging posts of the Taklamakan towards the end of its wet phase were followers of the Nestorian Church.

The Nestorians were members of a breakaway sect of the early Christian Church whose teachings were denounced as heretical at the Council of Ephesus in 428 CE, partly for political reasons but also because of its founder's insistence on the essential manhood of Christ. These teachings took firm root in Syria in the fourth century and quickly spread eastwards through Persia and beyond. Merv, Sistan, Samarkand and Herat all became important Nestorian centres and although Arab conquests in Asia Minor in the seventh century destroyed its base, the movement continued to spread eastwards. A Christian king is known to have ruled over Kashgar at the start of the eighth century and Chinese records speak of a Nestorian priest from Syria named Alopen arriving in Xian, the first Chinese capital, in 635 CE. Two surviving letters written by Patriarch Timothy I, head of the Nestorian church of Chaldea between 780 and 823, refer to Nestorian teachings being followed and metropolitans being appointed for the lands of Turkaye (Turkestan) and Tuptaye, the Syrian word for Tibet.

Supporting evidence in the form of Christian documents written in Syrian, Sogdian, Turkic and Chinese has been found at a number of sites along the Silk Road: from Bulayiq and Sui-pang near Turfan and from Tun-huang, on the edge of the Gobi desert west of Lop Nor. Although mostly fragmentary, enough text survives in these manuscripts to reveal the Christian faith being expounded in Buddhist terms – almost to the point of losing its Christian identity. Further evidence of Nestorian activity can be found among the huge haul of texts and scrolls taken from the famous walled-up library in the Caves of the Thousand Buddhas near Tun-huang by Sir Aurel Stein in 1907. These include texts written in Tibetan during the period between about 781 and 848 when Tun-huang came under Tibetan rule. A number have a Christian content, most notably a book on divination which contains the following paragraph: 'Oh man, the god named Jesus Messiah is your friend and as Vajrapani Sri Sakyamunu [Gautama Buddha] and when the doors of the heaven with seven layers are opened, you will pursue the way of conduct that you receive from the right hand of God.'

Among the scrolls recovered by Sir Aurel Stein is a painting on silk of a bearded Caucasian Christ-like figure. His upraised right hand is shown with the middle finger touching the thumb in the Buddhist gesture of argumentation in debate and the nimbus round his head could be either Buddhist or Christian, but the pectoral cross on his forehead and more crosses on his collar identify him as a Christian icon.

Also found at Tun-huang but from a different source is a letter apparently written and sent from Tibet on which is drawn a complex cross in which each arm develops its own smaller cross, thus: ✚. This has no place in Tibetan Buddhist iconography but may be linked to Nestorian symbolism.

Further evidence of Christian activity within and around Tibet's western borders comes in the form of painted crosses on frescoes at Alchi monastery in Ladakh, as well as petroglyphs found at three sites in the western Himalayas, all located at campsites beside trails. One of these is near Gilgit, where a number of Jerusalem crosses have been chiselled on boulders beside the Hunza river. A second site is at Donkhar in lower Ladakh, where an upturned rock carries an incised Calvary cross on a graded pedestal together with a partly obliterated Tibetan inscription. However, most impressive of all are the rock carvings found near the village of Tangtse in upper Ladakh.

Tangtse is in the Shyok valley at a point where four trails converge: from Kashgar and Khotan to the north and north-east; from Leh and Ladakh to the west; and from western Tibet to the south-east. Close by a lakeside campsite is a cluster of half a dozen large boulders all covered in graffiti left by passing travellers. The largest of these boulders carries hunting scenes, swastikas, stupas, crosses and inscriptions. One face of the rock carries a row of Maltese crosses supported by stalks and flower patterns; a single word inscribed in Sogdian above one such cross transliterates as *Ysaw* (Issau, or Jesus). Another carries a two-line inscription in Sogdian which reads (Sims-Williams, 1992): 'I Uri Turkhan have come in the name of God'. The expression 'in the name of God' is found on the Nestorian documents recovered from Tun-huang, which suggests that this too is Christian.

The largest of the inscriptions has been deciphered (Sims-Williams, 1990) to read:

In the year 210
we [were] sent
[we, namely] Caitra
the Samarkandian
together with the
monk Nosh-farn
[as] messenger[s] to
the Tibetan
Qughan.

This can be accurately dated to the year 841–2 CE. Samarkand had come under Moslem rule in the previous century and, since Moslems were in general far more hostile to infidel religions such as Buddhism than they were to a religion 'of the book' such as Christianity, it seems reasonable to suppose that Nosh-farn the monk was a Nestorian Christian rather than a Buddhist.

Further evidence of Christian activity in this same area comes from an unlikely quarter: Nicholas Roerich, the Russian mystic and artist who spent several years travelling through Ladakh, Tibet and central Asia in the 1920s. In his book *Himalaya* Roerich writes of Nestorian crosses seen in the Leh valley and of Kashmiri legends that Jesus the Nazarene spent his missing years there. 'In Leh,' he writes, 'not far from the bazaar exists a pond which stood under an old tree. Here Christ preached!' Roerich also examines an intriguing claim made by a Russian traveller named Notovitch that a life of Jesus written in Tibetan had been shown to him at the nearby monastery of Hemis. According to Notovitch, a lama brought out 'two large bound volumes with leaves yellowed by time and from them he read to me in the Tibetan language the biography of Issa, which I carefully noted down in my *carnet de voyage* as my interpreter translated what he said'. This two-volume biography was said to give a detailed account of Jesus' life and preaching in Kashmir.

Roerich attempted to track down the two volumes at Hemis monastery but had no success. Notovitch could well have been spinning a traveller's tale, but it is also possible that he was shown a Nestorian testament.

None of this helps to pin down Prester John's kingdom. What it does show is that the Nestorian Church was a significant cultural force in inner Asia from the sixth century onwards. We also know that the Nestorians enjoyed considerable success in north-west China in the eighth century because a stone pillar set up in Xian in 781 CE tells us so; it states that Christianity is now so popular in the region that numerous churches and monasteries have been established.

This success was shortlived. Within a century Christianity – along with a number of other 'foreign' religions – had been banned throughout China and replaced by Buddhism as the only foreign religion worthy of imperial patronage. However, the Nestorian faith continued to be practised north of the Great Wall, and it is here, among the Mongols, that the first positive link between Prester John and the Nestorians can be established.

In 1245 an elderly Italian Franciscan friar named Giovanni di Plano Carpini left Lyons at Pope Innocent IV's command to enter Tartary – the name by which the entire land mass of Central Asia east of the Caspian Sea came to be known to medieval Europe – to make contact with Batu Khan, Genghis Khan's grandson and chief of the khanate known as the Golden Horde, which now controlled the steppes east and north of the Black Sea. Setting out from what was then Mongol territory in Russia, the Franciscan emissary began a 5,000-mile journey that took him to the court of the Great Khan at Karakoram in central Mongolia.

Brother Giovanni's brief was to 'know the Tartars' attitude and intent', so as to avoid further massacres of Christians. His account of his travels, *Historia Mongalorum Quos Nos Taratoros Appellamus* ('The Story of the Mongols Whom We Call the Tartars') is the first detailed report by a European of a visit to inner Asia.

The Mongols turned out to be thoroughly un-Christian pagans who followed the ways of shamanism: 'The Tartars practise a great deal of divination, augury, magic and incantations, and when demons respond they believe God himself is speaking to them.' However, Brother Giovanni did find Nestorians among both the Mongols and the other nomadic tribes conquered by Genghis Khan half a century earlier. Indeed, Nestorians were to be found in senior positions at the court of the Great Khan himself: 'Christians who were of the emperor's household told us they firmly believed he would become a Christian and that they had an obvious sign of this because he himself supported Christian clerics and paid their expenses, and he always had a Christian choir before his largest tent, and they sang publicly and openly, and rang the hours according to the Greek custom.'

Of the Christian Emperor Prester John, Brother Giovanni had disappointingly little to say, except that he had been a king of 'Greater India' and had fought against the first Great Khan, Genghis Khan.

Eight years after Brother Giovanni a second Franciscan brother, a Frenchman named Gulielmus de Rubruquis, was sent out to Tartary. He reached Karakoram, had an audience with the Great Khan and returned to France with a quite different account of Prester John and his kingdom. Brother Gulielmus quite patently loathed the heretical Nestorians, whom he found enjoying considerable influence among the Mongols, and in his *Itinerarium* he loses no opportunity to rubbish their claims. Of Prester John he had this to say:

The Catai dwelt beyond certain mountains across which I wandered, and in a plain in the midst of the mountains lived once an important Nestorian shepherd [i.e. pastoralist nomad]

called Nayman, who ruled over the Nestorian people . . . The
Nestorian people raised this man to be king, and called him
King John, and related of him ten times as much as the truth.
And in like manner the story got about that there was a great
King John. However, I traversed his pastures, and no one
knew anything about him except a few Nestorians . . . This
John had a brother, a famous shepherd named Unc, who lived
three weeks' journey beyond the mountains of Caracatais.

The 'Catai' and the 'mountains of Caracatais' refer to the
Kara-Khitai, a nomadic people whose territories – extending
west of the Gobi and south of Lake Balkhash as far as the Tarim
basin – had been absorbed into the fast-expanding Mongol
Empire in about 1218. In 1141 they had taken on and defeated the
forces of the Seljuk Sultan of Persia on the Qatwan plain near
Samarkand, a rare victory against Moslems that reverberated
through inner Asia and beyond for many decades. The
'Nestorian shepherd called Nayman' suggests a link with the
Naiman, a proto-Mongolian tribe of Central Mongolia absorbed
into Genghis Khan's Mongol federation in the early 1200s. The
'shepherd named Unc' can be identified with the khan of
another Mongolian tribe, the Kerait – as we shall see.

No further light was shed on the great Christian emperor of
Asia until Marco Polo wrote (or dictated or copied from Arab
sources) his account of his travels to Cathay and beyond. The
Venetian traveller claimed to have lived at the court of the Great
Khan of the Mongols, Kublai Khan, for two extended periods
between about 1260 and 1292. So many versions of *Description of
the World* went into circulation, with so many discrepancies, that
doubt continues to be cast on Marco Polo's veracity, but all speak
of Nestorian communities scattered through inner Asia, and of a
region called 'Tenduc', once ruled over by Prester John but now
part of the Mongol empire:

The people are subject to the Great Khan, for so also are the descendants of Prester John. The province is ruled by a king of the lineage of Prester John, who is a Christian and a priest and also bears the title 'Prester John'. His personal name is George. He holds the land as a vassal of the Great Khan – not all the land that was held by Prester John but a part of it. I may tell you that the Great Khans have always given one of their daughters or kinswomen to reigning princes of the lineage of Prester John.

It is in this province that Prester John had his chief residence when he was chief of the Tartars and of all these neighbouring provinces and kingdoms; and it is here that his descendants still live. This is the place which we call in our language Gog and Magog; the natives call it Ung and Mungul.

'Tenduc' has been identified as the country immediately north of the Great Wall occupied by the Ongguts, a Mongol tribe which did indeed embrace Nestorianism and whose khan in Marco Polo's day – improbable as it sounds – was indeed named George. We know this because Khan George was converted to the true Catholic faith in the late 1290s by a papal legate to the Mongol court named Giovanni di Montecorvino.

So, if Tenduc was the khanate of Prester John's grandson George, what happened to the old man himself? Marco Polo says he was overthrown by Kublai Khan's grandfather, Genghis Khan:

The Tartars [in this context, Mongols] used to dwell farther north, in the region of Chorcha and Bargu [near Lake Baikal] . . . They were a lordless people, but were actually tributary to a great lord who was called in their language Ung Khan, which simply means Great Lord. This was that Prester John, of whose great empire all the world speaks. The Tartars paid him a tribute of one beast in every ten. Now it happened that their population increased greatly. When Prester John saw how their numbers had grown, he realised that they might be a danger to him; so he resolved to divide them among several countries.

The Mongols responded by choosing a leader 'whose name in their language was Chinghiz Khan'. Genghis Khan raised a great army, conquered eight provinces and then in 'the year of Christ's nativity 1200' sent emissaries to Prester John telling him that he wished to marry his daughter. His request was rejected and an angry Genghis Khan then assembled 'the greatest armament that was ever seen or heard of'. Prester John also gathered his forces and the two armies met on the plain of Tenduc.

Before the battle Genghis Khan summoned his court astrologers, 'Christian and Saracen', and ordered them to predict the outcome. The Moslems refused but the Christians responded by writing the names of Prester John and Genghis Khan on opposite sides of a rod and then splitting it lengthwise with a name on each piece. They then 'took the psalter and read certain psalms and performed their incantation. Thereupon the wand that bore the name of Chinghiz Khan, without anyone touching it, joined itself on to the other and came to rest above it. And this was seen by all the bystanders. When Chinghiz Khan saw it, he was overjoyed.'

Two days later 'the greatest battle that was ever seen' was fought and Prester John was killed: 'From that day he lost his land, which Chinghiz Khan continued day after day to subdue.'

Support for Marco Polo's version of events comes from the *Syric Chronicle* of the Jacobite Primate Gregory Bar-Hebraeus (1226–86), which states that 'in the year of the Greeks 1514, of the Arabs 599 [1202 CE], when Unk-Khan, who is the Christian King John, ruled over a stock of the barbarian Hunns, called Kergt, Tschingys-Khan served him with great zeal.' King John grew to distrust Genghis Khan and planned to kill him. Genghis Khan outwitted him and – as in Marco Polo's account – defeated him in battle. 'We must consider that King John the Kergtajer was not cast down for nought,' continues the *Chronicle* sanctimoniously. 'Nay, rather, because he forsook the religion of his ancestors and followed strange gods, therefore God took the government from him.'

These four Western testimonies – all written within half a century of each other but at least a century and more after the arrival of Prester John's letter in Europe – all add weight to Prester John as a genuine historical figure, but they also give us four different candidates. Giovanni di Plano Carpini identifies Prester John simply as king of Greater India; Gulielmus de Rubruquis suggests he was a khan of the Naiman tribes and a brother of Unc; Màrco Polo that he was Ung Khan, ruler of the Tenduc country; and Gregory Bar-Hebraeus that he was Unk-Khan, ruler of the Kerkt (Kerait).

Their combined evidence suggests that Prester John belonged to the Nestorian Church; that he was a priest king who wielded considerable influence over certain nomadic tribes of inner Asia; and that his power (or the power of his descendants) ended with the rise of Genghis Khan.

None of this, it has to be said, is supported by Eastern testimony. Mongolian and Chinese sources have absolutely nothing to say on the subject of Prester John – nor Marco Polo, for that matter.

The great Mongol warlord's rise to power is well documented in *The Secret History of the Mongols*, begun within a few years of Genghis Khan's death in 1227. The two dates given in our four occidental sources – 1200 and 1202 – relate to a period when Genghis Khan, under the name of Temuchin Khan, was in the process of uniting the Mongols before he began his conquests of China and central Asia as Genghis Khan.

Temuchin became chief of the Kiut and Taijiut Mongol sub-clans of eastern Mongolia in 1188, when he was twenty-six. In 1192 he joined forces with the powerful Kerait tribe of central Mongolia, which was ruled over by an elderly khan named Toghril. In 1201 Temuchin and Toghril together overcame an opposing alliance of Mongol clans which included the Naimans of western Mongolia. This victory earned them the gratitude of the Chinese emperor, who conferred on Toghril the title of Wang, 'king', which Mongolises into Ong. It now becomes apparent that the 'shepherd named Unc' of de Rubruquis, the 'great lord Ung Khan' of Marco Polo and the 'Unk-Khan' of Bar-Hebraeus are all one and the same: Toghril Khan, ruler of the Keriats.

Temuchin became warlord of the eastern Mongols and so powerful that he threatened the Keriats and the western Mongols under the aged Toghril. A confrontation was inevitable – and ended with the death of Toghril in about the year 1203. In 1206 Temuchin took the name Genghis ('ruler as far as the oceans') and embarked on the first of the military campaigns that within twenty years would make him ruler of all central Asia from the Black Sea to the China Sea.

It would have been quite feasible for the aged khan whom Genghis Khan overthrew, Toghril Khan, to have been the same man who some forty years earlier wrote that extraordinary, vainglorious letter to Pope Alexander and the crowned heads of western Europe as Presbyter Johannes, Lord of Lords and ruler of the three Indies. Nothing in *The Secret History of the Mongols* suggests that Toghril Khan was anything other than a non-Christian Mongol chieftain, even if he had Nestorian subjects and Nestorian neighbours – but until a more likely candidate is discovered, he remains the only serious contender for the title of Prester John. The mystery remains unsolved.

Despite the discovery of Christian emperors in Africa in the fifteenth century, the legend of a Christian civilisation lost somewhere in Asia persisted. Besides Prester John, stories also began to circulate in Christendom of a King David, Christian king of India, possibly the son or grandson of the great presbyter. So seriously did the Portuguese take these tales that Henry the Navigator sent ships down to and round the Cape of Good Hope with the express purpose of reaching India and opening trading links with the apparently ageless priest emperor or his descendants. Vasco da Gama asked after him and his Christians almost as soon as he had set foot on India's Cormandel coast. And when the first Portuguese Jesuits came to attend the court of the Great Mugul Akbar at Agra in 1580 they too lost no time in enquiring after the whereabouts of Prester John's kingdom.

To their delight, they were told of a land beyond the Himalayas where priests and people followed the same religious observances as the Holy Roman Church. The first report they wrote on this kingdom was based on accounts taken from Indian yogis and sadhus who had visited this country and could affirm that 'there are still surviving Christians there'. The land was said to be made up of 'mountains steep and difficult to climb but flat on the summit and suitable for habitation. On the banks of a certain lake there, which the local people call Lake Mansaruor, a certain tribe inhabits a very old city.'

Accompanying this same manuscript is a crude sketch map measuring some five inches by four. Beyond the great arc of the 'Imaus' mountains – the Himalayas – is drawn a large circular lake identified as 'MANSARVOR Lacus' and beside it the inscription '*Hic dicunter Christiani habitare*' (Here it is said Christians live).

This information led to intense speculation among the Jesuits in India that Prester John's long-lost kingdom was indeed waiting to be rediscovered and brought back into the Christian fold. As a result, a mission was despatched by way of Lahore in 1603 but it came to grief somewhere north of Tibet in the wilds of the Koko Nor desert. A more carefully planned second expedition set out in 1624, led by the leader of the Portuguese mission in India, Antonio de Andrade. He and his lieutenant, Manuel Marques, disguised themselves as Hindu pilgrims and attached themselves to a party of devotees bound for the Himalayan shrine of Badrinath. Following the ancient pilgrim trail that runs alongside the Alaknandu tributary of the Ganges, they made their way through the foothills of Garhwal and reached Badrinath without difficulty.

Leaving Marques to negotiate with local officials who were objecting to their going any further north, Andrade hired a local guide and pressed on. Despite suffering from snowblindness, frostbitten feet and 'noxious vapours' that made it almost impossible to breathe, he reached the 17,900-foot saddle of the Mana pass. Seeing only 'an awful desert' ahead of him, he turned about and went back to Badrinath.

A month later, now well acclimatised to the altitude, with permits to proceed in their pockets and with the passes cleared of snow, the two men crossed the Mana La and entered far western Tibet. Within a few days they stood on the southern rim of a deep canyon split with immense ravines. Before them lay what they believed to be the long-lost kingdom of Prester John.

Andrade and Marques did indeed find a kingdom here, along with a priest-king and subjects much given over to religion. It was not Prester John's kingdom, nor were its subjects Nestorian Christians. But it was, in its own way, an equally extraordinary discovery, which was set down by Andrade in two letters quickly published in Lisbon in 1626 under the grand title of *Novo Descobrimento do Gram Cathay, ou Reinos de Tibet* – and equally quickly forgotten. This is, of course, one of the books which Glory Conway spots on the shelves in the High Lama's library in the lamasery of Shangri-La, and which the author James Hilton lists in *Lost Horizon*.

What Andrade and Marques saw in far western Tibet was an ancient civilisation in final decline. It was the Buddhist kingdom of Gu-ge, centred on the rock fortress of Tsaparang, at the southern end of the gorge of the Garuda valley. Within forty years the kingdom would be overthrown, the fortress-city and its surrounding monasteries abandoned.

Three centuries later a German Buddhist by the name of Lama Govinda came to the spot where the two Jesuits had stood when they first looked down on the Garuda Valley and set down a graphic description of the 'paradise' spread out before him:

An enchanted world of rock formations which had crystallised into huge towers, shooting up thousands of feet into the deep blue sky, like a magnetic fence around an oasis, kept green by the waters of springs and mountain brooks. A great number of these nature-created towers had been transformed into dwellings – nay into veritable 'skyscrapers' – by the people who had lived here many hundreds of years ago. They had ingeniously hollowed out these rock towers from within, honeycombing them with caves, one above the other, connected by inner staircases and passages, and lit up by small window-like openings . . . The centre of the crest was crowned with temples, stupas, monasteries, and the ruins of ancient castles, whence one could get a beautiful view of the valley, bordered by phalanxes of rock-towers rising up, row after row, like organ pipes and perforated by hundreds and hundreds of cave-dwellings and their windows.

The greatest surprise, however, was to find the main temple not only intact but actually covered with a golden roof that gleamed in the wilderness of rocks and ruins like a forgotten jewel – a reminder and symbol of the splendour and the faith of a past age, in which this valley was inhabited by thousands of people and ruled by wise and pious kings . . .

That the Jesuits' intrusion into the hidden kingdom of Gu-ge helped to inspire James Hilton's Shangri-La, there can now be little doubt. What is far more difficult to assess is the impact of Nestorian Christianity, with or without the priest-king Prester John, on inner Asia and Tibet. A few metal buttons marked with crosses found by the shores of Mapham Tso and elsewhere in the Ngari region really do not add up to much. What is intriguing, however, is the survival within the two oldest religious sects of Tibet – in Bon and among the Nyingpa school of Tibetan Buddhism – of a ritual known as Tshe-bang or 'life consecration'. The central element of this rite is the distribution by the officiating priest among the attending congregation of wafers of consecrated bread and wine sipped from a chalice — or rather, barley-flour distributed in the form of small pellets and chang (fermented barley-beer) drunk from a common bowl. The rite is represented as a strengthening of the bla or life-force of the participants rather than an act of shared communion. How or when it became part of Bon ritual we will never know — but there can be little doubt that it had its origins in Nestorian Christianity.

6 *The Kingdom of Kanishka*

> We stayed a short time at the top, looking out over the
> Badakshan mountains towards the mysterious Central Asia
> which attracts by the glamour of its past history, by the veil
> that shrouds its future. Balkh, Bokhara, Samarkand, what
> visions come trooping as their names arise! The armies of
> Alexander, the hordes of Gingis Khan and Timur go glittering
> by; dynasties and civilisations rise and fall like the waves of the
> sea; peace and prosperity again and again go down under the
> iron hoof of the conquerer; for centuries past death and decay
> have ruled in the silent heart of Asia.
>
> Algernon Durand, *The Making of a Frontier*, 1899

FEBRUARY 1998

Fast-forward to the first month of the Year of the Fire-Ox.

I have felt it necessary to explore a side avenue which could
turn out to be a cul-de-sac; not Tibet this time but Pakistan and
Afghanistan. I have a theory that needs to be put to the test in the
field. Dick has volunteered to come with me on what will be our
third foray together in two years.

Which is how we come to be out one evening walking over
the ruins of Bhir, on the border between Pakistan's Lahore and
North-West Frontier Provinces. We are 'eating the air', as they
say in these parts, while half the lads from the local village play
scratch cricket among the ruins.

Bhir was the first city of Taxila. The young prince Ashok

ruled here as a viceroy on the outskirts of the Mauryan empire and returned again in about 260 BCE both as emperor and as a probable convert to Buddhism. The site was partly excavated in the early years of this century by Sir John Marshall before he moved to a second site a mile to the north and uncovered Taxila's second city, Sirkup, laid out in neat squares by the Graeco-Bactrians towards the end of the second century BCE, with a wide main street running north and south.

Marshall spent more than three decades digging here and elsewhere within the Gandhara region but he missed the third and fourth cities of Taxila. These lie under a modern village and orchards just five minutes' ride in a pony tonga from Sirkup. Trial trenches have been dug which suggest that both were founded in about the first quarter of the second century CE, a period of particular interest to me. But lack of funds and, I suspect, a lack of will have prevented their further excavation, and they now provide a good income for the local villagers who, if they strike lucky, can make more from one night's work with a pick-axe than they can ever hope to earn in a year. All the good stuff is taken away by dealers while the locals, for the most part, stick to selling poorly made fakes to tourists. Practically everyone we meet seems to carry genuine Bactrian, Kushan and Sasanian copper coins in their pockets like loose change.

Taxila has its own museum, a small beacon of excellence among the gloomy, neglected mausolea which pass for museums in Pakistan. It has a fine collection of stone and plaster statues, of which the best are Buddhist and date from between the first and fourth centuries CE. In its beautifully laid out grounds is the bungalow which John Marshall had built for himself and lived in while he supervised his digs. Thanks to the kindness of the museum curator, Dick and I have been given permission to spend the night there.

It is 1920s Raj in aspic. The bungalow's resident kansamah will 'do' for us. He proudly displays Sir John's original cutlery, crockery and other bits and bobs and then serves English-style tea and biscuits on the lawn, among orange trees heavy with fruit, while we bask in the late afternoon sun.

With an hour of daylight left we explore the grassed-over mounds of Taxila's first city and then wander down a lane to look at the Dharmarajika stupa, the largest Buddhist sanghrama in Taxila. It is dominated by the main stupa which is over 110 feet in diameter and has four sets of steps at each cardinal point. This is surrounded by a well-laid processional walkway and a ring of small chapels which contained shrines. More temples are laid out nearby, together with a number of buildings which served the monks as living quarters, kitchens, refectories and baths. The stupa came first – probably thrown up at the time of Prince Ashok – but was much glorified and added to five centuries later. We will see the same pattern reflected in a dozen and more complexes in the next few days.

Dusk falls suddenly as we make our way back through the fields, heralded by the cawing of rooks and then the calls to prayer of the local muezzins, first from one mosque, then another and then a third, spreading like ripples over the surrounding countryside.

That night, asleep in Sir John's bedroom, I am woken by several loud bursts of automatic gunfire. It is the season of weddings, we are told at breakfast. Dick claims to have slept through the lot.

A week later and I am standing on one of a cluster of mounds in a wide plateau flanked to north and south by mountains dusted with snow. Dick is some distance away taking photographs and trying not to think too hard about anti-personnel mines. We are now in the Afghan province of Ningrahar, through which flows the Kabul river on its way east to join the Indus river above Attock. About five miles to the north are the outskirts of Jelalabad.

A group of locals – all men, of course – have climbed up with me, including the headman of the nearest village, Tapa-i-

Shoter, which lies about 300 paces to our east in the middle of a second cluster of mounds. More clusters are visible to south and west. We are walking over the ruins of the Kushan town which the Chinese monk Faxian knew as He-lo and where he came in the year 400 to inspect the fragment of Gautama Shakyamuni's skull. Somewhere hereabouts – most probably under the huge orchard which the Russians planted outside Jelalabad in the early 1980s as part of their effort to collectivise the Afghan peasantry – are the foundations of the monasteries which housed the Buddha's tooth, staff and robe.

It is just possible to make out that the bumps we are standing on are the drums of small stupas. Like every other mound we can see from here, they have the characteristic bite in the side where treasure-seekers have dug into them. But these mounds at our feet have additional cavities: semi-circular indentations like the marks of ringworm.

'This is where the Russians were,' explains the village headman. 'They dug a trench for their soldiers up here' – he indicates · the pit I'm standing in. 'They had a tank over there' – he points to a larger pit to our right – 'and another tank on this side.' To strengthen their entrenchment, the Russian infantrymen knocked down the first stupa – the one we're now standing on – and burrowed into a second.

'The mujahideen attacked from this side' – the headman points to the south – 'and the Russians had to hide in the orchards. But they fought back and pushed the mujahideen out. Then the mujahideen came back again and killed many Russians.'

Our escort has been listening to all this from a distance without comment but now he nods. He was himself once a mujahideen, one of the Afghan anti-communist freedom fighters who fought the Russians for many years. Although the Russians finally withdrew from Afghanistan in 1989 it was not until four years later that the mujahideen finally overthrew the communists in Jelalabad. Now he is no longer a mujahideen. He sports the bushy beard, the black turban and the Kalashnikov which are the identifying marks of the Taliban, the ultra-orthodox Islamic movement which currently rules most of southern and western Afghanistan as far north as the Salang Pass.

The village headman and the others treat him with respect. As well they might, for the talib has himself admitted to us earlier that he is not welcome in these parts; he was recently involved in an exchange of fire with a man from the village who was raiding the orchard at night and shot him dead. So now he keeps his distance, and this allows us to talk more freely with the villagers.

'The excavations were just over there,' says the headman, pointing to what looks like a patch of waste ground adjacent to the village. This was the site excavated by the French in the 1970s. Their dig revealed a classic Kushan stupa and vihara, with linked assembly hall, cells round an open courtyard, refectory and kitchen. A wealth of statuary was uncovered: a score of large stucco figures and hundreds of smaller ones, together with many sculpted friezes. It was the finest Buddhist site yet excavated in Afghanistan and so it was decided to leave the finds in situ and turn the entire excavation into a museum. But when the mujahideen took over Jelalabad they had other ideas.

'The mujahideen commander did not like these statues,' explains the village headman. 'They set fire to them. Now there is nothing left.'

What the Sasanids and the Huns started, the mujahideen and the Taliban are helping to finish today.

Our plan is to proceed from here to Begram, forty miles or so north of Kabul, to inspect the ruins of Kapisha, the summer capital of the Kushans. Perhaps even visit the Bamian valley and see the two giant statues of Buddha. Faint hope.

We reach Kabul a day later. Most of the city is in ruins. Huge sectors are bombed out, rocketed and shelled into mere fragments of buildings. Entire districts have been abandoned piecemeal and show not a single sign of life. Every lamp-post seems to have taken a hit: some are pocked with bullet marks or shrapnel; others hang drunkenly at various angles or have snapped in two; many are no more than stumps. Kabul museum is just one more burned-out shell. Ironically, the former royal palaces – including the buildings which the Old Carthusian attempted to bomb eighty years ago – seem relatively undamaged. A blanket of snow covers the city but cannot hide the scars of ten years of pitiless civil war.

We are surprised – astonished, even – to find that the Taliban are widely perceived as a great blessing. True, the male population may have been deprived of their beloved weaponry and the female population of their liberty but this, together with untrimmed beards and chadors – which look like lace tablecloths dropped over the female form to cover everything down to the shin-bone – is regarded as a small price to pay for peace.

But we also discover that there is no question of proceeding either to Begram or Bamian. The former is now on the front line between the warring Taliban and the anti-Taliban mujahideen alliance. A mujahideen army, led by General Wali Masud, also stands between the Taliban and Bamian. When the general falls – as he surely will – the Taliban will carry out their declared intention of picking up the torch dropped by Genghis Khan and removing these last vestiges of idolatry from Afghanistan.

We head back towards the Khyber Pass and Pakistan.

After a few days in Peshawar and a depressing visit to the worst-kept museum in Asia we head north in a smart green taxi to Swat. This will be our last excursion before flying back to London.

Just short of the mountain range which separates the Vale of Peshawar from the Swat valley is a triangle of hills. We turn off the main road after Mardan and follow a dirt track which climbs into a hidden cul-de-sac. Perched high on a series of terraces which climb up the hillside are the ruins of perhaps half a dozen monasteries, all Buddhist. This is Takht-i-Bhai, the most extensive of all the Buddhist sites of Gandhara.

It is a puzzle why none of the four Chinese travellers who came to India between the fifth and seventh centuries came here or, if they did, never wrote about it. The excavations of Marshall and others show that the main stupa and the surrounding two-storey quadrangle of cells at the heart of the complex were raised in the first century CE and torched four centuries later, with evidence of some subsequent occupation on a lesser scale for perhaps a further century. Other Buddhist temples and monasteries in the surrounding plains were also sacked in the early 500s but show no signs of further occupation. What can one infer from that? Perhaps that Takht-i-Bhai served as a haven for Buddhists forced off the Peshawar plain, who held out here for as long as they could before being driven deeper into the hills?

The midday sun is already hot enough to make us sweat hard as we clamber up the ridge above Takht-i-Bhai. From the top you can make out that every point of high ground hereabouts had its own stupa. The hills must have fairly bristled with them.

We leave the dusty plains behind at Dargai and climb up to the Malakand pass. Half an hour's drive and we are in a quite different country, 2,000 feet higher and breathing alpine air, before us the Swat valley in the pale livery of early spring.

The Swat river curls down from the north, with broad alluvial flats on either side planted with wheat, barley, maize and even rice. Above the fields the hillsides are covered with deciduous woods well stocked with fruit trees: apple, apricot, almond, walnut and cashew. Higher still are alpine meadows which give way to pine and silver birch woods. The valley is well watered, well protected, warmed by long hours of sunshine in winter and cooled by the mountain breezes in summer. In sum, here is an ideal habitat for man. Today in Pakistan they refer to Swat as the granary of Pakistan's North-West Frontier Province. I can fully understand why in the distant past it was called the 'garden'; in Sanskrit, Uddiyana.

Uddiyana has long been revered among Tibetan Buddhists

as Orgyan, the tantric power-place in which the highest, most esoteric teachings of the Vajrayana and Dzogchen evolved before being exported east through the mountains to Tibet. Here, as the most famous prayer in Tibet tells us, was born the saint who brought those teachings, the great magus Guru Rinpoche:

Hom! In the north-west of the land of Orgyan
On the pollen-bed of a lotus flower
Endowed with the miraculous supreme realisation
Appeared Padmasambhava the lotus-born . . .

Lovely as the valley undoubtedly is, I find it hard to believe that this was the cradle of tantric Buddhism. The physical remains are disappointing, to say the least; a let-down after what we have seen and clambered over at Taxila and Takht-i-Bhai. In the fifty-mile stretch of valley between Malakand and Tirat perhaps half a dozen scattered stupas, the same number of carved Buddha figures on rocks and only one excavated site of any real size. I have with me a copy of *Buddhist Shrines in Swat* (1993) by Dr Ashraf Khan, curator of the Archaeological Museum at Saidu Sharif, the central museum of Swat. Armed with what we presume to be a fairly authoritative guide, Dick and I work our way northwards up the valley, examining the ruins first surveyed by Sir Aurel Stein in 1926 and excavated by Dr Tucci and others from 1956 onwards. One surprising and highly significant common factor starts to emerge, and the further north we go the more striking it becomes: none of the approximately 400 Buddhist shrines and settlements so far excavated in this valley show signs of occupation beyond the middle of the seventh century. No Buddhist artefacts have been recovered which can be dated into the eighth century. All the sanghgrama have lain in ruins long before then, their occupants long gone. Hinduism has taken over in the valley.

This is absolutely baffling because the author of *Buddhist*

Shrines in Swat frequently refers to the occupation of Buddhist sites 'lasting until the 7th–8th century AD'. He sites as evidence of this late occupation the records of the Chinese monk Xuanzang (Hsuan-Tsang). 'Hsuan-Tsang,' he writes, 'who graced this valley by his presence in the seventh century AD, said that there were 1,400 monasteries in Swat, which eloquently confirmed the extensive remains of the Buddhist period.'

The contradiction nags at me all through the afternoon. That night, as I'm lying snug in my bed in a government tourist lodge at Miandam, high above the Swat river, with a late fall of spring snow settling down outside, it occurs to me to check sources. In my pack I have a copy of Xuanzang's account of his visit to Swat in the year 629, and when I read it everything falls into place. This is what Xuanzang actually writes: 'On both sides of the river Su-po-far-su-ta [Swat] there are some 1,400 *old* Sanghramas. They are now generally waste and desolate; *formerly* there were some 18,000 priests in them, but gradually they have become less, till now there are very few' [my italics]. Those few Buddhist monks are followers of Mahayana, but neither tantricists nor scholars of the Law: 'They practise the duty of quiet meditation, and have pleasure in reciting texts relating to their subject but have no great understanding of them. They lead a pure life and purposely prohibit the use of charms.' What Xuanzang is describing is a Buddhist culture on its very last legs, its days of glory long since gone.

The evidence on the ground and Xuanzang's words now match. The implications hit me with the force of a revelation: it means that Swat/Uddiyana/Orgyan ceased to be the power-house of tantric Mahayana at least before the end of the sixth century – and what *that* does is seriously undermine the credibility of Tibetan Buddhism's greatest saint, Guru Rinpoche. The temerity of these thoughts sends me back to bed thoroughly shaken.

The Tibetan histories state that although King Trisong Detsen despatched messengers to Uddiyana to invite Padmasambhava to Tibet these messengers actually met the Blessed Guru at Mangyul, on the Tibet–Nepal border. The king then received the Buddhist teachings from Padmasambhava in his twentieth year, 762 CE. This means that Padmasambhava came to Tibet at least 120 years after the Chinese monk Xuanzang had written of the Buddhist sanghramas of Swat being 'now generally waste and desolate'. The archaeological evidence on the ground supports Xuanzang's observations. The conclusion is inescapable: Padmasambhava did not come from Swat.

The next morning we breakfast in bright spring sunshine. The overnight snow has soon melted away. Driving back down the valley we pass a number of side valleys to our left. The first of these leads up to the Shangla pass and then on over the mountains to the Indus river. In ancient times this modest little valley was the short-cut between Gandhara and Gilgit and all points north. We know of the Chinese and Tibetan pilgrims who came down this valley from the north from the fifth century CE onwards looking for a Buddhist paradise – but of those who travelled in the opposite direction, carrying revolutionary teachings in their heads, very little is known.

I cannot now accept that the Blessed Guru was one of them – which begs the question: if Padmasambhava could not have come from Swat, where *did* he come from?

The circumstantial evidence suggests that, if Padmasambhava came from anywhere, he came from Gilgit – Bru-sha, as it was – the neighbouring country most likely to have absorbed refugees and teachings from Swat. Chinese records show that in the year 736 Bru-sha – which the Bonpo claim as theirs at this time – was attacked both by the Tibetans and the Tang Chinese. In 740 a pitched battle took place between the Chinese and Tibetans which ended with the Tibetans being driven out of Bru-sha. Could it have been this exodus from Bru-sha rather than a royal summons that brought Padmasambhava to Tibet? And could this be why so many of his teachings seem so closely allied to those of Bon?

This is the first revelation that comes to me in Swat: that, wherever Guru Rinpoche came from, it wasn't here. The second is more in the nature of a confirmation: Swat today is a quiet, peaceful paradise. But how much more of a paradise it must have appeared all those centuries ago, when it was filled with shrines and monasteries, and so much learning, devotion and meditation.

In May 1993 a number of rockets fired by one of the warring factions among the Afghan mujahideen crashed into the walls of the National Museum in Kabul, setting the building on fire. The museum curator rescued what he could and transferred the most precious items to the vaults in the museum's basement, but the steel doors of the vaults were later breached by anti-tank rockets and explosives, and their contents systematically plundered. Over 90 per cent of the museum's contents have now disappeared, including the collection known as the Begram Treasure, which has been described as 'the most spectacular archaeological find of the twentieth century'.

What used to be the village of Begram lies thirty-five miles north of Kabul, above the confluence of the Ghorband and Panjsher rivers. It now forms part of the largest air base in Afghanistan, built by the Russians in the early 1980s in their fruitless attempt to bring the Afghans into the twentieth century. It is said that the sandy soil hereabouts used to give up more than 10,000 copper coins every year. This was once Kapisha, the summer capital of the Kushans – probably the least known and the most undervalued of all the many dynasties of kings who ruled in Asia.

The village itself stood on a long mound encircled by high walls. Only a fraction was ever excavated: digging in the bazaar area of the old city in 1937 and 1939, French archaeologists unearthed two hoards in adjoining rooms at the foot of a tower in the outer wall. Both rooms had been hastily walled up as though in an attempt to hide the treasures of what was obviously an extremely wealthy – if not royal – household. The Begram Treasure added up to some 2400 objects, including exquisitely carved ivories from central India, painted glassware from Alexandria, Han dynasty lacquer ware and Roman bronzes.

In the same month in which the rockets struck the National Museum in Kabul a British aid worker named Tim Porter, working in northern Afghanistan for a landmine-clearance charity, was shown a stone tablet which had been dug up on a hill known as the 'Kaffirs' [Unbelievers'] Castle', about eighty miles north of the Salang tunnel. It was a white limestone slab about three feet wide and twenty inches high, one face covered by an inscription written in Greek letters over twenty-three lines. Porter sent photographs to the British Museum, where the inscription was identified as being in the Bactrian language and dating from the first half of the second century CE. The discovery opened up a new era in studies of the Kushan kings of Gandhara.

We now know there were twelve Kushan kings: seven absolute rulers who spanned two centuries from about 30 CE to 242 CE and another five who ruled for approximately another century and a half as tributaries of the Sasanians. They were the rulers of the first great empire in central Asia, a commonwealth that at one time included all the countries south of the Aral Sea as far as the Arabian Sea and extended as far east into the Gangetic plain as Emperor Ashok's old capital of Pataliputra (now Patna). For three and a half golden centuries this corner of the Indian subcontinent and the high Pamir became the central marketplace of Asia, where religion, learning and the arts blossomed hand in hand with trade, and where peoples and ideas mixed freely to a degree which has rarely been seen elsewhere in Asia.

The origins of the rulers of this highly successful trade mart – the Kushans – are still matter for conjecture.

The Persian-speaking peoples of the upper Oxus or Amu Daria are known as the Tajiks, a name preserved in the former Soviet republic and now state of Tajikistan, which borders the northern shores of the Oxus. The name 'Tajik' carries a special resonance for followers of Bon because, as Tzag-zig, it is linked inextricably with Olmo-lungring, the homeland of their religion.

The Tajik country is set against the almost impenetrable mountain barriers of the Hindu Kush and the Karakoram but softened by broad, fertile valleys which give access from the west. These valleys form the main migratory and trade routes of the region, a frontier between the settled agricultural peoples of the south and the nomads of the inner Asian steppes. For those seeking to break through the mountains and plunder the fertile Indian plains they provided a natural gateway, which is why they have so often been shaken by the passage of invaders. Between about 500 BCE and 500 CE this Tajik country – known to the Chinese as Ta-hsia and to the Greeks as Bactria and Sogdiana – was ruled over in turn by the Achaemenid Persians, Mauryans, Alexander's Greeks, Parthians, Scythians, Sasanid Persians and Huna – as well as a nomadic people known to the Chinese as the Yuezhi, who came to call themselves the Kushans.

According to ancient Chinese bone inscriptions, the inner Asian steppes were for centuries inhabited by a number of cattle- and horse-breeding tribes – of which two have relevance to the story of Gandhara and its civilisation: the Yuezhi and the Xiongnu.

The most aggressive in Chinese eyes were the Xiongnu, who many centuries later would become notorious as the Huns/Huna. They are known to have spoken an eastern Iranian language and to have been animists who worshipped the sun, the moon and the stars. They made sacrifices and offerings to the heavens, the earth, the spirits and their ancestors. Their chiefs were spoken of as being 'born of heaven and earth, brought forth by the sun and the moon'.

These characteristics were very probably shared by their western neighbours, the Yuezhi, whose homeland appears to have been the region of the Kunlun Shan mountain range and the Tarim basin, which we would today call western Xinjiang (Sinkiang). The Chinese *Book of Kuan-Tẓu* states that jade, *yue*, came from the country of the Yuezhi – and the traditional source of Chinese jade has long been the region of the Khotan-Daria and Keria-Daria rivers which drain the northern slopes of the Kunlun Shan and then disappear into the sands of the Taklamakan. They may well have been the sun-worshipping, horse-sacrificing Massagetae of Herodotus.

In the third century BCE Yuezhi territory extended all the way from west of Gansu to the Tarim basin. According to a Chinese general named Zang Qian, they were then driven westward by the Xiongnu: 'Formerly they were strong and treated the Xiongnu with contempt but when Maotum [ruler of the Xiongnu] had come to the throne he attacked and defeated the Yuezhi and finally Laojang, chieftain of the Xiongnu, killed the king of the Yuezhi and made a drinking vessel from his skull. At first the Yuezhi had been living in the region between Tunhuang and Chilien [Western Kansu] but when they had been defeated by the Xiongnu, they went far away.'

The Yuezhi tribes split into two. The smaller group, the Little Yuezhi, settled in northern Tibet in the region of Nan Shan, the southern mountains which separate the upper waters of the Yellow river from Mongolia. The remainder, the Great Yuezhi, moved further west and by about 130 BCE had displaced the Scythians in the upper Amu Daria valley – the Greek Bactria: 'They passed through Tayuan [Ferghana] and to the west they smote Ta-hsia [Tajik/Bactria] and subdued it.'

Shortly after their conquest of the Tajik country the Great Yuezhi were visited by General Zang Qian, who reported that they were cattle-rearing pastoralists who could muster an army of between 100,000 and 200,000 archers, almost certainly bowmen mounted on what the Chinese came to know as the 'heavenly horses' of the Amu Daria, exceptionally sturdy chargers which gave their war bands unrivalled striking power.

Excavations on the north bank of the Amu Daria reveal that the Yuezhi soon developed a hybrid culture which mixed elements of their nomadic traditions with local Bactrian practices. In the wake of Alexander's invasion, a local syncretic Graeco-Iranian culture had evolved, practising Greek arts and crafts, employing the Greek script and taking up a number of Greek religious cults. The Yuezhi followed the same line; they adopted the Bactrian language and Greek script as their own, along with a number of local Graeco-Iranian deities whose attributes had affinities with their own beliefs.

These beliefs would have reflected Iranian dominance over much of inner Asia northeast of Iran since the fifth century BCE, so we may assume that the Yuezhi brought to Tajik their own forms of the dominant Iranian deities: the male gods of the sun (Hvare-Kshaeta), fire (Atar/Athsho), wind (Vata), time (Zurvan) and light (Mitra/Mithra), the goddesses of the moon (Mah/Mao) and water/fertility (Apo/Apsu/Anahita/Ardochso) and, quite possibly, the god Ahura Mazda, patron of Iran's Achaemenid rulers, usually represented by a solar disk born by a pair of eagle's wings. Of these deities one requires further explanation: Mithra, god of light.

This was not the Westernised Mithras known to us through the Mediterranean cult of Mithraism, with its cave temples and bull sacrifices, but a primal Iranian deity with strong pastoralist sympathies: Mithra the 'possessor of vast pastures'. Blood sacrifices, the drinking of the dark juice of the gods known as haoma/soma/ambrosia and fire worship were at the heart of early Mithraism, with the keeping of the fire charged to a clan of specialists who wore long white robes and carried a mace or wand. It was a mystery religion, its teachings revealed only to initiates.

Recent research by David Ulansey has shown that even in 'Mediterranean' Mithraism so loved by Rome's centurions the god Mithra is much more than a bull-slayer: drawn from an egg-shaped cosmic rock, he controls the heavenly sphere and the rotating zodiac. Figures carved in abundance along the lower tiers of stupa platforms in Gandhara, previously assumed to be those of Atlas supporting the sphere of the world on his shoulders, must now be seen as images of Mithras. Images of putti holding up garlands and wind gods holding up capes may well be representations of Mithras containing the stars within his cloak.

In Sanskrit Mithra means 'friend' and 'covenant', in Iranian 'sun' and 'mutual love', in Greek 'bond' or 'headband' (hence our word 'mitre'). He is an arbiter between god and man, upholder of truth and of contractual obligations. The earliest representations of Mithra are as solar images, with rays radiating the sun's life-giving heat, but over the centuries he gains qualities associated with his Iranian half-brother Varuna, lord of magic and light. He acquires a cudgel or a thunderbolt, the Sanskrit vajra, and he becomes an increasingly warlike god, sol invictus.

He can be seen in this persona on a fresco in the niche behind the famous 35-metre-high Buddha statue in the valley of Bamian, in central Afghanistan (which, as I write, has just been captured by the Taliban, who have publicly declared their intention to destroy these last vestiges of idolatry). Here he rides as a warrior king in a solar chariot attended by wind gods, winged maidens of dawn and gryphons. In another fresco – a mere fragment found in what was probably a monastery in Tajikistan – Mithra stands side by side with his partner the Iranian moon god Mao. He carries a sword and the sun is now his shield.

In Iran itself Mithraism declined as increasingly militant Zoroastrianism became promoted as a state religion. Its mysticism was no match for the teachings ascribed to the Zoroastrian prophet Zarathrustra, who introduced five revolutionary religious concepts: monotheism; free will; the struggle between opposing forces of good and evil; resurrection after death; and a divine judgement leading either to heaven or hell. A struggle between the old and the new, between the multifarious gods of the nomadic Iranians in the hills and the patriarchal god of gods of the settled cultivators of the plains, appears to have come to a head during the reign of Xerxes. Persecution of the followers of Mithra in eastern Iran during the fourth century BCE may have been the stimulus behind an apparent migration of nomadic tribes out of the Zoroastrian sphere and eastwards deeper into inner Asia. These may well have formed the people which the Chinese came to know as the Yuezhi. If so, then the Great Yuezhi were returning to reclaim their ancestral lands when they invaded Bactria towards the end of the second century BCE.

Over a period of about a century and a half the Great Yuezhi gradually extended their authority to cover a wide area on both banks of the Amu Daria. This gave them control over the western outlets of the trading routes that even then linked China with the western world. They may even have co-operated with the Han Chinese against their mutual enemies – the Xiongnu to the north and the proto-Tibetan tribes to the south – to further develop these trade routes both north and south of the Taklamakan desert. Soon after the start of the Christian era the Chinese built and garrisoned a series of forts at oases and other strategic points starting at Jiayukuan on the Chinese border and ending at a crossroads known as Tashkurgan, the 'tower of stone', which became a great bazaar where caravans from the east exchanged their burdens of silk, jade, spices and other precious cargoes for Roman gold and silver.

This and the other towers of stone became the cornerstones of the staging posts, caravanserai and, in time, city-states of what many centuries later came to be known as the 'Silk Road', a romantic but inappropriate term coined by Baron Ferdinand von Richtofen (uncle of the Red Baron) to describe the east–west trade routes through inner Asia linking China with the West. Inappropriate because the Silk Road was never a pukka road in the Roman sense but was more of a web of interlinking trails used as politics, changing markets and the seasons dictated. As a conduit of ideas just as much as trade goods it was hugely important.

The earliest trade route probably followed the southern edge of the Lop Nor from Tun-huang to Tashkurgan by way of Yu-men-Kuan, Cherchen, Niya, Kucha, Khotan and Yarkand. At Tashkurgan the route divided: one course crossed the Pamir plateau then descended down through the Wakhan valley to Balkh and Bactria, another ran south towards India through the Karakoram range, along more or less the same route followed by the Chinese and Pakistani engineers building the Karakoram Highway in the late 1970s.

It was always said that the Karakoram ranges formed an insurmountable barrier. But rock carvings and inscriptions discovered during the building of the highway at river crossing points at Hunza, Gilgit, Chilas and Chatial now make it clear that even invading armies have passed by. Drawings of their cavalry and inscriptions bearing the names of Scythian rulers show that Scythian troops came south this way after they were ousted from Bactria by the Great Yuezhi, probably the same Scythians who displaced the Greek rulers of the Indian Punjab in about 75 BCE and who then went on to rule a large parcel of northern India for about a century before once again being bumped on by the Great Yuezhi.

By then the Great Yuezhi had metamorphised into the Kushans. Settlement in Bactria had placed them at a cultural crossroads between the Greek and Persian worlds to the west and the Chinese to the east, a juxtaposition from which their five tribes benefited hugely as middlemen. One of the five tribes, the Kushans, either did better than the rest or simply fought its way to a position of authority. According to a report submitted by General Zang Qian to the Chinese emperor in about 125 CE, the Kushans – as they now called themselves – had united under a chieftain named Chiu-chiu-chueh (in Bactrian Greek, Kujula Kadphises). After proclaiming himself king of the Kushans, Kujula Kadphises had gathered his horsemen together and invaded Anhsi (Parthia) and Kao-fu (Kabul). He or his successor Vima Takto then went on to lead the Kushan tribes down into the plains of what is now northwest Pakistan, overwhelming the Scythians and setting up a new dynasty of rulers, the Kushan kings.

Under the patronage of the Kushans, a phenomenal explosion of trade and commerce occurred throughout Central Asia in the second and third centuries CE, to the further material benefit of the Kushans and the people they ruled over. This wealth creation provided the wherewithal for a winter capital to be built at Purashapura, outside modern Peshawar north of the Kabul river. It also funded the erection of a huge copper and gold stupa over 500 feet high which came to be regarded as one of the wonders of Asia – the most ambitious of hundreds of Buddhist monuments and sanghrama founded at this time within the Vale of Peshawar and in the surrounding hills.

This hub of the Kushan empire came to be known as Gandhara. It extended for about 250 miles on all sides of Purashapura: north over the Malakand pass into Uddiyana in the Swat valley, south across the Indus river as far as the Jhelum and westwards up the Kabul river valley, past the fertile valley of He-lo (now Jalalabad) and deep into Afghanistan as far as Kapisha, the summer capital of the Kushans (now the Russian air base at Begram).

Control of the Silk Road not only bankrolled Gandhara, but also allowed the flow of new ideas, telegraphed up and down the line. Each staging post became as much a religious centre as a caravanserai, as missionaries of every faith followed hard on the heels of the traders. Every artefact recovered from the sands of the Taklamakan and the caves of the surrounding mountains confirms that a quite unprecedented intermingling of ideas, both sacred and profane, occurred here. They also demonstrate the speed with which one faith in particular became the dominant religion of the Silk Road: carried out of India by Kushan traders from Gandhara, the Dharma fairly raced through inner Asia, Mongolia and China and on to Korea and Japan.

Much of what we know about Gandhara comes from the testimonies of three Buddhist travellers from China who journeyed along the Silk Road into India between the fifth and seventh centuries CE. Their journals were edited by other hands some centuries later and published in China as the *Records of the Buddhist Kingdoms*. These were intended for a Buddhist readership and what they don't say is perhaps as significant as what they do.

The first of these travellers was the Buddhist monk Faxian, who set off from China in the year 399 charged with a mission to bring back authoritative Buddhist texts to update those received in earlier days.

After surviving 'evil demons and hot winds' of the 'river of sand' – the Taklamakan – and enduring 'sufferings unparalleled in human experience', Faxian and his party reached Khotan, the most important of the staging posts of the southern route of the Silk Road. Here they found hospitality among a large community of Buddhist monks, mostly belonging to the Mahayana, the Great Vehicle, the more esoteric of the two major forms of Buddhism, the other being Hinayana, the Lesser Vehicle. They then went west to Yarkand, where they met more followers of the Mahayana path before travelling south into the mountains of the Kunlun Shan. A month later they entered upper Ladakh and began to follow the course of the Indus all the way downstream from somewhere in the region of today's Leh.

Faxian provides a vivid description of the passage of the 100-mile Rongdo gorge between Skardu and Shanglus:

The way was difficult and rugged, a bank exceedingly precipitous, which rose up there, a hill-like wall of rock 10,000 cubits from the base. When one approached the edge of it, his eyes became unsteady; and if he wished to go forwards in the same direction, there was no place on which he could place his foot;

and beneath were the waters of the river called Sindhu [Indus]. In former times men had chiselled paths along the rocks, and distributed ladders on the face of them, to the number altogether of 700, at the bottom of which there was a suspension bridge of ropes, by which the river was crossed, its banks there being eighty paces apart.

The monk followed the Indus down river as far as modern Beglam, where he climbed westwards out of the Indus valley and crossed the Shangla pass to enter the enchanting valley of Swat – the ancient country of Uddiyana. 'The Law of Buddha is very flourishing,' Faxian noted here. 'They call the places where the monks stay or reside permanently sanghramas; and of these there are in all 500.' This tallies with archaeological excavations which show that the hillsides of the Swat valley are studded with over 400 known Buddhist sites mostly dating from the second to the fifth centuries CE. The only puzzle is that, according to Faxian, these 500 sanghramas were all filled with students of the Hinayana form of Buddhism.

Faxian spent the summer of the year 400 in Uddiyana before crossing the Malakand pass and emerging, at last, on to the plains of India and the heartland of Gandhara.

By now the Kushan empire's golden years had already turned to silver. Gandhara had become an outlying province of the Regnum Sasanidarum, the Sasanian empire founded by Ardashir I, and its Kushan kings ruled in name only. But this was holy ground as far as the Chinese Buddhist was concerned and he spent many months here, wandering from one monastery to the next to inspect and worship the many monuments and relics associated with Gautama Shakyamuni and the early Buddhist saints. At Purashapura he marvelled at the great tower built by King Kanishka, noting that 'of all stupas and temples which they saw in their journeyings, there was not one comparable to this in solemn beauty and majestic grandeur'. He visited the nearby monastery built to house the most famous relic in the Buddhist world: the alms bowl of Lord Buddha, brought back in triumph from Pataliputra by the Kushans as war booty and now displayed to the public twice a day, at noon and in the evening. 'It may contain rather more than two pecks,' noted Faxian. 'And is of various colours, black predominating, with the seams that show its four-fold composition clearly marked. Its thickness is about the fifth of an inch, and it has a bright and glossy lustre.'

From Purashapura Faxian travelled west through the Khyber Pass and up along the course of the Kabul river to the Gandharan city of He-lo, a few miles south of the present city of Jalalabad. Here he attended a public viewing of a large fragment of the Buddha's skull, before moving on to worship further relics: one of Gautama Shakyamuni Buddha's teeth, his robe and his staff.

The former Gandharan summer capital of Kapisha now lay within Sasanid country so at this point Faxian's party turned back and travelled south across the Indus into the Punjab. Everywhere they saw signs of a flourishing Buddhist religion. 'They followed the course of the P'oo-na [Jumna] river,' recorded Faxian. 'On the banks of which, left and right, there were twenty monasteries, which might contain 3,000 monks; and the law of Buddha was still flourishing. Everywhere, from the Sandy Desert [Thar], in all the countries of India, the kings had been firm believers in that Law.'

The Chinese monk returned to China to paint a glowing but misleading picture of Buddhism flourishing in Gandhara and in much of India. He also did much to strengthen the legend of a mighty king – King Kanishka – who had been a great protector and disseminator of the Dharma.

It was under Kanishka's aegis that Buddhism became a religion and Gautama Shakyamuni a god.

Within the mixing bowl that was Kanishka's Gandhara, Buddhism was reshaped in an extraordinary cultural exchange in which a torrent of exotic and already well-developed religious ideas from Iran, Bactria, Sogdiana and beyond flooded into its bazaars along with Roman gold, Chinese silk, Indian ivories, Sogdian mares and Khotanese jade.

It is in Kushan Gandhara that the first representations of Gautama Shakyamuni appear in stone. Such representations had been frowned upon by the great sage himself as having no place in a teaching which emphasises the illusory nature of all things. Under the influence of Greek and Roman art, with its fondness for the human figure and its many portrayals of the gods in human form, symbols of the Awakened One as pillars, wheels of law, lotuses, stupas, empty thrones and bodhi trees gave way to representations of Buddha Shakyamuni both as a man and as a god, complete with the nimbus of fire round the head that was first developed in Gandhara to indicate divinity.

By King Kanishka's time – the latest evidence suggests that he ruled for twenty-three years between the years 100–123 CE – human images of the Buddha on carvings and in paintings had already become widespread throughout the Gandhara region. Buddhist legend has it that the first portrayal in the form of a statue carved out of sandalwood was ordered by a ruler named Uddayana, which suggests that the first statues were carved in Uddiyana. This prototype was said to portray the Buddha standing and with his right hand raised in the gesture of reassurance known as abhayamudra. A number of such statues dating from the first and second centuries can be seen today in museums in Mathura, New Delhi, Lahore and Peshawar. One of the finest is a lifesize statue of the Maitreya Buddha in the National Museum in New Delhi. It shows a heroic, virile young man whose male member is prominently and deliberately outlined under a scanty dhoti, a regal figure but one very much of the flesh, an earthly man whose hair falls over his ears in long locks to rest on his shoulders. A huge nimbus blazes like the sun behind his head and shoulders.

But side by side with such heroic images can be seen numerous carvings of Gautama Buddha in classic meditative yogic posture. This very quickly became the abiding image in the iconography not only of both Mahayana and Hinayana Buddhism but also of central Indian Jainism.

This transformation exacerbated divisions among the many monastic schools of Buddhism which now existed both throughout the Indian sub-continent and beyond. What had started out as an exclusive, essentially atheistic philosophy of life which regarded gods as expressions of illusion was fast evolving into a popular, cosmopolitan religion in which the worship of divine and superhuman beings played an ever growing part. The historical Buddha no longer stood alone as the Enlightened One but was increasingly seen as but one of many emanations of a greater celestial power, a supreme Buddha far removed from earthly matters. These superdeities and their many manifestations were proving to be too remote for ordinary folk to relate to, so an additional category of lesser deities was now coming to the fore in the form of bodhisattvas, saintly beings who delayed their own progression towards buddhahood in order to help others, serving as role models and sources of gaining merit. Their greater approachability would in time promote them from attendants flanking the Buddha into godlike figures of far greater potency. Thus Avalokiteshvara, originally protector of travellers, would grow in stature over the centuries to become Tibet's favourite and most important deity, Chenresig, the protector of the nation. Other lesser forms of superbeings and spirits, both human and celestial, were also being added to an ever swelling, ever welcoming pantheon, including a rich variety of fertility figures in the form of yakshis (svelte female spirits), yakshas (bulkier male guards) and nagarajas (serpent kings).

There are said to have been eighteen different Buddhist schools at this time, with almost 500 points of disagreement. King Kanishka, so the *Records of the Buddhist Kingdoms* say, 'found the different views of the schools so contradictory that he was filled with doubt, and he had no way to get rid of his uncertainty.' In order to resolve these differences he convened the Fourth Buddhist Council, which was probably held in Kashmir in about the year 120 CE. Part of its brief was to harmonise what were known as the three pitakas or baskets of Buddha.

Made up of Gautama Shakyamuni's sayings, sermons and teachings assembled by his first disciples soon after his death, the baskets formed the Buddhist canon. They had been committed to memory by generations of monks, and inevitably, major variations had developed over the seven centuries since his death. Kanishka's Council was given the task of setting down all these oral transmissions as written texts and then sorting out the many differences of interpretation that had been placed on them.

The Kashmir Council concluded that the differences between the major schools of Buddhism were irreconcilable. This led to the division of the Buddhist Sangha into two main camps: the Path of the Elders, properly known as Theravada but more commonly referred to as the Hinayana or Lesser Vehicle, whose followers clung to the original teachings of Gautama Shakyamuni; and the Mahayana or Greater Vehicle, with its stress on personal enlightenment, its willingness to explore ever more esoteric paths as means of achieving the goal of enlightenment and its acceptance of a multiplicity of deities and attendants.

By some process not yet fully understood there developed out of Mahayana a form of esoteric Buddhism which came to be known as Vajrayana, the Thunderbolt or Diamond Vehicle. It drew its philosophy from mainstream Mahayana, without a doubt, but developed a complex system of ritual known as tantra, involving meditation, the chanting of mantras and hand gestures, in which secret knowledge is imparted by a guru (in Tibetan, lama) or personal mentor who directs the initiate by the acquisition of quasi-magical powers towards salvation. A central element in tantra is the union of compassion – found in the male figure – with wisdom – found in the female – often represented in paintings as sexual embrace. The Diamond Vehicle, Vajrayana, would become in time the established Buddhism of Tibet following its (supposed) introduction from Uddiyana by

Padmasambhava in 720 CE. Its origins remain very much in the dark. It shares more features with Hindu tantra than it does with Buddhism, but it is equally true to say that it draws heavily on the elemental aspects of inner Asian shamanism. These two strains came together in the mixing bowl that was Gandhara.

To read the accounts of Faxian and the Chinese travellers who followed him one would think that Gandhara was an entirely Buddhist kingdom with Buddhist rulers. This may well have been the writers' intention but is very wide of the mark. A provisional translation (by Nicholas Sims-Williams) of the twenty-three lines of Bactrian inscribed in Greek letters on the stone recently uncovered at Rabatak in northern Afghanistan shows it to be an edict set up by order of King Kanishka, described as 'the righteous, the just, the autocrat, the god worthy of worship, who has obtained the kingship from Nana and from all the gods' (lines 1–2), and as 'king of kings, the son of god' (line 14). This makes it plain that the Iranian model of divine rule and the divinity of kings lay at the heart of the Kushan political system.

The inscription sets out the extent of King Kanishka's realm and then goes on to explain that the king has ordered a sanctuary to be built and a number of images of gods erected in honour of King Kanishka's forebears. Of these gods, 'the glorious Umma leads the service here' (line 9). The others are then listed as 'the lady Nana and the lady Umma, Aurmuzd, Mozdooano, Sroshard, Narasa, [and] Mihr' (lines 9–10).

The two most important deities are goddesses: one is 'the lady Nana', daughter of the moon god and sister of the sun god, the Kushan form of Anahita, Zoroastrian goddess of fertility; the other is 'glorious Umma', most probably the consort of the fourth god on the list, Mozdooano, whose name translates as 'gracious one', a placatory title for Oesho, the Bactrian lord of demons and wind god of the Kushans. Oesho has a close tie-up with the yogic god Shiva, whom we tend to think of as an essentially Hindu god, but who shares a common Iranian ancestry

with Oesho in the elemental god of wind and thunder, Oado or
Rudra, 'the howler', the hurler of the thunderbolt vajira, symbol
of destruction. With Aurmuzd, Sroshard, Narasa and Mihr, we
are on safer ground because all are Zoroastrian deities: Aurmuzd
is the supreme god of light, Ahura Mazda; and Mihr, the sun
god, is linked with the Iranian Mithra.

Exactly the same non-Buddhist, polytheist picture emerges
when we look at the coinage of King Kanishka. He was the first
ruler in history to use the device of the halo or nimbus on his
coinage to emphasise his own divine status. He was also the first
ruler in Asia to employ a monetary system based on gold rather
than silver, a clear indication of the extraordinary wealth that
flowed into the Kushan state coffers during his reign.

Of the twenty-nine staters or half-staters of the British
Museum's collection of Kanishka I gold coinage, all display the
same standing image on the obverse: King Kanishka the nomad
warrior-chieftain, long-bearded, helmeted, dressed in a belted
topcoat with baggy leggings and boots, a sword at his waist and
a lance in his left hand. He is turned towards a small altar upon
which he makes an offering with his right hand. Flames burn on
his right shoulder, proclaiming him and his line to be fire gods
associated with the Zoroastrian fire god Athsho. Every coin carries the inscription *BASILEUS BASILEON* ('KING OF
KINGS') – together with the king's name in Greek letters.

On the reverse are shown the chief gods of the Kushans. Five
of the twenty-nine gold coins show Nanashao (the 'lady Nana'
of the Rabatak stone), who is portrayed with a nimbus about her
head, a forked sceptre in her right hand and a sword at her waist.
Another five coins are of the three-headed, four-armed demon
lord Oesho (Mozdooano on the Rabatak stone). He is shown
with erect phallus, armed with a trident and trailing an animal-
skin over his left arm. Four coins show Miiro (Mihr on the
Rabatak stone), the Mithraic sun god, with the sun's rays radiating from a nimbus round his head. Another four show Mao,
goddess of the moon and partner to Miiro/Mihr, helmeted with

curved wings showing above her shoulders, right hand out-stretched to make a V-sign.

A single gold coin in the collection carries on the reverse the inscription BODDO in Greek letters. It shows Gautama Shakyamuni standing with a nimbus behind his head and a larger aureole behind his body. In this collection of twenty-nine coins he is the only deity of indisputably Indian origin. All the others have Iranian, Bactrian or inner Asian roots.

Of the twelve Kushan kings only Kanishka I issued coins with Buddhist images – and even he produced very few. Two pairs of deities dominate Kushan coinage: the sun and moon deities Miro and Mao and the rather more complex god and goddess Oesho and Nana.

Oesho and Nana are seen by a number of Indian scholars as evidence of Hindu influence on the gods of Gandhara, with Oesho being identified as Shiva and Nana as Shiva's consort in the wrathful manifestations of Parvati/Durga/Kali. When you consider Oesho's appearance on Kushan coinage – the phallus, trident, animal skins and, very often, an accompanying bull standing at his shoulder – you can understand why. But Shiva and Parvati as we know them today emerged not from the Gangetic plains but from the mountains to the north. It is the conjunction of the destructive Oesho and the creative Nana in sexual union, the joining of opposite forces to create oneness, which leads to liberation. Out of this develop the cults of shakti and tantra, with the destructive vajra transformed into an instrument of creative (and tantric) energy.

The site of Kanishka's great pagoda outside Peshawar was excavated by British archaeologists between 1908 and 1911. A square pit at its centre contained a small copper casket. Inside was a crystal reliquary containing a clay seal showing the figure of an elephant – an early pre-Kushan representation of Gautama Shakyamuni Buddha – and three fragments of bone.

Casket and contents now sit on the lower shelf of a display case in the darkened recesses of the Peshawar Museum. On the lid of the casket are three figures cast in metal: Buddha Shakyamuni seated cross-legged on a mushroom-like lotus, flanked by standing figures of two bodhisattvas. Running round the base of the casket is a frieze which shows Roman-style putti

holding up a garland which frames a number of figures: the donor, a Kushan dressed in the nomad's garb of belted topcoat, baggy pants and felt boots associated with Kushan royalty, guarded on either side by two floating figures, identified as the Kushan sun and moon deities Miro and Mao. The associated coins show the donor to be Kanishka I. The message is unequivocal. King Kanishka gave his support to the Buddhist faith but retained his own beliefs in the elemental gods and goddesses of the steppes: the deities of fire, sun, moon, wind and fertility.

Gandhara, in sum, was far less Buddhist and far more polytheist than the *Records of the Western Worlds* would have us believe. The numismatic and archaeological evidence shows that the Kushan empire was a rainbow empire, whose subjects embraced a wide spectrum of beliefs. The picture that emerges is of Zoroastrian and various Iranian/Bactrian religions, including Mithraism, dominating the regions west and north of the summer capital of Kapisha; of Buddhism strongly influenced by these same ideas from the west dominating the Gandharan heartland in the centre; and of Buddhism, Hinduism and Jainism battling for supremacy in India south and east of Mathura, with Hinduism growing ever stronger further down river along the Ganges and Indus plains.

The break-up of the Kushan empire preserved these regional variations. In about 233 CE the Sasanian Persian king Ardashir invaded Bactria, overran and sacked Kapisha (while missing the hidden Begram Treasure) and incorporated this western sector of Kushan territory into his Persian empire. With their control of the valuable east–west traffic now lost, the Kushan kings of Gandhara were no longer major players on the international trading scene. Their territories east of the Indus fell to the Parthians and the Guptas. Only at the centre, Gandhara, were they allowed to remain in power, though as vassal-princes of the Persians.

Under Ardashir's rule, Zoroastrianism underwent a second major revival. With the magi as its zealots, it was transformed into a fundamental, uncompromising dualism in which Ormuzd, the god of truth, battled against the devil Ahriman in a constant struggle between good and evil, light and darkness. It was soon challenged by the syncretic teachings of the Babylonian teacher Mani, who added to this dualism the gnostic traditions of some of the early Christian sects, preaching that Jesus, Zoroaster and Buddha were all manifestations of God sent to rescue man from darkness.

This heresy resulted in Mani's execution in about 250 CE. Even so – or perhaps in consequence – the new religion of Manichaeism won many converts in Turkestan and along the Silk Road. In China its successes so troubled the Emperor Hsuan-tsung that in 732 he issued a prohibition order, condemning it for passing itself off as a form of Buddhism. In central Tibet, too, its popularity so concerned King Trisong Detsen that he had it banned, declaring: 'The great Persian liar Mar Ma-ne [Mani] of insatiable heresy has borrowed from all systems in order to fabricate a system deviating from all others.'

Whether introduced within reformed Zoroastrianism or Manichaeism, dualism added a further dimension to the many religious ideas already circulating within inner Asia.

In 519 CE, about 120 years after Faxian's visit to India, a second Chinese Buddhist monk, Sunyun, set out along the Silk Road. Now everything had changed dramatically for the worse. Khotan and Yarkand were no longer Buddhist states and 'the king of Khotan is no believer in the Law'. Sunyun gives no clue as to the new religious affiliations of the inhabitants of the Taklamakan oases.

Sunyun arrived at Gandhara to find a country overrun by barbarians and at war with its neighbour: 'This is the country which the Ye-the destroyed and afterwards set up Lae-Lih to be king over the country, since which events two generations have passed. The disposition of this king was cruel and vindictive and he practised the most barbarous atrocities. He did not believe the Law of Buddha but liked to worship demons.' These

'Ye-the', now 'receiving tribute from all the surrounding nations, more than forty countries in all', were the descendants of the Yuezhi's old rivals, the Xiongnu, but now transformed into the Huna or White Huns.

Although the Sasanids of Persia were soon able to recover their territory west of the Khyber, the Huna held on to their gains in the Indian plains. Buddhism appears to have been their chief target: one of the few scraps of information to survive this dark age is a statement that the Huna ruler Mihirakula presided over the demolition of 1,600 Buddhist institutions in northwest India.

One hundred and ten years after Sunyan's visit it fell to another Chinese monk, Xuanzang, to write what was to all intents the obituary of the once great civilisation of Gandhara. 'The royal family is extinct,' he wrote in his extensive and meticulous account. 'The kingdom is governed now by deputies from Kapisa. The disposition of the people is timid and soft. Most of them belong to the heretical faiths; a few believe in the true Law.' In the Vale of Peshawar Buddhism had been all but replaced by militant Hinduism:

> There are about one thousand monasteries which are deserted and in ruins. They are filled with wild shrubs and solitary to the last degree. The stupas are mostly decayed. The heretical [e.g. non-Buddhist, presumably Hindu] temples, to the number of about one hundred, are occupied by heretics. Inside the royal city, towards the northwest, is a ruined foundation. Formerly this was the precious tower of the alms-bowl of Buddha, where it was worshipped during many centuries. It has gone now to Persia.

The alms bowl now disappears into legend, rather like the Holy Grail in western Europe. It is said to have rested briefly in Karashahr, the capital of the Kalmuks, before that city was over-run by the Moslems — and then silence. Popular legend among the Kalmuks has it that Buddha's alms bowl lies buried and awaits the arrival of the Maitreya, the Buddha still to come.

It is highly probable that the impact of the Huna on Gandhara, starting in about 500 CE, coupled with the advance of militant Hinduism from the south, had the effect of squeezing the Buddhist faithful in the Vale of Peshawar, leading to a wave of Buddhist migration northwards and eastwards into – and through – the Karakoram ranges and the western Himalayas.

The easiest option would have been to go due north over the Malakand range to Uddiyana in the Swat valley, and this would explain why Tibetan Buddhist texts make so much of Uddiyana/Orgyan, the home of tantra and its greatest exponent Guru Rinpoche. But there is a mystery here, because it is now beyond dispute that Buddhist Orgyan was already in terminal decline a century and a half before Guru Rinpoche's dramatic overthrow of the demons at the building of the temple of Samye. As I have shown, the Chinese monk Xuanzang, who was so meticulous in recording the details of Buddhist settlements elsewhere, could find almost nothing to say when he toured the Swat valley in 629 BC. By contrast, when Xuanzang travelled south–east to Kashmir he was received with open arms by the Buddhist local ruler, who sent his son together with a large escort to meet him at the border. So warm was the welcome, in fact, that the monk lingered in Kashmir for two years 'to learn the scriptures and commentaries'.

Finally, we have the second-hand testimony of a fourth Chinese traveller, Hueichao, a monk who visited the Indo-Iranic borderlands in the year 726:

> North-east of Kashmir are the kingdoms of Great Bolor [Baltistan], Yang-tung [Shang-shung] and So-po-tzu [unidentified but probably Bru-sha or Gilgit]. These are under the rule of the Tibetans. Their people believe in the Triple Jewel and [there] are monks and monasteries. Their dress, language and customs are completely different from those of the Tibetans.

The Tibetans do not follow the Buddhist teachings and there are no monasteries in Tibet. Hu [Iranic tribes] are the population inhabiting these three countries.

This is hearsay evidence but it suggests that pockets of the western Himalayas and far western Tibet were inhabited by Buddhist refugees from Gandhara in the first quarter of the eighth century. This is confirmed in part by recent finds at Naupur in the Gilgit valley, where shepherds digging into the ruins of what was probably a library uncovered a cache of manuscripts made up of some fifty different Buddhist Mahayana texts, dating from the sixth and seventh centuries. Some of these texts are linked through orthography and names with Khotan, 300 miles to the north, which indicates links between Gilgit and the Silk Road states to the north.

The Indus and Gilgit river passages would have been an obvious escape route for refugees retreating before the Huna. Many would have continued beyond Gilgit, either continuing north through the Hunza gorge and risking the Khunjerab crossing or taking the easier but longer route by turning east and continuing up the Indus valley into the country of Ladakh. It is not stretching supposition to its limits to suggest that at least some of these refugees would have continued to follow the trade route further eastwards still – to emerge in due course on the high plateau of the Chang Tang.

It is also highly probable that the post-Huna migration from Gandhara was preceded by at least two equally significant waves of migration from west to east.

The earliest of these probably followed the religious persecutions instituted by Emperor Xerxes in Persia in about 500 BCE and saw Mithraist pastoralists migrate eastwards from the land of Tajik, the upper Amur Darya valley, into the Taklamakan region and beyond.

The second took place much later and followed the conquest of the Zoroastrian/Mithraic sector of the Kushan empire – the

Bactrian/Tajik country north of Begram – by the Sasanians in about 233 CE. As a direct consequence of this conquest east–west trade along the Silk Route ceased for the better part of a century. However, Khotan, Kashgar and other caravanserai in the Taklamakan basin survived as predominantly Buddhist independent city-states, obvious places of shelter for Buddhist refugees fleeing from the Sasanians. Strong evidence of this migration exists in the sudden influx of Gandharan influences on Silk Road art at this time. One striking example survives in the form of a fragment of fresco uncovered by the archaeologist Sir Aurel Stein at Miran, one of the desert outposts of the Taklamakan, and now in the Museum of Antiquities in New Delhi. Dating from the third century CE, it shows a group of smart and rather smug-looking young men with curly black hair and neat Clark Gable moustaches. With their round, staring eyes and direct gaze, they recall the figures of the Roman mosaics found at Pompeii and Herculaneum. They appear astoundingly modern and out of place, and their illustrator signs himself 'Vito' or 'Vita', which suggests that the artist may have been an itinerant painter from the Roman world. But perhaps the most astonishing thing about this little fragment is that it portrays Gautama Shakyamuni Buddha and half a dozen of his disciples.

Every form of religion from Zoroastrianism to Nestorian Christianity found a welcome in the desert states, but at this period it is possible that Mithraists and other non-Buddhists would not have been so welcome in these already vulnerable oases as fellow Buddhists. If they were asked to move on they would have had no option but to continue eastwards – into far western Tibet.

These three waves of migration, I suggest – in about 500 BCE, 230 CE and 500 CE – laid the foundations for the pre-Buddhist and proto-Buddhist culture of Shang-shung that developed into the Bon religion.

7 The Kingdom of Shang-shung

Les vrais paradis sont les paradis qu'on a perdus.

Marcel Proust

OCTOBER 1997

The ninth month of the year of the Air-Mouse. I am returning to Tibet with the single objective of getting to the Garuda valley, Kyunglung, and exploring Kyunglung Ngulkar Karpo, the Silver Castle of the Garuda, capital of Shang-shung.

Between the end of the Indian monsoon in September and the start of the Tibetan winter in November, there is a travellers' window of four to six weeks when the rivers that drain the melted monsoon snows are low enough to be forded by vehicles with high suspensions and the high passes are free of snow. But if the snows come too soon the rivers will rise again and we'll be in trouble. It'll be a race against the weather.

Dick has agreed to come with me again, on the condition that we cover more of Tibet, so our plan is to fly to Lhasa and drive west.

The flight from Kathmandu to Lhasa in a China Southwest Airlines passenger jet is a dream. Fifteen minutes out of

Kathmandu the plane does a hard left turn and floats over Makalu, with Everest seemingly so close I find myself searching the summit for climbers. A minute or two later the snows drop away and everything turns brown. Now we have a god's eye view of Tibet and the legend of the giant ogress straddling the land falls into place. It is a landscape utterly devoid of order. No symmetry, no form; only an endless squeezing and piling together of rocks, hugger-mugger, with the occasional splash of deep turquoise in the form of lakes. Twenty minutes of this chaos and then the first natural feature that has definition: the east–west corridor scoured out by the Tsangpo. The valley broadens and to our right the puddles of water that make up Yamdok Tso, the Scorpion Lake, glint in the sun. Somewhere beyond is the Yarlung valley and the tombs of the first Tibetan kings. As the plane circles to land we catch a glimpse of Tibet's most famous oracle lake, Lahamo Latso, where the regents of Tibet came in 1933 to seek visions in its waters of the whereabouts of the present Dalai Lama.

The airport is spick and spanking new, dazzling in the bright sunlight, the air clean and deceptively bracing. Scores of tiny Chinese officials in neatly pressed green uniforms and peaked caps one size too big, as if they're not really theirs, appear hostile in their dark glasses, but then who doesn't? One of the smallest looks the fiercest but she waves us through with a beaming smile and says, in English, 'Welcome to Tibet'.

We are met by a young Tibetan from TIST, the largest of the government travel services which look after foreign travellers in Tibet. I shall name him Pasang. He is a huge improvement on Sonam and has the directness of manner that sets Tibetans apart from Chinese. We both take to him. This is his last job before the winter, with a long lay-off until the end of May.

Lhasa is an hour's drive away on a fine metalled road. On either side fields are being ploughed by yak with smart red tassels on their horns, while tractors seem to be used mostly to transport produce and people. What looks like yak-baiting turns out to be something more innocent. They are threshing the barley: half-a-dozen yak are made to trample on the corn by being chased about by people standing in a circle and waving their arms in the air. It looks fun but inefficient. Beside the river the leaves of the poplar trees and willow are turning gold.

Lhasa is a dream ended by the Chinese occupation. At floor level it is a Chinese town made up of cheapjack public buildings and wide boulevards, but at its heart is that steep-sided hill out of whose summit and slopes grow the white walls and the russet-brown upper citadel of the Potala. At a distance its grace as architecture takes your breath away. Come a little closer and you begin to see how huge it is. The double stairway that zigzags up the front facade serves to emphasise its height. It was built to astound, and it does. Its effect on those who saw it as a celestial palace made manifest on earth must have been overwhelming. Even now, drained of its life-force, the Potala is still a little out of this world.

In the old days the Potala kept its secrets to itself. Now you drive round to the back and follow the custodian along galleries and up and down steep wooden stairs from one darkened room to another. He has fifty or so keys on a keyring attached to his belt and every room has to be unlocked to let us in and then locked again before we move on to the next. The complex divides into the outer White Palace, which served as the Whitehall or administrative headquarters of the country, and the inner Red Palace, which was the centre of worship and contains the reliquary tombs of eight past Dalai Lamas. But as you work your way round and up and then down again you become aware that the interior of the Potala does not match the scale of its exterior. It is mostly a facade joined to a rock with a comparatively small number of rooms in between. For all its statues and reliquaries, today the Potala is just a museum. The air is still heavy with the incense of centuries, but it is an empty shell, nothing without the presence of a living Dalai Lama.

This hasn't stopped the Potala from being the focal point of pilgrimage in Lhasa. Like all devotional objects in Tibet, the Marpori hill on which it stands has its own khorlam which pilgrims follow as they circle the edifice. Lhasa valley was once richly ringed with these circuits, large and small, and a pilgrim would spend weeks trudging round them all. Now only the two that really matter are the Potala and the Barkhor khorlams.

The Barkhor is the last quarter of the old town that hasn't been pulled down and rebuilt along Chinese lines. It must be the despair of the Chinese authorities. Prayer-wheel-spinning pilgrims cram the marketplace. Its stone flags are polished and worn by prostrations, the smoke from juniper twigs rises from incense fires at every street corner. At the heart of the Barkhor is the Jokhang temple, and at its very core the three-storey inner temple built over the heart of the supine ogress. It is still the main repository of Tibet's religious history, all the more precious after what was lost elsewhere in the Cultural Revolution. Sticking out like sore thumbs among the thousands of Tibetan pilgrims are a number of smart-suited Chinese officials and their even smarter wives. The wives crack first. They giggle self-consciously as they pull out a pendant or a photograph and place it for a moment or two on the altar below a large image of Wopame or Chenresig. Their men tend to stand back and smile indulgently, taking a photo or two. But by the time they reach the high-roofed chamber which contains the image of the Jowo Rinpoche, lit brightly by countless butter lamps, the couples have fallen silent. If they think they're not being observed they bring their hands together in a furtive sort of way that suggests, if not silent prayer, at least a gesture of respect.

Dick and I seem to be the only guests in a plush hotel called the Himalaya. It is staffed by half a dozen young women who have nothing to do except stand behind the reception desk and stare at you with incredulous open mouths whenever you approach them. They are younger, prettier and better-dressed versions of the guest-house keepers we met in Purang and Darchen last year. These are the de luxe models, so staggeringly useless that you can only stand back and admire. Where do they find these women, who are so unlike the robust, down-to-earth and good-natured women you meet everywhere else in Tibet? Do the authorities employ some form of terton, who scours the country in search of semi-catatonics who are then deprogrammed of all social skills? We devote hours of speculation to this subject on the long journey westwards.

Our permits have to be cleared. We have made it absolutely clear in our applications that our main object on this journey is to spend several days trekking downstream from Tirthapuri to the ruins of Kyunglung Ngulkar in the upper Sutlej gorge. Ever since the Italian Tibetologist Dr Tucci passed by this troglodyte city in 1932 the site has been known and noted on the map, even though no one has since paid it much attention. With Pasang to interpret for us we spend a lively half hour in the TIST offices explaining exactly where Kyunglung is and pointing it out on the tourist map. During these exchanges I catch sight of our original visa applications from Kathmandu: a little trimming has taken place. Under 'Occupation' Dick had written 'Architectural photographer' and I had written 'Civil servant'. These entries have been shortened to 'Architect' and 'Servant'.

The following day Pasang emerges from the TIST offices all smiles and waving our permits and passports. We are cleared to go. To take us the thousand or so kilometres to Tirthapuri we have the two great workhorses of modern Tibet: a Toyota Landcruiser and a Chinese Dong Feng four-tonner. This may seem a little over the top but as the days pass the need for a back-up vehicle becomes clearer.

A new road has been built from Lhasa to Shigatse which follows the course of the Tsangpo upstream through a twisting gorge. We emerge on to a broad valley with the river stretching away into the distance. On the far bank we can see a village and a partly restored monastic settlement which my map identifies as Yungdrungling, 'Swastika Park'. The name is pure Bon, which is hardly surprising since this area used to be a major centre of

Bon. Menri, once the largest Bonpo monastic centre in Tibet, is just a day's walk away to the northwest. We stop beside the river for a photograph and while Dick sets about his business I walk back down to the road to where another Landcruiser has parked. Two male Westerners are doing more or less the same as us but they behave so extraordinarily furtively as I approach that I have second thoughts and turn back.

A little further down the road we stop in a little village above the river so that Dick can chase a boatman who's walking tortoise-like down the road under a yak-hide coracle. Pasang and I are drinking tea with our two drivers in a tea shop when a handsome young couple enter and start singing. He scrapes on a primitive one-stringed fiddle but she has the voice of an angel. She transmutes a simple melody into two minutes of the sweetest sound you could ever wish to hear. When their song ends the couple drop their eyes and stand motionless, with grave faces. Everyone in the room puts something in their hat. They take our money as their due and leave without a backward glance. Pasang tells me that they are itinerant musicians, a very ancient and respected profession.

We reach Shigatse in time to see the gilded roofs and finials of Tashilhunpo monastery glinting in the last rays of the sun.

At the Shigatse Hotel the staff confound our prejudices by being charming and helpful. Our room is de luxe and everything works. There's a TV set in the corner and when we turn it on we find ourselves watching *Laurel and Hardy Join the Foreign Legion*, with Stan and Olly's voices dubbed into Mandarin. In the banqueting hall we run across the Western travellers who were behaving so mysteriously by the river earlier that afternoon. They turn out to be Michel Peissel, the French explorer, and Charles Guinness, a film-maker. We cautiously exchange notes, only showing our respective cards when it becomes clear that we won't be treading on each other's toes. We'll be on the same road for another day but after the town of

Raga Peissel and Guinness will turn north on to the Chang Tang while we continue westwards. Their aim is to follow old trade routes as far north as they can go.

A month later Reuters will publish a press release from Peissel in which he will claim to have found the lost kingdom of Shang-shung. He will be some 500 miles wide of the mark.

On the first day of driving we covered 170 miles in half a day. This lulls us into thinking that we have time to spare. We spend half the morning exploring Tashilhunpo, former stronghold of the Panchen Lamas, full of toothless old Gelugpa monks shuffling around like residents of an old folks' home.

Soon after leaving Shigatse we pass a couple of Chinese Army trucks parked by the roadside. They're being loaded with green juniper bushes. Parties of young Chinese soldiers are working their way across the mountainside chopping down every bush they come to, not just a branch or two but the entire sapling. To the Tibetans the juniper bush is a living treasure. What use can it be to the Chinese? We wonder if they're after the berries, so that they can drown the sorrows of their exile in barrack-made gin.

Among the many hundreds of religious structures in Tibet the most remarkable in architectural terms are probably the great multi-tiered chortens built at Gyantse and a number of other sites. All were thought to have been torn to bits until Roberto Vitali announced in 1987 that one had survived the great destruction more or less unscathed. This he has located near an isolated village named Riboche, beside the Tsangpo. On the map Riboche appears to be not so very far off our route and Dick is very keen to see and photograph it, so we decide to track it down. We locate the side road and all goes well for the first two hours as the track leads us up and over a high mountain and then down through a narrow ravine which brings us out beside the Tsangpo. It is utterly tranquil here and the scenery gets lovelier by the minute as the evening shadows lengthen.

Then we meet a party of shepherds on the track and they tell us that Riboche is still half a day's journey away.

Nonsense, we cry. Look — it's here on the map! It must be just around the corner!

So we drive on, round the next corner and the next after that and so on, past many, many bends in the river, bouncing over sandbanks, rattling across stony river beds till dusk settles and then darkness, while Pasang and the drivers grow ever more restless and agitated. Finally, in the pitch dark, at about eight o'clock Nepalese time — which means after eleven o'clock local time — I crack. I'm not going any further. I know that Dick is deeply disappointed but he takes it very well. We turn the vehicles about and use our headlamps to retrace our tracks.

One of the great mysteries of the Orient now unfolds: our truck driver announces that he has a relation living in a nearby village and he can take us there. In fact, it is the *only* village for miles and miles. The astonishing capability of the Chinese lorry is now demonstrated as the driver, after several attempts, finally succeeds in forcing it up a steep sandbank and into his relative's village. Our noisy approach has woken the entire population. I step out of the Landcruiser into the pitch dark and the moment my foot touches the ground my hand is seized and I'm dragged away from the car. I have no idea where I'm being taken or who's got hold of me but whoever it is has no intention of letting go. Dick is grabbed in exactly the same way and together we are rushed through the narrow streets of the village with much shouting, pushing and bumping. Then we are made to duck into a small courtyard and bundled up some stairs into a large room with a stove burning at the centre.

My kidnapper is revealed as a grandmother with a one-year-old child strapped to her back. We are to be her guests for the night. So we eat round her fire, surrounded by her family, and when we've finished and the chatter and laughter has died down, we stretch out head to toe on the raised bunks that extend all round the room and go to sleep. Rarely have I been made to feel so much at home as in that village, the name and exact location of which I never found out.

*

The east–west highway keeps more or less parallel to the Tsangpo but some miles to its north. After the large township of Saga the road becomes no more than a track, where it's good going to cover more than fifteen miles an hour or to reach third gear. We start driving soon after sunrise and usually carry on long after sunset.

The country is a mix of wide, flat valleys and low mountain ranges that rise perhaps 1000 feet or so above the plateau. The larger valleys extend for thirty or forty miles: some contain shallow lakes and are covered in what is now rich grazing grass, others are little more than deserts with the sand piling up at one end into great dunes. The snowpeaks of the Himalayan chain provide a constant backdrop over to our left, only falling back when we approach Mustang. Here we spot several pairs of the increasingly rare Siberian crane. They have crossed the Chang Tang and are now resting and watering before the next stage of their journey. They will fly across Mustang and then down through the Kali Gandaki gorge between the Dhaulagiri and Annapurna ranges. By this time next week tourists may be photographing these very same birds in the bird sanctuary at Bharatpore. Somewhere among those brown ranges is the gap through which the valiant little Japanese monk Ekai Kawaguchi stumbled into Tibet on his pilgrimage to Kangri Rinpoche a century ago. And somewhere up this same trail, covering exactly 31½ inches with each stride and counting off every hundredth step on his beads, marched that great pioneer explorer-spy known simply as the 'Pundit', Nain Singh Rawat of Garhwal. It seems extraordinary that the road system is no better now than it was in his day. Perhaps the Chinese prefer to keep it that way. No communications means fewer foreigners and foreign ideas.

One sharp night under canvas is enough to remind us that

winter is fast approaching. From then on we stick to caravanserai. The best of these is the Yak Hotel at Paryang, a tiny settlement surrounded on all sides by open prairie. The women here are charming and most helpful. After supper Pasang and the drivers disappear and we make assumptions. Only next morning do we discover that they went to a movie, a Chinese film about Colonel Younghusband's invasion of Tibet in 1903–4. They didn't invite us to join them because they thought we might be upset. Paryang wins five stars because it has the best privy in western Tibet, high in a tower with a hole in the floor. Dick uses it as a vantage point for a session of early-morning sunrise photography and in so doing creates a tailback of would-be users.

Settlements here are few and far between but the valley floors are dotted with herds of yak, sheep and goats. Full-bred yak sport slightly absurd Viking helmet horns. They stand their ground with heads lowered like bison, whiffling through their noses and looking thoroughly menacing. If you continue to approach they suddenly and dramatically toss their heads and buck to one side, and then entirely spoil the effect by skipping off with their forelegs raised like trotting ponies.

Descending into one valley we see far below what looks like the advance of Napoleon's Grande Armée: four regiments of sheep, marching in neat formation one behind the other, munching their way across the grass in extended line. This is a time for feeding up the livestock and some of best pastures in the higher valleys have deliberately been saved till the end of autumn. Several times we spot little clouds of dust moving fast across the skyline. These turn out to be pairs of horsemen racing each other.

Our last day's drive is the longest. It takes a whole morning for our two vehicles to work their way up and out of the Tsangpo watershed. We snatch a quick lunch beside one of its highest sources, just a mile or so short of the saddle of the 16,900-foot Maryum La. An overnight fall of snow has left the pass and the surrounding mountain with a thick white pall which gives us a few problems on our descent. This is a real worry; if the snows come again and settle over the next few days we could be stuck on the wrong side of the pass – and that could mean a very long, very cold winter in Ngari until the road opens again in the spring.

The descent into Ngari province and the Sutlej river basin takes us down through a valley which has a long narrow lake stretching down one side. This is Gung-ghyu Gulmo, the lake which the Bon texts speak of as resembling 'a large piece of blue silk stretched on the ground', and the first of the four central lakes of old Shang-shung. The floor of the valley is mostly covered in small boulders which slow us down to a wearing, bumping grind in low gear. Very little livestock is grazing here, which may account for the abundance of wildlife: several species of duck bobbing about in the streams, a number of small herds of Tibetan antelope and a great many larger herds of the Tibetan wild ass, the kiang. They indulge in classic kiang behaviour, galloping parallel to us rather than away and in several instances changing direction to cut across in front of our Landcruiser.

The deer are far more timid and when Dick attempts to approach a herd on foot they keep retreating higher up the slopes. While he's doing one such stalk my eye falls on a low line of boulders not far from the car. This turns out to be the remains of a mani wall several hundred feet long. The mani stones have been scattered and nearly every one has been smashed but this and a number of low mounds round about point to human settlement here at some time in the past.

We arrive at Darchen long after dark. The Nine Stacked Swastikas Mountain is hidden behind thick cloud. Snow storms have closed the pilgrim circuit. When it opens again two German tourists, travelling illegally without a guide, will be found dead at the upper end of the Lha Chhu valley; one in his tent, the other caught out in the open apparently while trying to make his way back to fetch help.

We had hoped to bypass Darchen and its squalor altogether but Pasang is required to report to the Public Security Bureau office with our passports and permits. He returns after an hour looking shame-faced. After a little hedging the truth emerges. We are denied permission to go to Kyunglung.

This is awful news. When it sinks in we begin to protest. Kyunglung is why we're coming here! That's why we've spent the last five days bouncing across Tibet on our backsides! Look, it's written on our permits!

Only then does Pasang admit that Kyunglung never was listed on our permits. He didn't have the heart to tell us earlier.

I never do discover why Lhasa refused us permission. It's easy to fall back on Chinese conspiracy theories but it was probably a cock-up based on ignorance: they didn't know where Kyunglung was and so they played safe. It is a sad reality that the young Tibetans who now fill many of the junior posts in central and local government in Tibet are strangers to their own culture. Many have been educated outside Tibet or in Chinese-dominated eastern Tibet. They may have sentimental feelings about Buddhism but no real understanding. They know even less about Bon.

To understand Bon you have to go back to its origins:

In the beginning of the beginning the Father Khri-Sher Karpo held the Essence of the Five Causes to his body and breathed the sound 'Ha!' which became cold wind. As the wind circled faster and faster it formed into a wheel of light, from which came fire. The heat of the fire and the coldness of the wind produced dew drops upon which clustered atoms. These were stirred and blown about by the wind to form particles of matter which became as large as mountains.

The dew and the cold wind also united to form a lake like a

mirror, out of which came a membrane that shaped itself into an egg. Out of this egg were hatched two eagles, one white and one black. The first was called 'The One Provided With Light That Shined'; the other 'The One Provided With Darkness and Torment'.

The birds mated to produce a clutch of three eggs; one white, one black and one speckled. From the yolk of the white egg came the Realm of Light; from the white of the same egg came a white dru (hybrid yak–cow); and from the shell came three levels of gods headed by the world god White Light. From the black egg came the black Proud Man and the Heap of Black. From the speckled egg hatched the all-handsome Wish-requesting Man.

Wish-requesting Man lacked every sense except that of imagination. Nevertheless, he named himself the world god Sangpo Bumtri. He then created a gold mountain and a turquoise valley for the Cha race, a conch mountain and a cornelian valley for the Mu race and a crystal mountain and iron valley for the Tzug race. The Tzug developed into animals, the Cha turned into black-headed men, and the Mu race became the enlightened Bonpo.

Here in its essentials is one of the cosmogonic myths of Tibet as told by the Bonpo. For those looking for signs of Iranian influence, the evidence is there: in the heavy emphasis on primordial light and fire (elements of Mithraism); the dualistic element (features of later Zoroastrianism and Manichaeism); the joining of two antagonistic, opposite forces in an act of creation (another echo of Manichaeism) to produce the cosmic egg (as in early Iranian mythology); and the beauteous Sangpo Bumtri (again, close parallels with the primeval man King Yima the Glorious, born of a cosmic egg in Iranian mythology). Even the word 'Bon' can be construed as deriving from the Iranian *bwn*, meaning 'construct', although the Bonpo interpret it as 'unwavering' or 'protecting', which gives it the same meaning as

A Bonpo map of the paradise of Olmo-lungring: a woodblock from western Nepal reproduced by Professor David Snellgrove in his pioneering study of Bon, *The Nine Ways of Bon*. The Tibetan commentary at the bottom states that it is known by many names: 'The people of Uddiyana call it Sukhavati (the Paradise of Amitabha). It is also called the Land of the Unchanging Swastika, the Land of the Initiation Circles and the Land Where Desires are Fulfilled. The Indians call it Shambhala, the Chinese call it the Treasure Continent, the Kashmiris know it as the Indestructible Vajra Continent, in the Gesar tradition it is called the Land of the Turquoise-winged Cuckoos, in Nepal they speak of the Continent of Wish-granting Trees and the Tibetans call it Ol-mo-lung-ring.' (Translation by Amy Heller, courtesy of Martin Brauen.) The map represents a giant four-sided pyramid or ziggurat rising in a series of steps. Forty-eight outer countries surround eight inner countries, approached through doors or gates. At the centre is the holy land of Olmo-lungring or Shambhala, and at its heart the nine-storey Nine Stacked Swastikas Mountain reaching up to heaven.

the Tibetan word Chos, used by Tibetan Buddhists as an equivalent of the Sanskrit word Dharma.

The founding father of Bon was Shenrab Miboche, better known as Tonpa Shenrab, the Teacher of Knowledge. The Bon biographies tell us he was born 2,500 years before the persecution of the Bonpo in Tibet by King Trisong Detsen, which gives us a date of 1720 BCE (although some versions say he was born some 15,000 years earlier). His birthplace was a city called Barpo Sogye, the capital of a country called Olmo-lungring, which was either part of a larger country called Tajik or simply another name for Tajik. 'Ol' symbolises the unborn, 'mo' the undiminishing, 'lung' the prophetic words of Tonpa Shenrab, and 'ring' his everlasting compassion, so Olmo-lungring – the Place of the Unborn, Undiminishing, Prophetic Words of Tonpa Shenrab the Ever-Compassionate – may be seen to be a conceptual rather than a physical place, whereas Tajik is very much of this earth. Even so, Olmo-lungring is always spoken of as being to the west of Tibet and having the form of an eight-petalled lotus. At its centre rises a great mountain named Ribo Yungdrung Gutseg, the Nine Stacked Swastikas Mountain, with four lesser mountains to north, south, east and west.

Lying some distance to the south-west of Olmo-lungring/Tajik is the land of Shang-shung – which also has its own duplicate Nine Stacked Swastikas Mountain at the centre. The Bon manuscript known as *Mdo-dus*, said to have been rediscovered as terma in the late tenth century and the earliest of the three biographies of Tonpa Shenrab, provides a basic geography of both Olmo-lungring and Shang-shung. The former is described as many times larger than Shang-shung: 'It is cut by the rivers Pag-shu and Si-ti; [and] cut by the Nine Dark Mountains. In the west is the country of Dmu [Mu]. In the east is the country of China. In the south is the country of Mon. In the south-east is the country of Jang. In the north are Li [Khotan], Bal and Phrom. In the north-east is the country of Hor [and] Snowy Tibet [Gang(s)-can Bod].'

This account makes clear that Olmo-lungring is set at some unspecified distance north-west of Shang-shung and bounded by the four countries of Mu (?), Balkh, Khotan and Turkestan. We are told it is cut by nine dark mountains, which suggests nine mountain ranges without summer snow or without glaciers, and also by the rivers Pag-shu and Si-ti.

The Tibetologist Dan Martin and other scholars have done their best to make some sense of this geography – so far, without success. Geographical accuracy is not a feature of Bon literature: one text frequently contradicts another or even contradicts itself. Bon's enemies would say this is because they have been made up or stolen from Chos texts, but to me it suggests that these are records patched together from several sources – sources which may have been verbally transmitted in the old languages of Shang-shung but then translated and set down in Tibetan. My own interpretation of the Olmo-lungring geography as given in the *Mdo-dus* is that the rivers Pag-shu and Si-ti are the Amur-Daria and the Tarim. Thus the heartland of Olmo-lungring was somewhere in the Pamirs and Karakoram between Persia and Tibet.

More information on the roots of Bon can be drawn from the language of Shang-shung. No document written entirely in the Shang-shung language has yet come to light other than a medical text from Tun-huang. But sufficient non-Tibetan Shang-shung words have been retained in surviving Bon texts to point to an earlier language which falls into the category of Tibeto-Burmese, the language base underlying many of the local dialects spoken along Tibet's southern and western borders.

The Bon text *Ma-rgyud* states that there were four languages of Shang-shung. The first was the language of lesser gods and was spoken in the Innermost Realm. This was also called the language of Ka-pi-ta. The second tongue is spoken in the Intermediate Realm, north-west of Tibet. The third was the language of the Gateway Realm, spoken in the lands of the upper Indus from Leh along the western Himalayas as far as Garhwal.

The fourth language was spoken by the people in five districts of far western Tibet, inlcuding Gu-ge and Purang.

The 'language of Ka-pi-ta' immediately brings to mind Kapisha, the summer capital of Kushan Gandhara outside Kabul. This suggests that the language of the Innermost Realm was Bactrian and Sanskrit the language of the Intermediate Realm. These would have been the languages in which the first teachings of Bon were received in Shang-shung, in much the same way as the first scriptures of Buddhism were received without being understood in Yarlung and Lhasa. And if Ka-pi-ta is indeed Kapisha, could this have been the city of Barpo Sogye, where Bon's founding father Tonpa Shenrab was born?

Whatever the location of Barpo Sogye, this is where Tonpa Shenrab was born as a prince of the royal lineage of Murigtrul. It is often claimed that he is little more than a smudged carbon-copy of Gautama Shakyamuni, but even the most cursory reading of his biographies will show that this is not the case.

Tonpa Shenrab is placed on the throne of his kingdom at the age of one. He rules his kingdom as its monarch for thirty years, during which time he journeys far and wide to spread the teachings of Bon and to carry out the elaborate rituals which make up the basic ceremonials of Bon practice. He builds numerous chorten and temples but no monasteries, the ideals of celibacy and of celibates gathered together within one institution only becoming part of mainstream Bon culture after the Buddhists had started to set up major monasteries in Tibet in the eleventh century. Indeed, Tonpa Shenrab himself has ten wives who bear him eight sons and two daughters. The former become his chief disciples and go forth, each armed with a specific skill, to spread his teachings.

Tonpa Shenrab becomes an ascetic at the age of thirty-one. Only at this stage of his life does he have sufficient spiritual merit to take on his greatest opponent, the demon king Khyabpa Lagring. The protracted struggle between the two has been portrayed as the Bon attempt to come up with an equivalent to Guru

Rinpoche's vanquishing of the demons of Tibet. But the similarities are superficial: Guru Rinpoche moved through Tibet conquering and converting the local spirits area by area, and his story is a metaphor for the spread of Buddhism through Tibet, whereas the confrontations between Shenrab and Khyabpa are a long-drawn-out battle between the champions of good and evil on the Zoroastrian/Manichean model.

In seeking to undo the good work being undertaken by Tonpa Shenrab all over the known world, Khyabpa Lagring leaves his demon castle and tries to trick Shenrab into killing himself. When this fails he seduces Shenrab's daughter and takes her back to his castle, where she gives birth to twins. Shenrab then rescues his daughter and takes both her and her children back to Olmo-lungring.

Tibet only comes into the picture when the demon king kidnaps Shenrab's seven horses and takes them to Kongpo in eastern Tibet. Tonpa Shenrab sets out in pursuit, with Khyabpa Lagring and his demonic minions doing all they they can to halt his advance. At Zahor (Jallandra, in the western Himalayas) they block his progress with snow, and Shenrab pauses to impart the 'Bon of Spells' to the Bonpos of Zahor, Kashmir and Gilgit. Then, at the frontier between Tajik and Shang-shung, his way is barred by fire. Here Shenrab pauses to impart the 'Bon of Bombs' before loosing off an arrow that carves a passage through the mountains, so opening an 'arrow-way' linking Shang-shung to Olmo-lungring. Shenrab then proceeds to the sources of the four great rivers in Shang-shung, which Khyabpa Lagring has turned into a vast lake. He finally enters Shang-shung after overcoming one last obstacle in the form of a desert of sand. This progress suggests that the Teacher of Shen started from somewhere in the Gandhara region and crossed into far western Tibet either by way of the upper Indus or the upper Sutlej.

Tonpa Shenrab is described as arriving at Shang-shung 'astride the blessed garuda'. This most curious hybrid plays a major role in the culture of Shang-shung. It possesses the head and wings of an eagle and the body and limbs of a man, and is usually portrayed with red wings, golden limbs, a white face and a pair of short, curved horns. It is the king of birds and the enemy of all serpents. At birth it was so brilliant that it was thought to be the god of fire. It went on to steal the water of life, amrita, which was only recovered by the god Indra after a fierce fight in which the garuda smashed Indra's thunderbolt.

Images of the garuda perch on the eaves of Buddhist monasteries in the role of guardians. This is said to be because of the garuda's links with the Hindu god Vishnu, but the garuda has a far older association with Tibet through Bon. It can be traced back to the Mesopotamian lion-headed bird of stone called Zu, or Imdugud, which steals the tablets of destiny from the god Enli. In the old language of Shang-shung the word for the garuda is shang, which suggests that 'Shang-shung' itself, usually given to mean 'Gateway of the Gods', translates more accurately as 'Gateway of the Garuda'. In the Tibetan language garuda translates as kyung, and it is in this Tibetan form that the garuda usually appears on Bon texts. The kyung is the protector of the land of Shang-shung. It 'destroys like fire and water all the princes of the stationary and the moving', and is the 'long presence of [guards over] the five families [clans of Shangshung] and the five wisdoms [of Bon]'. It gives its name both to the innermost region of Shang-shung – Kyunglung, the valley of the Garuda – and to the capital of Shang-shung within that valley – Kyunglung Ngulkar Karpo, the Silver Castle of the Garuda Valley. The symbol of royalty worn by the kings of Shang-shung was a crown known as byum or 'bird crown', which incorporated a pair of curved horns similar to the horned head-dresses of the Sasanid rulers of Persia. The same horned crowns can be seen on early portraits of the Mongol khans.

At Shang-shung Tonpa Shenrab lingers for a while, staying at a site directly under the southern face of the Nine Stacked Swastikas Mountain, where the Gelugpa monastery of

Gyangdrak now stands. Here the founding master imparts the basic Bon rituals to the local ascetics: 'Shenrab gave to the Bonpos as Bon [Doctrine] the inspired teaching concerning prayers to the gods and the expelling of demons. As ritual items he showed them various small aromatic herbs, the use of barley as a sacrificial item and libations of chang [fermented barley]. By summoning all gods and demons by means of Bon, the Bonpos gained their protection; by worshipping them, they sent them about their tasks; and, by striking them, they prevailed over them.'

From Shang-shung Tonpa Shenrab continues eastwards into Tibet proper in his pursuit of the demon king and his stolen horses. After further trials he gets his horses back and secures Khyabpa Lagring's submission. This is only a feint to try to catch Shenrab off-guard and further adventures follow, but eventually the demon king admits defeat and is converted to his conqueror's cause.

Because the Tibetan plateau is not yet ready to receive his words, Tonpa does not impart all his teachings but prophesies that these will flourish in Shang-shung and Tibet when the time is ripe. He then returns to Olmo-lungring and dies there at the age of eighty-two.

The Bonpo themselves accept that there were three distinct stages in their religious evolution, beginning with an undeveloped Bon which included Dud Bon, the Bon of Devils, and Tsan Bon, the Bon of Spirits. Both these rites made extensive use of animal sacrifice in their rituals. When Shenrab Miboche came to Shang-shung he introduced substitutes for blood sacrifices in the form of dos, rituals involving statuettes rather than animals, and yas, offerings in the form of cakes. He laid the ground for – but did not himself directly transmit – the teachings of Yungdrung Bon, Eternal or Swastika Bon, which came after him.

According to Samten Karmay's translation in *The Treasury of Good Sayings*, the full teachings of Tonpa Shenrab were brought to Shang-shung two generations later by Krilde Odpo, a disciple of Tonpa Shenrab's immediate successor, Mucho Demdrug:

> The sage K'ri-lde Odpo of sTag-gzig transformed himself into a vulture and flew into the presence of the holy master Od-kyi Mu-sans at gNas-brtan Rin-po-c'e Palace which was situated on the slope of Mount Ti-se in Zan-zun [Shang-shung]. Thereafter, a religious community of 16,000 practitioners flourished at the A-ti gSan-ba Yung-drun Cave, which is located left of Mount Ti-se. The king who ruled at that time was K'ri-wer La-rje of Zan-zun, the Holder of the Golden Horn-like Crown, who dwelt at Ga-ljan Yu-lo Castle situated in front of Mount Ti-se.

Krilde Odpo's disciple, Danba Yidren, founded a second religious community on an island on the lake south of the Nine Stacked Swastikas Mountain, Langak Tso. His disciple in turn founded a third community at another location, and so the teachings of Bon were passed from shen to shen and from one foundation to another, first throughout Shang-shung and then westwards into Tibet, down through the generations for two thousand years: 'In Zan-zun, during these two thousand years, the religious masters had long-lasting lives, the ruling kings increased their power and wealth, and the holy doctrine was diffused everywhere.'

As well as listing the dynasties of the priests of Shang-shung, *The Treasury of Good Sayings* also gives the names of its kings. Eighteen kings together ruled over the Eighteen Great Countries which made up the eighteen kingdoms of Inner, Middle and Outer Shang-shung. Within Inner Shang-shung eight of these kings together ruled over three regions: Gyanri Hill, immediately to the south of the Nine Stacked Swastikas Mountain; the Kyunglung valley, forty miles to the west; and Purang, south of the two main lakes. Six kings ruled three regions in Middle Shang-shung named as Tsi-na, Ta-rog and Ta-sgo, and four kings ruled four countries in Outer Shang-shung, listed as K'a-skyor, K'a-yug, La-dvags (Ladakh) and Ru-t'og (Rudok).

'During the lifetime of the kings,' adds *The Treasury*, 'the eighteen districts of Zan-zun covered most of the Eighteen Great Countries. Besides, the holy doctrine of the Yun-drun Bon spread in every place, the life of human beings reached a span of two thousand years, and supreme realisation was also attained without leaving the physical body behind.'

Lifespans of two thousand years seriously complicate matters when it comes to attempting a realistic chronology of events, but this inordinate longevity helps to explain what seems to be a substantial gap of more than two generations between Tonpa Shenrab's visit to Tibet and the subsequent arrival of his teachings. The first citizen of Shang-shung we can date with some confidence is the great wizard who took on Guru Rinpoche in Lhasa, and converted to Chos during the later years of the reign of King Trisong Detsen in the last quarter of the eighth century: Gyerpung Drenpa Namka. He belonged to the clan of Gu-rib – a family name still found in northern Tibet even though these families are no longer followers of Bon.

Gyerpung Drenpa Namka is acknowledged as the first great master of the Shang-shung oral tradition and the codifier of the meditational doctrines of *Zhang-zhung snyan-rgyud*, the 'Oral Transmission of Shang-shung'. The Bon texts state that Gyerpung had 'perfect knowledge of the nine vehicles, studying with great constancy'. However, 'he had not yet perfectly accomplished the supreme realisation' and was 'very proud of himself'. A Bon sage-deity then appeared to him: 'He overcame in him pride and ego attachment. He taught him the method of meditation and dissolved all the chains that bound him. Thus he could contemplate his own mind in the condition of equanimity.' The deity then transmitted to him 'all the doctrines in the sacred texts of the *Zhang-zhung snyan-rgyud*'.

From Gyerpung to the present day the secrets – secret in the sense of being accessible only to initiates – of the Shang-shung oral tradition have passed down from master to disciple in an unbroken line in the process of teaching known as 'direct transmission'. They include the teaching known as the Dzog-pachen-po Zhang-zhung Nam-Gyud. Widely known today as Dzogchen or the Great Perfection, these esoteric beliefs include the doctrine of Bardo Thodol, known in the West as the Tibetan Book of the Dead.

The dating of the wizard Gyerpung Drenpa Namka to the second half of the eighth century makes it possible to speculate on when and how the Bon religion might have come to far western Tibet and Shang-shung. I believe it came in three stages, which correspond to the three stages of development traditionally ascribed to Bon – and to the three migrations described in the previous chapter.

In stage one the Mu tribe, part of the Yuezhi nation, migrates from the Khotan/Taklamakan region into far western Tibet in about 500 BCE, bringing its own form of mi-chos, the religion of humans, which includes elements of Mithraist sun and fire worship and blood sacrifice. These are the blood-sacrificing Bonpo whom Tonpa Shenrab encounters when he first comes to Shang-shung and to whom he imparts 'inspired teaching', as well as introducing the use of barley and chang in sacrifices.

The arrival of the Teacher of Shen in Shang-shung marks the start of stage two. This is precipitated by the conquest of western Gandhara and the overthrow of the Kushan's summer capital of Kapisha by the Sasinians in 233 CE. Those not wishing to follow King Ardashir's hardline Zoroastrianism migrate westwards. Under a charismatic shaman who is both prince and priest, they make a long, hard journey through the Karakoram and eventually arrive at Shang-shung. Some settle here but their leader pushes on across the Tibetan plateau to Yarlung before turning back. Some of his followers remain in Yarlung as shen to the Tibetan kings and are regarded as magicians with great powers.

The final and most important stage follows the conquest of

eastern Gandhara by the Huna in about 500 CE. A number of what might be termed proto-Vajrayanists with strong tantric beliefs make their way from Uddiyana up the Indus by way of Gilgit and Balti. Led by the guru Krilde Odpo, they bring with them complex, orally-transmitted meditational doctrines as well as Sanskrit and Bactrian texts. In Shang-shung these new teachings acquire the patronage of the existing Iranian–Bactrian deities imported two and a half centuries earlier. Out of this fusion emerges Yungdrung Bon.

The core teachings of Yungdrung Bon can be found in the major text known as *Bon theg-pa rim-dgu*, the Nine Ways of Bon. The first four of the ways or stages are known as rGyui-theg-pa, the Four Ways of Cause, and concern themselves chiefly with rites: how to worship the gods, expel demons, collect treasures and pray for good fortune. The second four are Brns-bu'i-theg-pa, the Ways of Result, and concern themselves with the practice of good works as a means of attaining the status of arhatship: the practice of compassion, tantric worship through the invocation of a tutelary deity and the application of mystical practices. The last of the nine is Khyad-par chen-po'i-theg-pa, the Unsurpassable Way, also known as Dzogchen, the Great Perfection. This teaches the doctrine of the 'great and all-round fullness' as the means of attaining unification with the Ultimate Truth and thus release from the cycle of birth, death and rebirth.

To this day unreconstructed Bonpo continue to follow the old ways of undeveloped, shamanistic Bon. All through Tibet and along the Himalayan overspills where Tibetan culture intrudes into Nepal, Sikhim and Bhutan, strong local traditions persist of a form of shamanism which goes by the name of Bon nag or Black Bon. Such shamans can be found co-existing quite comfortably alongside Buddhist and mainstream Bon priests, usually passing their powers down through the generations, mostly from father to son but occasionally from father to daughter.

The Bon nag take on two quite distinct roles. As Nagpa or sorcerers, they counteract evil spirits, cure sicknesses and make weather, perhaps by averting hailstorms or by bringing rain. Their chief instrument is the phyed nga, a half-drum held by a short handle in the left hand close to the face and beaten with a curved stick which is struck upwards rather than down – a style of drumming ridiculed by other Tibetans, who say that the nagpa hold their drums up to their faces to cover their shame since the day their deity Naro Bonchung got thrown off the Nine Stacked Swastikas Mountain by the yogi Milarepa.

In western Tibet these shamans are known as dhammi or jhankri. They include Hindu deities in their invocations but their links with Bon are demonstrated by the fact that many initiates travel over the Himalayas to Mapham Tso to bathe in the waters and be possessed by the Nag spirits of the lake.

The second group of Black Bon shamans practise a more powerful and even sinister form of magic. They call themselves pawo ('heroes') and use as their main ritual instrument the small double-faced rattle-drum called the nga chung (known outside Tibet as the damaru) which has two short cords with little balls on the end attached to its handle. Rapid twisting of the hand causes the balls to strike the drumskin alternately on either side, producing the characteristic rattle sounded throughout much of south Asia by both Hindu and Buddhist mendicants.

Mainstream Bonpo call such practices 'straying' Bon. However, they were sufficiently popular in Tibet in the first quarter of the twentieth century to require the politically powerful Thirteenth Dalai Lama to issue an edict forbidding its members to carry out acts of sorcery, which were reportedly terrifying the inhabitants of some regions of eastern Tibet.

It is beyond the scope of this book to go any deeper into Bon theology and practice other than saying that the religion which today calls itself Yungdrung Bon shares the same ultimate goal as all schools of Buddhism: the striving towards ultimate buddhahood through study, the practice of ritual and meditation. Clearly, Bon and Chos have more in common than not.

But the differences are significant, as Per Kvaerne has shown in his groundbreaking study *The Bon Religion of Tibet*, published in 1995. Compare the chief deities of the two belief systems and you will see why.

At the centre of the Buddhist mandala is the primordial Buddha, Sangs-gui. From him emanate outwards the five cosmic or meditation Buddhas known as the Buddhas of the Five Families. One of these – Nampa Dangze, better known by his Sanskrit name of Vairocana, Creator of All Appearances – remains at the core. The other four have their places at the four cardinal points. On the east is Michopa, known outside Tibet as Aksobhgya, the Unshakeable One. To the south is Rinchen Jungden or Ratnasambhava, Being of Jewels. To the west is Opame or Amitabha, god of Infinite Light. Finally, to the north, Tonyo Drupa or Amoghasiddhi, Perfect Power.

From each of the five cosmic Buddhas further emanations extend outwards into the class of deities known as bodhisattvas. The bodhisattva manifestation of Amitabha, for example, is Avalokiteshvara (in Tibetan, Chenresig), Lord of Compassion and Protector of Tibet. The next circle of the mandala can be said to be taken up by the Mortal Buddhas, who come in various numbers according to cult. Here we must mention the Buddha of the Present Age, Gautama Shakyamuni (Bodh), who is also regarded as a manifestation of Amitabha/Avalokiteshvara; and the Buddha of the Future Age, Maitreya (Champa), manifestation of Amoghsiddhi/Vishrapani.

Now to the greater gods of Bon. At the centre of the Bon mandala, occupying the places which in Chos are taken by the Buddhas of the Five Families, are the Four Transcendent Lords. But there are striking differences. Here the prime figure is a female deity: Yum, the Mother, surrounded by three male divinities in their most primordial form: Lha, the God; Si-pa, the Protector; and Tonpa, the Teacher. In the present age this tetrad is manifested by the goddess Satrid Ergang, the gods Shenla Wokar and Sangpo Bumptri and the teacher Shenrab Miboche.

In the Shang-shung language Satrid Ergang means Purified Wisdom. Her two instruments are the swastika, symbol of time and the sun, and the mirror, representing the moon and the warding off of evil. She is spoken of as 'the Mother, from whom the Enlightened Ones of the past, present and future come forth'. She has no parallel in Chos.

Shenla Wokar translates as White Light. His symbol is a hook-like wand which represents his chief attribute, compassion. He also personifies Bon ku, the Body of Bon, and for this reason is known as the God of Priests. He is the original teacher of the lineage of teachings known as Dzogchen, the Great Perfection. His main emanation is Kuntu Zangpo, the All-Good, who is regarded as the supreme Bon deity in matters of ritual, particularly within the meditational tradition of Zhang-zhung snyan rgyud. He personifies Ultimate Reality and, as such, plays an important role in the closely allied Chos tantric school known as Nyingmapa.

Sagpo Bumptri is the Lord of a Hundred Thousand Beings. Lauded as 'the subduer through skilful means of living things', he takes on a wide range of manifestations and appears in Tibetan cosmogonic mythology as the semi-demonic Yemon Gyalpo.

Finally, Shenrab Miboche or Tonpa Shenrab, the Teacher of Shen and father of Bon in this present age. He appears on Bon thankas and paintings as a monk, yogi or supreme deity enthroned in splendour, depending on what stage of his life-cycle is being portrayed. As a yogi, he is coloured dark blue or black but when shown enthroned he is supported by wheels of universal dominion similar to the Chinese yin-yang symbol, his right hand touches the ground in the gesture of enlightenment usually associated with Gautama Shakyamuni, and his instrument is the Bon sceptre, a dumbbell-like instrument made up of two swastikas joined by a short column. As in all Bon iconography, these are counter-clockwise swastikas of the unorthodox model.

How these two sets of major deities evolved and who took what from whom is still very much open to conjecture. Draw up an iconographic chart of the Four Transcendent Lords and all their avatars and set that beside a similar chart of the Buddhas of the Five Families and no startling links emerge – with the possible exception of Shenla Wokar and Amitabha, who share literal names associated with light, the quality of compassion and the role of protectors; the one of the Dzogchen tantra and the other of Tibet.

The cult of Amitabha/Avalokiteshvara became hugely popular along the Silk Road, so much so that by the seventh century he had all but eclipsed the other Buddhist deities, possibly because he took over from an earlier non-Buddhist god sharing many of his qualities. A tantalising clue into this same deity's origins can be found in a ninth-century silk scroll painting from the Tun-huang caves. This shows Avalokiteshvara with a book resting on the palm of the most prominent of his right hands. Painted in red on the cover is the counter-clockwise swastika of Bon. Another curious feature of the early Amitabha/Avalokiteshvara is that the further east he travels, the more feminine he becomes, until eventually in Japan and Korea he is transformed into an entirely female goddess.

The safest conclusion to draw is that Shenla Wokar and Amitabha have common roots in Tajik and Iran: from Mithra and Zurvan by way of Zoroaster and Mani.

In both Chos and Bon, the middle and outer rings of their respective mandalas are filled with numerous classes of protectors. Numbered among the protectors of the Dharma are the benevolent Arhats and angry tutelary deities known as the Yidam. The latter are the wrathful gods of tantric ritual and meditation: angry, grimacing gods with many heads, arms and legs. They trample on their enemies, locked in yab-yum (father–mother/male–female) sexual embrace with their consorts and surrounded by haloes of fire.

In Bon the benevolent protectors are represented by the Six

Subduing Shen, the Thirteen Primeval Shen and the Twelve Ritualists; the wrathful tutelaries by a range of Yidam known as Bon-khyun. As in Chos, these Bon-khyun play a major role in the rituals and meditations of tantra.

From this point outwards both deity mandalas become extremely complicated. In Chos places have to be found for various groups such as the Eight Medicine Buddhas; the Thirty-Five Confession Buddhas; the Six Sages of the Six Realms; the Eighty-Four Mahasiddhas; the Sixteen Elders; the Eight Deities of the Transmitted Precepts; the Seventy-Five Great Protector Deities; the Protectors of Doctrine; the Hundred Peaceful and Wrathful Deities; the Eight Awareness Holders; the Ten Wrathful Kings, the Four Guardian Kings, the Two Gatekeepers – to say nothing of female divinities such as the Twenty-One Taras and the fairy sprites known as Dakinis.

The Taras deserve a special mention as female deities represented in their own right. The most powerful is Drolma, whose five manifestations are known by their colours. They include Drolma Karpo, the White Saviouress (incarnated in Brikuti Devi, princess of Nepal) and Drolma Jang-gu, the Green Tara (incarnated as the Chinese princess, Weng Chen).

Bon also has its supporting lesser deities, including the sages known as the Drubtob shen, or 'priests who have obtained spiritual perfection'; Tuwoche, or 'great magicians'; Gyerpung, or 'Teachers of Bon'; and Khadroma, the female fairies known as 'skywalkers'.

Where Bon outshines Chos is in the multiplicity of its local gods and goddesses, many of whom have been appropriated by Chos after being subdued by Guru Rinpoche. Of these, two categories have a particular relevance to our story: a class of male deities known, rather delightfully, as gekho – potentially harmful spirits bound by oaths to protect the Bon doctrine – and their female opposite numbers, drapla. There are no less than 360 gekho, one for each day of the lunar year, and all reside on the Nine Stacked Swastikas Mountain. The king of the gekho is Welchen Gekho, or 'All-Piercing Gekho', also known as the 'Secret, Great, Violent One' and 'Subduer of Demons'. In the Bon invocations he is always spoken of in awestruck tones, as in the following excerpt (as translated by Per Kvaerne):

> Gekho, king of gods, subduer of demons,
> With great magic power, terrifying, with nine heads and
>   eighteen arms,
> Blueish-black, furious, an awe-inspiring, blazing wonder –
> His form has a violent, haughty posture.
> With his fierce nine heads he subdues the arrogant, black
>   demons:
> The faces to the right are shining white,
> Those to the left are flaming red,
> While the faces in the middle are blueish-black.
> All nine heads are furious, with the face of a demon.
> The topmost head has the face of a garuda.
> His hair is yellowish-black,
> Like a mass of fire filling the universe.
> Lightning, hail and snow-storms whirl around him,
> His eyebrows are like flashes of lightning,
> Shooting forth hail and thunderbolts.
> His eyes, forming a triangle, are filled with rage;
> Thrown back by his eyes, red with fury,
> Gods and demons swoon from fright.
> Violent claps of thunder resound from his ears,
> Adorned with turquoise dragons as beautiful earrings.
> His nose has terrifying wrinkles;
> From it swirls an apocalyptic snowstorm.
> His greedily gaping mouth devours and destroys the demons;
> From his tongue flashes of lightning penetrate the Three
>   Realms.

Welchen Gekho's consort – with whom he is always locked in yab-yum embrace – is no less terrifying. She is Logbar Tsame, the Lady of Flashing Lightning and queen of the drapla. In her invocation her links with the sun, moon, sky and planets are constantly emphasised:

> She is the wrathful lady in the sky, shining like the sun.
> To the right her face is that of the water-crystal moon,
> To the left, that of the fire-crystal sun,
> While the middle head glows like molten gold . . .
> On her bracelets which shine like the sun and the moon,
> The twenty-eight lunar mansions are engraved . . .

This terrifying duo are far from alone. Also dwelling on the Nine Stacked Swastikas Mountain is Nyipangse, an emanation of Welchen Gekho, who guards the teachings of Dzogchen. Nyipangse was the supreme lord of the local mountain-spirits until subdued by the Bon shen Gyerpung Drenpa Namkha, who hurled a bomb at him while in the process of subduing all the spirits and demons on the mountain.

It is impossible to think of these two Bon deities, Welchen Gekho/Nyipangse and Logbar Tsame, enthroned in their mountain domain, without being reminded of Shiva and his fierce consort Parvati. Why should these two pairs of deities, both so closely identified with tantra and yogic practice, share the same mountain, if not for the reason that both, Hindu and Bon, have a common ancestry in the Kushan/Bactrian god and goddess Oesho and Nana?

Just as the Nine Stacked Swastikas Mountain has its Bon protectors, so too do the surrounding four lakes and four rivers. The lakes are looked after by the Tsobi rungma, a class of female spirits; four Chubi rungma or river-protectors watch over the sources of the four great rivers.

The many place-names of cities, palaces and temples given in the Bon texts make it appear that the people of Shang-shung were settled all over Ngari – but what little we know from evidence on the ground suggests that the main centres of population were confined to three areas: the comparatively exposed open valleys around Rudok, in the area that is now known locally as Senge Khambab; the well-sheltered Mapcha Khambab valley, centred on Purang; and the eighty-mile-long canyon of the Lanchen Khambab, the Garuda Valley.

Of these three regions, the Garuda Valley is today the least inhabited and the hardest to enter. It appears to be so hostile an environment that you wonder how this wilderness of stark canyons and bleak, windswept plateaux could ever have been a centre of civilisation. But Bon history tells us this was so, Chos history supports this claim – and information gathered on the ground over the last decade by Western back-packers such as the inestimable Victor Chan and the sadly deceased Brian Beresford confirms it.

There was indeed a pre-Buddhist civilisation centred on the Garuda Valley.

8 The Kingdom of Gu-ge

> There is still much to learn of the great age of Totling, when its golden monastery radiated light and learning through all Tibet from Kashmir to Assam . . . Today it looks as if the strong wilderness were climbing upwards from the valley with a slow but inexorable advance that is engulfing in its naked yellow throat the last vestiges of a great past. We descended to the camp sad and disconsolate, like men who have looked upon death.
>
> Dr Giuseppe Tucci, *Secrets of Tibet*, 1933

LATE OCTOBER 1997

'Look at it this way,' says Pasang after a fruitless attempt to get the PSB officers to soften their attitude. 'You cannot go to Kyunglung but you can go to Tholing.'

We never asked to go to Tholing but back in Lhasa that's what they wrote down on our permits in place of Kyunglung.

In my present black mood I can only think of getting out of Tibet with all speed. But Dick has a Candide-like capacity for seeing the best in people and situations. He regards Pasang as no less a victim of the system than ourselves. Since we're here, with a guide and two vehicles at our disposal, we might as well make of it what we can. We have nothing to lose by going to Tholing. As it turns out, we have a lot to gain.

Tholing lies at the far, south-western end of the Garuda valley. To reach it from Darchen we have to drive on west for another half day until we cross into the watershed of the upper Indus. We then leave the east–west highway and turn south, zigzagging up to the high pass, the Bogo La, to cross the mountain range that separates the upper Sutlej from the westernmost tributary of the upper Indus. This is a newly made road and the best we have seen for days; just as well, since it takes us up to over 17,000 feet and the drops are horrendous. The Italian Tibetologist Dr Giuseppe Tucci came this way in 1932 – the same year in which James Hilton wrote *Lost Horizon* – and later described the approach to the Bogo La as 'terribly wild and mournful'. In his day there were wild yak grazing on the mountainsides and packs of wolves.

Tucci crossed the mountains a little further west and higher up and was rewarded with extensive panoramas of both the Kangri Ti-se range to the north and the Himalayas to the south. Our view is a little more restricted but when we finally begin the descent towards the Langchen Khambab the sight is more than breathtaking: it is stupendous almost beyond belief.

Fifty years ago Lama Govinda saw this same gorge laid out at his feet and wrote of its 'awe-inspiring monumentality, for which the word "beautiful" would be far too weak'. That 'the wonders of this Tibetan canyon country, covering hundreds of square miles, could have remained unknown to the world is almost as surprising as seeing them with one's own eyes,' he reflected.

Now Dick and I, standing in amazement beside the car and looking out across the void towards the Himalayas, ask ourselves much the same question: 'How is it that this extraordinary place isn't known and talked about as one of the wonders of the world?'

We are parked on rolling alpine meadow at about 16,000 feet. This extends for miles to left and right of us like the slope of a gigantic roof. Before us are the Himalayas, extending through a full 180 degrees from our far right to our far left: the snowpeaks of Ladakh, Lahoul, Kuli and Spiti to the west; then the mountains of Garhwal and Kumaon, dominated by the huge snow pillar of Mount Kamet almost directly due south and straddling the Indo-Tibetan border about 50 miles away; east of Kamet, majestic Trisul and the sharp white spur of Nanda Devi; and far, far away to the east the mountains of Nepal with Gurla Mandhata all but obscured by clouds at a distance of more than a hundred miles.

But midway between the alp we stand on and the Himalayas is a third feature and the one which sets this apart from all other mountain scenery: a vast chasm running from east to west which itself is split by many hundreds of side fissures, the Langchen Khambab gorge. Think of the Grand Canyon and add the Himalayas on top as a sort of side dressing. Then break the Grand Canyon into a thousand side valleys and serrate every cliff face with deep cuts set close running top to bottom to create a kind of ripple effect like curtains on every wall. Now add the buttes and spurs of Arizona and, finally, soften the top surfaces so that they appear like half-melted candles or sponge cakes that have been left out in the rain. The Langchen Khambab and its many side waters have dug deep into the soft pale clay to create a vast, bleached, alien moonscape. Ice and snow, sun and wind have done the rest: precipitation in the form of snow is melted off in the day, creating little runnels and softening the topsoil; then as the sun goes down the remaining moisture freezes and expands and opens up the already crumbly soil to build huge screes at the base of every cliff, spur and rock tower.

To us, as it was to Lama Govinda in 1948, this is more than mere landscape. 'It is architecture in the highest sense,' he wrote in *The Way of the White Clouds*. 'Whole mountain ranges have been transformed into rows of gigantic temples with minutely sculpted cornices, recesses, pillared galleries, bundles of bulging cones, intersected by delicate ledges, crowned with spires, domes, pinnacles, and many other architectural forms.'

We are soon working our way down into the gorge along a series of ever deepening ravines, just as Professor Tucci did with his yak caravan in the thirties. To Tucci it was like entering 'an intricate labyrinth' made up of deep gullies like 'corridors in fantastic castles; from time to time, wide spaces on which stand vertical towers and peaks – contorted, ponderous – or there rise solitary monolithic columns with enormous capitals'.

Tucci passed several deserted settlements, including the ruins of a 'gigantic castle', but was too intent on reaching Tholing to stop and explore. As recently as 1992 three caves were discovered in this area above a small village called Donggar which contain some of the earliest wall paintings to be found in Tibet, very similar in style to the eighth- and ninth-century paintings of Tun-huang. Many other discoveries will surely follow as the ravines of ancient Shang-shung and the kingdom of Gu-ge give up their secrets.

At last, we arrive at the valley floor and a sudden abundance of green vegetation on both banks of the still infant Sutlej. We cross the river just above a very ancient chain bridge which has stood here for many centuries and reach the ancient settlement of Tholing as dusk is falling. As we approach the town we pass a small Chinese cemetery whose walls enclose half a dozen headstones, the lonely graves of soldiers of the PLA who never made it home, part of the price of empire.

A modern mining settlement has been built not beside but on top of King Yeshe O's monastery complex of Tholing. Two blocks of concrete shoeboxes provide rooms for tourists and travelling officials, their foundations set into a raised mound of what seems like solid grey clay. In fact it is part of the old capital city of Gu-ge. By scrambling over a wall and through a couple of backyards Dick and I gain access to the main temple complex. Of the several temples raised here by Rinchen Zangpo at the king's behest, two – the Lhakang Karpo (white temple) and the Dukhang (assembly hall) – are more or less intact. We cannot find a caretaker, so all we can do is peer through the cracks in their locked doors. Of the famous Mandala Chapel of King Yeshe O, Tholing's Golden Temple, only the four guardian chorten that surround it are undamaged. They stand guard over what is really little more than a heap of rubble and mud, although it does look as if efforts are being made to do some restoration.

It snows in the night, the first snowfall of winter.

Early next morning we hear whistle blasts. All the soldiers in the settlement plus the older children of school age are taking part in a military-style morning run round the town. Large numbers of skivers at the back shave off a corner and run past us grinning and giggling.

After breakfast we drive south along the river bank for a few miles to the site where the kings of Gu-ge had their central citadel. When the rock fortress of Tsaparang comes into view it surpasses all expectations. From a distance it resembles a huge termite mound. Then it seems more like a giant sandcastle, but honeycombed with holes and tunnels rather than decorated with shells and pretty pebbles. It looks entirely man-made but when we draw up at its base we can see that it is really a huge pyramidal rock that rises up about 500 or 600 feet on the end of a long narrow spur. As well as caves, platforms have been carved out at many levels from top to bottom where small single-storey buildings have been raised. Three of these have walls of dried-blood-red and white but all else is the colour of baked clay.

The citadel divides into three areas. At its base was a settlement where the common people had their homes, leading up to two public temples, the red and the white chapels. The middle level and both sides were taken up with monastic accommodations. Then at the top – and reached by an extraordinary twisting staircase tunnelled through some fifty feet of rock – were the royal quarters. At the very summit is the summer palace. From here generations of kings and queens of Gu-ge and their courtiers must have stood beside its battlements and gazed out across their domain as eagles might look out from their eyries. This is where that last doomed royal couple stood in 1685 and watched as the Muslim mercenaries from Ladakh went about the business of sealing them in and starving them out. You can still see the siege tower that was raised at the foot of the citadel.

Also at the highest point is a small chapel where the kings and queens of Gu-ge worshipped in private. The frescos here and in the two far larger temples below are still among the most magnificent in Tibet, and now all the more precious for being so rare. They are in the charge of a single caretaker who lives alone in a small house at the foot of the citadel and does what he can to protect them from the ravages of the weather and the depredations of thieves.

The caretaker unlocks the doors of the glories of Tsaparang: the interiors of the Lhakang Karpo (white chapel) and the Lhakang Marpo (red chapel). We are overwhelmed by the beauty of what remains and by the tragedy of how much has been lost, not in the long distant past but in the madness of 1967. What we see now is not what greeted Lama Govinda in 1948:

> The over-life-size golden images, gleaming amidst the warm colours of the frescoed walls, were more alive than anything we had seen before of this kind; in fact, they embodied the very spirit of this deserted city: the only thing that time had not been able to touch. Even the conquering hordes that caused the downfall of Tsaparang had shrunk from defiling the silent majesty of these images. Yet it was apparent to us that even these last remnants of former glory were doomed, as we could see from the cracks in the walls and leaks in the roofs of these two temples.

Prophetic words. What the 'conquering hordes' failed to do, the Red Guards have completed. Every one of the forty or so giant bodhisattvas that lined the walls and stood above the high altars has been reduced to dust. Only the guardian deities remain standing, minus arms and with great holes gouged out of their torsos. Heaps of piled-up rubble and plaster that were once heads and limbs and bodies lie along the walls, together with scraps of sacred texts that were concealed inside these images when they were first assembled. The caretaker has done what he can to preserve the larger fragments, putting aside stucco and stone heads in smaller heaps for the day when the Chinese government comes to its senses or an outraged world demands that something be done to save and restore what is left.

For all the natural and human damage, the surviving frescos are still quite exceptional both in their age and quality. The earliest are in the Red Chapel but all derive their fluid, luminous style from the thirty-two Kashmiri artists brought to Tibet by Rinchen Zangpo in the late tenth century. Not all concern themselves with religious matters. One long frieze illustrates the building of the White Chapel. It starts with scenes of porters and animals bringing wood and building materials and ends with the temple's consecration, with tributaries gathered from various parts of the Himalayas in their regional costumes, musicians and dancers in attendance, the people of Gu-ge seated in rows before their king, flanked by his queen and the royal family, and all turning in devotion towards the central image of Amitabha, himself flanked by rows of teachers, scholars and monks.

On our way down from the summit Dick's eye is caught by a glint of metal underfoot. He pulls up a section of chain-mailed armour. The caretaker tells us that until recently there were caves here full of such armour as well as weapons left behind after that last fatal siege, all now taken by robbers. I ask him – through Pasang – if he knows about the cave that is said to contain the headless torsos of the last king and queen of Gu-ge and all their followers.

Yes, he replies. He knows of it, but it is hidden. He waves his hand vaguely towards the cliffs behind the citadel.

But does he know where it is?

No, he says. No one is alive now who knows its whereabouts.

Pasang is thoroughly mystified by this exchange. He has been taught that Tsaparang was destroyed by Colonel Younghusband and the British in 1904.

When I tell him the real story of the fall of Tsaparang he is amazed and moved.

Orthodox Tibetan history tells us that the assassination in 841 of the apostate, King Lang Darma, was followed by a 'dark age', a period of anarchy that lasted for 146 years during which no Buddhist activity took place within Tibet.

In about 919 the two grandsons of Lang Darma fled to far western Tibet with an army of 300 horsemen. The eldest, Nyima Gon, crossed the watershed of the Tsangpo into Ngari province – the former realm of Shang-shung – and settled in Purang. He built himself a redoubt above the valley, found himself a local wife and set himself up as the new ruler of far western Tibet. He extended his territory deep into Spiti and Ladakh, and at Sheh he ordered a giant image to be carved on a rock face in honour of his ancestors and for the religious benefit of the people of Ngari. This standing figure, dressed in a loincloth and wearing a three-pointed crown shaped like something out of a Christmas cracker, is said to represent the Maitreya Buddha but could just as easily have been a Bon deity. An early eleventh-century Tibetan text from Tun-huang states that King Nyima Gon and his three sons all 'realised the power of Mahayana'. However, Bonpo histories claim this region as theirs at this time and a Bon manuscript found in the 'library' hoard at Gilgit appears to confirm this claim, stating that three Bonpo kingdoms – Gilgit, Uddiyana and Tokharisk – were invaded by a Tibetan king who was captured and ransomed for his weight in gold.

Further support for the thesis that Nyima Gon may not have been a follower of Chos is found in a local Dard folk song which calls him the 'sun lord' and his son the 'moon lord'. We also know that foremost among the royal regalia inherited by King Nyima Gon's grandson was 'a crowned helmet with white horns made of khrom lightning' — metal from Iran/Tajik. This has a direct link with the bya-ru or 'bird-horn crown' worn by the Bonpo kings of Shang-shung.

When Nyima Gon died his kingdom was divided among the three sons to become the three kingdoms of Gu-ge, Purang and Maryul.

Our interest now focuses on Gu-ge, the 'land of caves', tucked away in the deep canyon of the Langchen Khambab. It is the same deep gorge — the Valley of the Garuda — which was already the setting for the rise and fall of Shang-shung. But the centre of power has now shifted from the Silver Castle of Kyunglung and the upper end of the gorge to the lower. The new king settled on the river plain at Tholing, at a point where the river could easily be spanned by a short bridge. Just a mile or two downriver at Tsaparang a fortress was dug out of the crags on the end of a 600-foot spur, guarding the southern end of the Garuda valley and providing a strong defensive position. For seven centuries they would serve the kings of Gu-ge as their central church and fortress.

Whatever gods Nyima Gon may have worshipped, the grandson who inherited the bird-horn crown of Gu-ge was an extremely devout Buddhist who early in adulthood was ordained as a monk and took the name Lama Yeshe O or Light of Knowledge. Under his aegis and that of the equally devout great-nephew who followed him, Gu-ge became the powerhouse of the revival of Buddhism in Tibet, over a period roughly contemporary with the first unification of England, which started with Athelstan and ended a century later under Edward the Confessor.

In orthodox Buddhist history it is the first diffusion of Chos in Tibet under Guru Rinpoche in the eighth century that is all important, but the truth is that this first diffusion failed; the Bon-supporting nobility resisted and the Buddhist teachings were all but extinguished. Chos as we know it today owes everything to the second diffusion – to Gu-ge, where it occurred; to King Yeshe O, who was its first patron; and to two great propagators of Chos, Rinchen Zangpo and Atisha.

The Buddhist version of events is that the fragmentation of the Buddhist church brought about by the wicked King Lang Darma had lead to the growth of all sorts of deviant practices in Chos. In particular, the tantric teaching of the Indestructible Vehicle introduced by Guru Rinpoche had become debased. These had degenerated into forms of 'left-handed' or baneful magic involving sexual rites and blood sacrifices. In an effort to return to the core teachings, King Yeshe O sent a number of young students over the Himalayas to India. Of these, only two survived, one of whom became known as Lochen Rinchen Zangpo – the Great Translator. He made three journeys over the mountains to the surviving pockets of Buddhist culture in the Himalayas and returned not only with the true teachings but also with Indian pandits, builders and artists. Armed with the king's support, he then embarked on the most ambitious building pro-gramme ever seen in Tibet, founding 108 religious buildings. The ruins of the earliest of these are scattered along the banks of the upper Sutlej and upper Karnali and their many side valleys.

Rinchen Zangpo's masterwork was the Golden House in Tholing, named after a golden stupa on its eastern side which reflected the rays of the rising sun in the morning directly into the sanctuary of the central structure. This central lhakang, known as King Yeshe O's chapel, took the form of a three-dimensional mandala guarded at each corner by conical stupas.

The Great Translator's building programme was accompa-nied by a root-and-branch reforming process focused on the tantras. Unreformed teachings classed as heretical tantra were replaced by new tantra which Rinchen Zangpo had brought back from in Kashmir. These were known collectively as the Sangba-blana Medpai-gyud-de, the Unsurpassable Secret Mantra, which have at their core the Dzogchen tantra.

Dzogchen draws on a philosophy which is still regarded within mainstream Tibetan Buddhism as essentially heretical, despite the fact that some of Tibet's greatest religious teachers have both studied and propagated it, including such famous figures in Tibetan history as the First Panchen Lama and his pupil the Fifth Dalai Lama, to say nothing of the present Fourteenth Dalai Lama. Dzogchen knits together three main tantric strands – the Primal Spontaneity tantra, the Primeval Purity tantra and the Great Yoga – together with a number of subtexts such as the Secret Union of the Sun and Moon tantra. The Great Yoga is believed to have been proscribed at the time of King Trisong Detsen following the Great Council of 790. Its teachings were preserved by secret adherents during the 'dark age' to reappear in Gu-ge two centuries later. These, together with the other Dzogchen tantras, provided the inner teachings of the first monastic school of Tibetan lamaism, the so-called 'unreformed' sect known as the Nyingmapa or the 'Ancient Ones'. The Nyingmapa claim Guru Rinpoche as their main inspiration but it is no accident that they share a number of teachings with the Bonpo – who, as we have seen, claim Dzogchen as the ninth and most important of the Nine Ways of Bon.

The Tibetan Buddhist tradition is that Dzogchen originated in the land of Orgyan, Uddiyana. Here the deity Vajrapani conveyed them by a process of direct mental transmission to a boy named Garab Dorje, who taught them to his disciple Manjusrimitra, who passed them on to his disciples in Uddiyana. Twelve generations after Garab Dorje they were learned by Padmasambhava of Uddiyana (Guru Rinpoche) who brought them to Tibet. Guru Rinpoche passed them on to twenty-five of his disciples but also took the precaution of burying Dzogchen texts on Mount Gamposhar, where they were rediscovered as terma in 1326 by the treasure-seekers of the Nyingmapa school. However, the Buddhist histories also inform us that one of Guru Rinpoche's Tibetan disciples was a young man named Vairocana, who was sent to Uddiyana by King Trisong Detsen and returned with the Dzogchen tantras and other secret texts. This, in brief, is the basis for the Buddhists' claim that the Dzogchen teachings are theirs – brought from Uddiyana by both Guru Rinpoche and his disciple Vairocana.

Part of this tradition is echoed – copied, the Buddhists would say – by the Bonpo. The Bon *Dzog-chen Zhang-zhung Snyabn-eGyud* states that after twelve generations of disciples of the Great Teacher Shenrab Miboche there came a tantric master named Garab of Shang-shung, and it was he who received by mental transmission the Dzogchen teachings that he then passed on to the Bon masters of Dzogchen, one of these by Gyerpung Drenpa Namkha.

A key link between these two traditions is Guru Rinpoche's disciple Vairocana, who is known to have been a tutor to the son of King Trisong Detsen and who was sent into exile in Bhutan because of his close links with Bon. In Vairocana's autobiographical text *The-grim* he writes of translating Bon texts 'from the Gilgit language' into Tibetan and of hiding Bon texts as terma. He adds that: 'I myself Vairocana made the translation of the great everlasting Bon without sparing myself and entrusted it to the king.' Thus it comes as no surprise to find the Buddhist Vairocana also featuring in Bonpo history as a disciple of Gyerpung Drenpa Namkha. In the Bon version of events he follows the example of his Bon master and adopts Chos in order to preserve Bon at a time of persecution. The newly converted Gyerpung Drenpa Namkha goes on to revise Bon texts so as to bring them more into line with Chos, and passes these teachings on to Vairocana, who is thus able to embrace both Chos and Bon.

What this means is that Bon and Chos drew on common sources for the Dzogchen teachings. The Chos claim that Guru Rinpoche brought the Dzogchen teachings from Uddiyana has to be thrown out; it is far more plausible to suggest that they originated in Bon-dominated Gilgit and were brought into Tibet originally by way of Shang-shung, and then reintroduced much later into Gu-ge from Kashmir by the Great Translator. This would explain the fierce disputes over the Dzogchen teachings, old and new, that developed in Gu-ge between the two religious groups.

After Tibet's conquest of Shang-shung and the persecutions instituted by King Trisong Detsen, the adherents of Bon had re-established themselves in a number of pockets in eastern Tibet and on the Tibetan borderlands. In the former territory of Inner Shang-shung or Ngari they had retained a small but very significant presence, probably as small communities of hermits belonging to the Bonpo Dzogchen school of meditative tradition of Gyerpung Drenpa Namkha.

With the publication in 1996 of Roberto Vitali's English translation and commentary of the history of Gu-ge from the tenth to thirteenth centuries, the fate of these Dzogchen Bonpo of Shang-shung has now been revealed. *The Kingdoms of Gu-ge Pu-rang According to mNgar'-ris Rgyal-rabs* is much more than just a genealogical history of the royal family of Gu-ge. It sets out the manner in which the foundations of Tibetan Buddhism as we now know it today were prepared and laid.

'For 146 years the doctrine in this sTod mNgar'-ris [kingdom of Ngari] was Bon, funerary rites were black, the living ones were practising heretical religion, dead bodies were carried to cemeteries.' This Bon primacy changed when Yeshe O was proclaimed king. He was born in 947 and died in 1024. Although the year of his accession is in doubt his reforms had certainly begun well before 996, the year in which the foundations of the Buddhist temple complex at Tholing were laid.

The Chos reformation was initiated by a stirring royal proclamation made by King Yeshe O in the year 986:

All lay people and monks have to safeguard the stability of the Buddhist teachings. From now onwards, the latest developments in terms of teachings and written sources, which are recommended by the monks of high knowledge and the full-time keepers of religious vows, all of them as well as medical and technical science, if they do not exist, should be brought from elsewhere. All monks and laymen have to stand as guards against the hazards [of] people at the borders of the kingdom. The population [has to learn] to shoot arrows, to run and jump and to wrestle [in various] techniques, to swim and to perform exercises of dexterity on horses, to read and write and make calculations, the nine kinds of male training. Moreover, all kinds of exercises of bravery have to be learned . . . In brief, no one is allowed to break the great laws of chos-khrims . . . All take a solemn oath. We also are bound in the future. The brothers, sons, the queens, the ministers, all of us in our turn take a solemn vow not to contravene the chos-rtsigs. We [swear] not [to fail] future generations [to do] the same. So it is declared.

This dramatic oathtaking and call to arms took place in an atmosphere of crisis, against a background of continuing suppression of Buddhism on every side of Tibet. North of Tibet the Turkic tribe known as the Qarakhanids, newly converted to Islam, had taken over southern Turkestan and were now pushing southwards, eventually occupying Khotan in 1006. In India the Law was approaching extinction after centuries of assault from enemies within and without. In Afghanistan the Hindu Shahi kingdom had been overthrown and Subuktuqin, the new Muslim ruler of Ghazni, had just launched the first of a series of raids into the Punjab which would lead led to the conquest of Lahore in 991. He would be followed by his rapacious son Mahmud who from the year 1000 onwards would undertake no less than seventeen invasions of the Indian plains, setting a pattern to be followed by subsequent Afghan and Persian rulers which would continue until every centre of Buddhist learning in India had been razed and every infidel within it either converted or purged from the earth.

Given these circumstances, the actions of King Yeshe O

become more understandable. This was not a time for religious tolerance or for half measures. If the Law was to survive it had to be cleansed of impurities. Any threat to its survival within the kingdom had to be removed.

That threat came, of course, from Bon.

The text is unambiguous. The second diffusion was achieved at the cost of the proscription of Bon and the destruction of the Bonpo community in Ngari:

> Since the Bon teachings were widespread in Zhang-zhung [Shang-shung], all Bonpos were gathered, thrown inside a house, which was set on fire. As all Bon texts were collected, they were thrown into rivers. Since the existing custom of burying the dead in cemeteries was abandoned, a righteous practice [possibly sky burial?] was introduced . . . As he [Yeshod] banned the practitioners of whatever was heretical, such as liberation through sexual union, meditation on corpses and, in particular, all practitioners of Bon, he brought [practice] back to the true path . . . For the sake of the greatness of Chos, he did not allow those leaning in favour of Bon to contaminate Chos by blending it with the old doctrines of Bon.

But the 'blending' of Chos with the old doctrines of Bon is exactly what did take place. We have, for example, a Buddhist account taken from the *Guru bKra-shis chos-byung* of a prince of Gu-ge finding Bon documents in the temple at Samye and passing them on to the Great Translator:

> He [Rinchen Zangpo] was especially interested because they were written in the language of Zhang-zhung. Lo-chen [Rinchen Zangpo] also paid attention to Bon-po for some time, which he disliked. As he was entrusted with them, he considered that they were worth spending time on, with the exception of *Pu-tra*. He returned to it, having [worked] a little time [then] achieved its translation except its mantras which

had been translated into the Zhang-zhung language. Since [the copy] which had been hidden as gter [treasure] by slob-dpon Padma [Guru Rinpoche] at bSam-yas was rediscovered, it thus benefited the subsequent generations.

In other words, Bon texts discovered as *terma* were translated by Rinchen Zangpo and accepted as the writings of Guru Rinpoche. King Yeshe O is popularly credited with sending Rinchen Zangpo on a final journey to India to secure the services of the most famous teacher of the age, the Bengali sage Atisha Dipamkara, better known in Tibet as Jowoje. Atisha had been initiated into the tantric rites but had then broken from Vajrayana to be ordained as a Mahasanghana Buddhist. His studies of the canonical and classical texts of Buddhism had led him east by sea to Suvanandavipa, the 'island of gold' – believed to be Srivajaya on the island of Sumatra – where he had studied for twelve years before returning to India to become the abbot of Vikramashila in Bengal.

The *mNga'-ris Rgyal-rabs* makes it clear that King Yeshe O died in 1024 and that it was his great-nephew King Phobrang Bhyangchub who brought Atisha to Tibet. As a ruler, King Phobrang appears to have been as fierce an opponent of Bon and the unreformed tantras as his great-uncle. This may explain why he was so determined to bring Atisha to Gu-ge; in the hope that he would put an end to heretical tantra and the unreformed Dzogchen teachings. If so, he may been seriously disappointed because Atisha – bless his tolerant heart – achieved a historic compromise.

Atisha arrived in Gu-ge in the year 1042. The Great Translator was still alive, aged eighty-two, and was present to welcome him to Tholing. Rinchen Zangpo very quickly realised the greater superiority of Atisha as a teacher and supported him in his reforms. Atisha's historic legacy is the lamaist doctrine that a Buddhist monk may still fulfil his monastic vows by following the sutras but at the same time can – and even should –

practise certain tantric teachings or mantras as a means of attaining buddhahood. We owe to Atisha, too, other hallmarks of Tibetan religious culture: the emphasis placed on self-discipline, compassion, tolerance and respect for all life.

Beginning with Atisha's own Kadampa school of the 'gradual path' to enlightenment, nearly all successive schools of teaching which came into being in the eleventh century accepted this middle way. Only the Nyingmapa and Bonpo have stayed outside by remaining pre-eminently tantrists and ritualists. But even they can be seen to be part of Atisha's legacy, which extends right across Tibetan culture.

After three years of teaching in Ngari Atisha moved on to central and southern Tibet where he helped to restore and revitalise Samye and many other Chos foundations. He died at Tsang in 1054, his death more or less coinciding with the resurgence of Lhasa as the central authority of Tibet.

The compromise achieved by Atisha came too late for the Bonpo of western Tibet and other unreformed tantrics. However, we can safely assume that some survivors of the purge initiated by King Yeshe O in the last decade of the tenth century sought refuge beyond the borders of Gu-ge.

This brings us back to the story of the origins of the Shambhala legend recounted in Chapter 1. In the year 1026 – two years after the death of King Yeshe O of Gu-ge – the teachings of the Kalacakra tantra were brought to Tibet from India.

We are told that, sixty years earlier, in the year 966, the young man known as Tsi-lu-pa had shown up unknown and unannounced at the gates of Nalanda, the ancient Buddhist monastic university on the Gangetic plain south of Patna. He had drawn the great mystic seal of Kalacakra over the lintel of the door and announced that he came from beyond the mountains to the north, from the country of Shambhala.

The esoteric teachings he brought with him, which so confounded the teacher Naropa, would come to be regarded as among the most precious in Tibetan Buddhism. But where did they – and he – come from? Where was this Shambhala?

The Bonpo would answer without hesitation: Shang-shung, their lost paradise, their Shangri-La, itself a manifestation or extension of the original western paradise of Olmo-lungring in Tajik. They have a good case.

The sixty-year lapse between the first arrival of the Kalacakra in Nalanda and its later arrival in Tibet has a special significance because it is Naropa who is said to have devised the Tibetan sixty-year cyclic calendar. So the sixty-year delay can be seen as more symbolic than actual. The date that matters is 1026, the year in which the Kalacakra tantra is received in Tibet.

What happened in the sixty years preceding 1026 that could have a bearing on the origins of Shambhala? With the exception of the isolated valley of Bamian in central Afghanistan, the whole of the Gandharan civilisation had gone. Pockets of Buddhism were holding out at a number of points along the Ganges such as Nalanda, but in the western Himalayas only the Vale of Kashmir, Spiti, Kulu and Ladakh still had communities of Buddhist or Bon monks. Here the retreat, as ever, continued towards the north-east, always deeper into the mountains.

A bright spark appeared in all the gloom when the young King Yeshe O came to the throne of Gu-ge. This was not entirely good news for the Buddhists of Gu-ge, because – as we have established – he regarded many of their tantric practices as heretical, and it was very bad news for the Bonpo. Let us suppose that a young man devoted to a particular tantric teaching associated with Dzogchen and brought from Uddiyana by way of Shang-shung wished to preserve these teachings. He had little option but to go south. So he crossed over the Himalayas by way of Spiti and reached the Vale of Kashmir, but here he found – as we know from the studies that the Great Translator Rinchen Zangpo undertook here from 986 onwards – that this was now a centre of reformed tantra. He was not welcome, so he pushed on into the plains of India – until he came to Nalanda. Here he met the great Naropa, who was happy to accept these unreformed tantra since they fitted in well with his own teachings.

In Tibet, however, as the *mNgar'-ris Rgyal-rabs* shows, the unreformed tantric teachings were still regarded as heretical when King Phobrang Bhyangchub came to the throne in 1042. They would be unwelcome in their form, so Naropa revised them and repackaged them as the Kalacakra tantra – and his disciple Atisha, in due course, welcomed them back to Shang-shung. And so the legend of the hidden kingdom of Shambhala, based on the lost paradise of King Kanishka's Uddiyana but now reinforced by the loss of Shang-shung, took root.

The kingdom of Gu-ge continued to prosper for another half century after the death of Atisha in 1054, but the advance of Islam to the north and west gradually reduced both its capacity to trade with its neighbours and its authority. A second invasion from the west in the early twelfth century was followed by another from the south in 1193, almost certainly a scouting party from the armies of Qutb-ud-din, the future Sultan of Delhi, who in the previous year had routed a huge Hindu Rajput army at Kanauj.

A century later Ngari, along with the rest of Tibet, was over-run by the Mongols of Genghis Khan. The country's leaders were forced to acknowledge Mongolian suzerainty and pay annual tribute, while at the same time providing spiritual advisers to the Mongol leaders. This political patronage greatly assisted the rise of the Sakya religious order until it was over-taken in the mid-fifteenth century by the Gelugpa 'reformed' school founded by Tsong Khapa. Ganden monastery was set up by Tsong Khapa in 1409, and his disciples in turn founded Sera monastery in 1419, Drepung in 1416 and Tashi Lunpo in 1447. Tashi Lunpo's founder was later recognised as the first Dalai Lama, whose successive reincarnations extended the power, prestige and land-owning wealth of the Gelugpas to a point where the Dalai Lamas became the de facto temporal and spiritual rulers of Tibet. From the fifteenth century onwards the monastic way of life dominated the culture of Tibet, extending its influence and its theocratic discipline into every corner of the land.

But there were still many who clung to the old, unreformed teachings. Two disciples of Atisha and Nalanda revised his doctrines by returning to the direct transmission of the esoteric teachings of the Indian sages; their followers founded the Kagyupa and Sakyapa sects. The teachings of Marpa embraced by the Kagyupa emphasised meditation, renunciation and extreme asceticism. It supreme exponent was Jetsun Milarepa, the poet-yogi who lived in caves on a diet of nettles and whose struggles with Naro Bon Chung for control of the Precious Snow Mountain form only a tiny part of an extraordinary life lived out between 1040 and 1123 on two planes, real and mythological.

Other religious groups such as the Nyingmapa clung to the tantras. Through the fortuitous rediscovery of concealed texts, they were able to reintroduce as the rediscovered texts of Guru Rinpoche what were to all intents Bon and other pre-reformation rites. To this day, the Ancient Ones continue to practise rites of tantra, spirit possession and exorcism which their Gelugpa critics deplore as heretical Bon practices, and there still exists a bond of fellow-feeling between Nyingpama and Bonpo. One of the many rituals these two sects have long held in common is the Bardo-Thodol, the guiding of the departing soul through the intermediate limbo between death and rebirth which lasts for forty-nine days.

In the same bedding-down process which followed the reforms of Atisha and led to the construction of mainstream Tibetan Buddhism, the Bon religion also underwent change. It synthesised, adapted and reorganised, and in the process evolved from a cult of shens into an organised religion modelled on the reshaped Tibetan Buddhist pattern. 'Developed' Bon formalised its canons, doctrines and practices until in many respects they mirrored those of their rivals. These included such core 'Buddhist' beliefs as the ideal of enlightenment, the wheel of existence, rebirth in the six states of existence, the six paths to salvation, the ten stages of perfection and the six virtues, and such concepts as the law of karma or moral causality, sansara and nirvana. In their application, many Bon rituals and meditational practices also follow 'Buddhist' patterns. Some Bon texts mirror Buddhist writings word for word.

At some early point in this reforming process the Bon's counter-clockwise swastika symbol was decreed to be anti-Chos by the Buddhists, who went for the clockwise symbol instead. The Bon stuck with the counter-clockwise swastika, but to make a distinction between their public actions and those of Chos they abandoned clockwise movement round religious objects for counter-clockwise circumambulation.

Other more fundamental differences remain. Buddhists attain enlightenment through the Buddha. Whatever sect they belong to, they share a belief in the philosophies contained in the sutras and in the practices of meditation linked with the tantras, all transmitted from India as the doctrines of the historical Buddha Gautama Shakyamuni.

Bonpos, reformed or otherwise, still believe in harnessing the forces of nature to combat evil and in controlling the basic spirit powers as a means to enlightenment. They still claim that their teachings come from Olmo-lungring and Tajik, by way of Shang-shung, and are derived from their own original pre-Buddhist Buddha, teacher Shenrab Miboche.

Towards the end of the eleventh century a cluster of Bon centres of learning were established in the upper Tsangpo river valley. Over the succeeding centuries many other Bon monasteries were built throughout Tibet, each with a thriving community of monks who undertook the same number of vows – 253 – as their Buddhist counterparts. Not that the vows were the same. Chastity, for example, is not required of a Bon priest, who often marries and raises a family.

The reorganised Bon which emerged not from Ngari but from Amdo and eastern Tibet in the eleventh and twelfth centuries was still sufficiently pervasive in the seventeenth century to cause the great Fifth Dalai Lama to request his Mongolian over-lords to send an army to destroy the Bonpo King of Kham. A famous quote attributed to the regent during the years of the Sixth Dalai Lama's minority runs: 'The Sakyapa, Gelugpa and Nyingmapa are the victory banners of the Buddha's teaching; the Karmapa, Brugpa and Bonpo are the robbers and thieves of the Buddha's teaching.'

In the 1770s a Manchu emperor helped to further elevate the authority of the Gelugpa by recognising it as the chief tradition of Tibet, while at the same time actively suppressing the Bonpo in far eastern Tibet and prohibiting Bon teaching. Nevertheless, Bon hung on and at the start of the twentieth century there were

said to be more than 330 Bon monasteries in Tibet. All were destroyed by the Red Guards between 1967 and 1970, although quite a number have since been rebuilt. It is impossible to estimate how many practising Bonpo there are in Tibet today. The Nine Stacked Swastikas Mountain is still their holy mountain but, to judge from my own observations, only about one in every hundred Tibetan pilgrims who complete the kora of the Precious Snow Mountain is a Bonpo (easily spotted because they circle the mountain the 'wrong' way). However, I am told that in certain areas of Tibet – the Menri area in the Shang valley, the Bonri mountain area of Kongpo, the Tengchen district of Kham and in the Ngawa and Zungchu regions of Amdo in the east – they constitute a sizeable minority. There are also growing communities of Bonpo at Dolanji in the foothills of Himachal Pradesh in India and in the Kathmandu valley of Nepal.

9 *The Search for Shangri-La*

> History is really a kind of consensus hallucination.
>
> James Cameron, producer and
> director of *Titanic*

The overnight snow in Tholing signals that winter may be coming early to western Tibet this year, just as it did in the disastrous winter of 1995–6 when so much snow fell in October that the yak were unable to feed and so died in their thousands. Dick is all for taking a chance and staying on for a few more days. I am not; no way am I going to risk getting stuck in Ngari province until next spring. I want out before more snow settles on the Maryam La and seals us in for the winter.

But we agree to visit one more site before we leave the area.

After completing their circuits of Mount Kailas and Lake Manasarovar, it has long been customary for Hindus and Buddhists to round off their pilgrimages in far western Tibet by visiting a third site: Tirthapuri. It lies thirty miles due west of the Nine Stacked Swastikas Mountain and about five south of the east–west highway.

To get there we recross the Bogo La and then strike off the

highway at Moincer, a bleak little mining township. A track leads down to the Sutlej at a point where the river ends its meandering across the prairie land and begins to dig deeper into the soft soil of the plateau. Tilled fields on both sides of the river mark the absolute upper limits of human cultivation. A cloud of steam and strings of damp prayer flags hanging over a gurgling, belching hot spring signal the site.

This is Tirthapuri, the 'place of death', one of the most important power-points in the whole of Tibet and the Indian sub-continent. It is a place of magic, spells and potions linked with death, sickness, healing and divination. The ground on all sides is pockmarked by little pits where pilgrims have dug into it in search of tiny pellets of lime the size of birdshot. These are swallowed as medicine pills and are said to ease that fatal transition of the spirit after death known as bardo.

The hot springs here are more impressive than those in the dry channel between the two lakes at Chiu Gompa. Until a decade or so ago a geyser would regularly blow every few minutes, sending an eruption of boiling water about twenty feet into the air. As with the Chiu channel, its sudden cessation is linked to the dwindling fortunes of Tibet. There is also a small monastery here and, as one might expect, relics associated with Guru Rinpoche in the form of footprints and caves. But, all in all, it's very hard to see what all the fuss is about, why this particular place should be set on the same exalted pedestal as Kailas and Manasarovar.

But there is an explanation. Tirthapuri stands at the gateway to the Garuda Valley. This is where the Sutlej cuts into its first chasm and begins its writhing – and still partly uncharted – passage through a series of canyons that only ends on the southern slopes of the Siwalik foothills in the Punjab. Here, surely, is the real reason for Tirthapuri's exalted position: it points the way to Kyunglung.

Tirthapuri is as far as our permit allows us to travel in this area, so Pasang and our two drivers become agitated when we ask them to follow the river downstream from Tirthapuri. 'There's no road,' they assure us, and we can see them thinking to themselves, 'Oh God, another wild goose chase.'

After a couple of miles we are faced by a long escarpment about 500 feet high. Here the Sutlej cuts into a tuck in the cliffs and disappears from sight. But the trail across the fields also seems to end here, and we are on the point of turning round and going home when a Landcruiser appears from the direction of Moincer. It bumps past us without stopping but we can see three monks in red and yellow robes bouncing around in the back seat. The vehicle swings out of sight to the right to skirt the boggy ground beside the river but eventually reappears beyond the fields, heading back towards the river to disappear out of sight through the gap in the cliffs. A lucky break for us: we now know there is something beyond the gap and we have a track to follow.

Our enthusiasm is not shared by Pasang and the drivers. Our relations have been strained ever since the revelation over the permit. Pasang was shaken to see how deeply upset I was and he has done his best since to make amends. He agrees, without further protest, to drive on for just another mile or two.

The Sutlej here is no more than twenty feet wide and no deeper than two feet. We drive along its right bank as it cuts through a narrow cleft with high cliffs on either side. Almost at once we emerge, with exclamations of surprise and pleasure, into a dream of a valley, hardly more than a quarter mile wide and half a mile long, ringed on every side by dark cliffs so that it seems cut off from the outside world. In the foreground is the base of what must once have been a giant chorten (very similar to the stupas that Dick and I will see three months later in Taxila, Afghanistan and Swat), surrounded by four lesser chorten. Above it rise two terraces piled with the rubble of ancient buildings and above them scores of caves cut into the cliffs. The valley floor itself has a carpet of green grass on which horses and yak are grazing. Set at the base of the cliffs so as to face south, the red and white walls of a monastery stand out in sharp contrast: the Bon monastery of Gurugem. A balm for sore eyes after days of endless, windswept vistas of steppes and mountain ranges.

We drive up to the monastery and park inside the courtyard beside a central darchen decorated with prayer flags. Two Bonpo monks open up the guest room and offer us Tibetan salt tea and sweet cakes. Luck really is with us today because the Landcruiser which showed us the way has also brought the abbot of Gurugem, who spends most of the year at Gartok, a day's drive away to the west. He is Rinpoche Tenzin Wangduk, one of Tibet's leading practitioners of traditional medicine.

Halfway up the cliff face above the monastery and linked to the valley floor by a decorated stairway is a large whitewashed splodge which marks the entrance to a cave. This I know to be the meditation cave of the eighth-century Bonpo master Gyerpung Drenpa Namkha. For centuries this was the home of Bon's greatest healers – and now that tradition has been renewed by the new abbot of Gurugem.

After tea Dick and I are led up the stairway to meet the Rinpoche. At the top is a wooden balcony lined with wind-powered prayer wheels. They have been constructed, most ingeniously, out of recycled tin cans. Everything here is newly built: the monastery may look as old as time but its reconstruction only began in 1989. From the balcony we clamber up through a tunnel dug into the rock which brings us out on to another platform about thirty feet higher up the cliff face. A few more awkward steps and we enter Drenpa Namkha's meditation cave, not much bigger than the interior of a camper van, where the Rinpoche has his home.

A small square window cut through the rock lights the cave. The Rinpoche is sat cross-legged on a slightly raised dais, with a small writing desk in front of him; a diminutive figure of great age with a smiling, wrinkled moon face. He reminds me at once of Yoda, the Jedi master in *Star Wars*, and has that same air of omniscience. Dick and I kneel in turn to present our kadak, which are immediately returned and draped over our own shoulders. Pasang interprets as we exchange the usual compliments and pleasantries.

We talk first about Gyerpung Drenpa Namkha and the Bon medical tradition which still underpins Tibetan medicine. I had meant to ask to see two holy relics kept in this cave – the great shaman's mortar and pestle which he used to make up his medicines – but somehow the conversation veers away on to the subject of my stomach and I end up with a small paper packet of grey powder which looks like gunpowder.

Then we talk about Shang-shung. To my great satisfaction the abbot confirms my view that this little valley is the gateway to inner Shang-shung. We tell him about our problems with the permit and how we had hoped to follow the river downstream from here to Kyunglung.

The Rinpoche smiles. 'But you have come to Kyunglung.'

Pasang's face is a picture of mixed emotions.

The abbot asks me to look out of the window. 'Do you see those ruins out there?' He indicates the giant chorten on the valley floor and its four surrounding lesser stupas. 'That is Kyunglung.' He points to the top of the cliff at the head of the valley where we can make out a prayer flag flying above a small building. 'Up there is Kyunglung Ngulkar, the Silver Castle of the Garuda. That is where King Ligmigya, the last king of Shang-shung, had his palace. The last three kings of Shang-shung lived there at the time of Gyerpung Drenpa Namkha. They were Gyalpo Rinchen Wreke Charuchen, Gyalpo Shiraksen Wreke Charuchen and Gyalpo Unchen Dunki Charuchen, also known as Ligmakya, who was killed in battle by the king of Tibet.'

This revelation takes a bit of time to sort out but gradually a picture emerges of two capitals of Shang-shung, both named Kyunglung Ngulkar. The last was here in this little valley, where strong fortifications were built to defend the entrance to the

Garuda valley from the Tibetans in the seventh century. But this was really only an extension of the original Silver Castle of the Garuda.

'So where is the old city of Kyunglung Ngulkar?'

Now the Rinpoche points out of his tiny square window towards the south. 'It is just over those hills, only one day's walk away – two days for a Westerner. You must climb over two passes before you can cross the river and reach the city. One of my monks will guide you.'

We explain that we are not permitted to proceed any further south – and that we have run out of time.

'Then you must come again.'

We arrange to meet next summer, just after the Saga Dawa festival.

'I will be waiting for you,' says the Rinpoche.

We bow and withdraw.

In the Kalacakra tantra the story tells that Shambhala fades from the sight of ordinary mortals as its inhabitants grow ever more enlightened. In far western Tibet its mundane inspiration – the land of Shang-shung – remained in full view but nevertheless slipped by degrees off the map of history until it too had all but faded out of sight.

The Ngari region became a cultural cul-de-sac, always a goal for pilgrims and those seeking the contemplative life as hermits, but too isolated from the rest of Tibet and the outside world to have any political clout, too far from the main trans-Himalayan trade routes to arouse any mercantile interest other than the purchase of pashmin goat's wool.

And all the while the Himalayan wall continued its inexorable rise. With each passing decade a tiny but calculable amount of monsoon precipitation was denied to the high plateau. The slow process of desiccation and desertification gathered pace.

The far western highland could no longer support large settled communities and monastic institutions. Pastoralism again became the sole sustainable means of life, but only for as many yak, sheep and goats as the infertile soil could support. Overgrazing and consequent loss of grazing accelerated an eastward population drift that continues to this day.

But dynasties of kings continued to rule. Indeed, the kingdom of Gu-ge experienced a brief renaissance at the end of the fourteenth century when many temples were rebuilt and restored. At the great citadel of Tsaparang a series of magnificent chapels were raised on small terraces carved out of the rock. The finest artists were brought from Kashmir and Kathmandu to paint their walls and ceilings and to mould their stucco statues. What remains of their artistry, on the walls of the Lhakang Karpo, Lakhang Marpo, Dorje Jigje Lhakang and – at the very summit, in what were once the royal apartments – the Demchog Mandala chapel, must be accounted among the most magnificent examples of mural painting in Asia, as well as the most unappreciated.

It was these same lhaking – each guarded by a pair of snarling, weapon-wielding, multi-armed guardians 10 feet high, lined by giant Buddhas and bodhisattvas seated on plinths, and every inch of pillar, wall and ceiling ablaze with brightly painted figures and scenes – as well as the ceremonies they witnessed therein, which must finally have dashed the hopes of the two Jesuits, Antonio de Andrade and Manuel Marques after their arrival in Gu-ge in the summer of 1624. Their hopes of finding the Christian flock of Prester John must surely have been dented by the time they reached the royal citadel. Father Andrade appears to have been shocked by what he saw as demonic rituals involving human skulls and thigh bones but he was also moved both by the kindness he was shown and by the religiosity of the local population. They were 'a tractable and upright people', he reported, and ripe for conversion to Christianity.

And indeed, the king and queen of Gu-ge received the two missionary explorers with open arms and went out of their way to make them welcome, perhaps out of genuine kindness, perhaps in hopes of receiving further infusions of Buddhism from across the Himalayas. Whatever the motives, it is clear that Andrade's missionary zeal made a strong impression on the king: he pronounced him 'Our Chief Lama' and gave the Jesuit a signed permit which authorised him to preach the Christian gospel throughout the kingdom of Gu-ge.

In the following summer the Jesuits returned to Tsaparang with reinforcements and built a church at the foot of the rock citadel, as well as establishing a second mission outpost 130 miles away at Rudok. Andrade's colleagues were full of optimism, one writing in 1627 that 'this country promises more than any other I have yet heard of'. However, everything hung on the king's conversion and, for all the royal goodwill, this was something that Andrade never achieved.

Andrade left Tibet in 1630 and within a few months of his departure the Jesuit mission was in disarray. The lamas had seen their authority gradually being whittled away by the king's evident enthusiasm for the new faith and they had turned to neighbouring Ladakh for support. What happened next is uncertain but it is known that the mission building in Tsaparang was pulled down and the five Jesuits in residence were imprisoned. They were then escorted to the border and expelled from Tibet.

In 1640 Manuel Marques led a new expedition over the Mana La in a vain attempt to reopen the Jesuit mission at Tsaparang. The party was attacked, Marques was seized and the others fled back across the border. A year later a pitiful letter from Marques was received at the Jesuit headquarters in Agra in which he begged for rescue. Attempts were made through intermediaries in Ladakh to secure his release but without success, and no more was heard of him.

It has long been said that this intervention by the Jesuits lead directly to the final downfall of Gu-ge. However, new evidence gathered locally by Gyurme Dorje and recounted in his *Tibet Handbook* (1996) suggests a very different, far more tragic ending.

It centred on a young king of Gu-ge who was deeply loved by his people. In the early 1680s his forces successfully repelled a series of invasions from Ladakh until finally, in 1685, the Buddhist ruler of Ladakh hired an army of Muslim tribal mercenaries to do his fighting for him:

> With this additional strength his army soon laid siege to the city, encircling the population of several thousand at Tsaparang town around the base of the citadel. With their army decimated, the people had no protection. The Ladakhi ruler then threatened to slaughter fifty people a day until the young king capitulated. From the heights of the royal citadel, impregnable and secure with its own secret water source, the king volunteered to renounce his position and depart from the realm, saying that he would devote himself to the anonymity of a monastic life. He promised never to lay claim to the throne in the future on the condition that his subjects be spared their lives and that his queen and family, along with the ministers of court, be guaranteed free and safe passage out of the land.

To the relief of the people of Tsaparang, these conditions were agreed to and so the king, together with his queen, their children and all the ministers and chief officers of their army, descended from the heights of the citadel and walked out through its gate:

> They presented themselves to the invaders and were all immediately bound and taken prisoner. The young king and his family were slaughtered in full view of the population. Members of the court, ministers and generals were led down the hillside where they were all beheaded, their bodies tossed

into the ravine below. Their heads were then impaled upon spears and poles, forming a circle around the entire town.

Whether it was in reaction to this horror or whether they were forcibly driven out by the Muslims, the fact is that Tsaparang and the greater part of the Garuda Valley was abandoned immediately after these tragic events. For over 300 years now the rock citadel has remained empty, its great painted chapels dark and unlit, the roofs of its royal chambers gradually falling in and lying open to the sky, a ghost palace, a monument to man's illusions.

Likewise the Valley of the Garuda. Then a green paradise, crowded with ideas and hopes, now a dusty moonscape, an empty quarter.

As the Dhammapada says: 'It is painful to be in the world. It is painful to be alone amongst the many. The long road of transmigration is a road of pain for the traveller. Let him rest by the road and be free.'

But the Dhammapada also says: 'When a man considers this world as a bubble of froth, and as the illusion of an appearance, then the king of death has no power over him.'

Envoi: The Sixth View

In my introduction I spoke of the mystery of the origins of the Bon religion. I quoted a passage from Dan Martin's book *Mandala Cosmogony*, in which he sets out five points of view – and I went on to suggest that I could come up with a sixth. That sixth view I would now summarise as follows: the Bon religion is a synthesis of a number of religions and religious concepts mostly of Iranian origin, and the first Bonpo originated from the high steppes of 'Tajik', lying between the Amur Daria and Tarim rivers: the Bon holy land of Olmo-lungring. They were drawn from the people known to the Chinese as the Yuechi, who later called themselves the Kushans. The Bon religion entered western Tibet in three phases and in the final phase restructured itself to conform more closely to Chos. Tibetan culture owes much to Bon, with Chos itself drawing on concepts common to both religions developed in the Gandharan mixing bowl and later claiming exclusive rights to shared transmissions, including the Dzogchen and Kalacakra tantras.

The Kalacakra tantra has its origins in Gandhara. After the invasion of the Huna the teaching was brought from Uddiyana to the Bon region of the western Himalayas and from there to Shang-shung. At the time of the persecution of the Bonpo which followed the founding of the Buddhist kingdom of Gu-ge, it was brought south to Nalanda monastery and from there back to Tibet, having been revised to bring it into line with current Buddhist orthodoxy.

The story of the hidden paradise of Shambhala contained in the Kalacakra was inspired by a combination of three lost paradises: Olmo-lungring, Uddiyana and Shang-shung. A thousand years later the Shambhala legend was picked up by the writer James Hilton and Westernised into Shangri-La.

In June 1998 I returned to far western Tibet with a film crew to make a documentary for BBC TV called *The Search for Shangri-La*. Funding and political difficulties prevented us from following my original plan but we were able to make a three-day foray into the Garuda Valley beyond Gurugem monastery. The Rinpoche failed to keep our rendezvous but we persuaded some yak-herders to show us the way. One day's march took us over the Tsaldot La and down to the Sutlej river, where we camped. On the second day we forded the river and reached the modern village of Kyunglung by midday. A building standing on a small knoll overlooking the village, identified by Professor Tucci in 1932 as a fort, turned out to be a small Gelugpa monastery, now fully restored but unoccupied. It pointed the way to an extensive complex of ruins, consisting of small temples and large numbers of stupas, lying about half a mile east of the village on the very edge of the valley among a series of ravines and ridges. Above these ruins were a number of caves in rows dug into the sides of cliffs and pinnacles. We were only able to explore these remains for a couple of hours before we had to turn back to our camp-site.

At the time I was able to convince myself (and the film crew) that these were the remains of Kyunglung Ngulkar, the Silver Castle of the Garuda Valley, and thus the original capital city of Shang-shung: Shangri-La, in fact. However, the villagers of Kyunglung had themselves pointed out to me that there were many more ruins and caves further south, a mile or beyond the village on the other bank of the river.

I shall always regret not making the extra effort and pushing on, but we had already run out of funds and time. I now believe that we reached only the outskirts of Kyunglung Ngulkar and that the main city itself lies deeper within the valley. So for the time being at least, 'Shangri-La' – if that is really what it is – remains 'undiscovered' and unexplored.

Charles Allen, November 1998

Glossary

(S) = Sanskrit

Amitabha (S): meditational Buddha of the west, Wopame; one of five meditational Buddhas, coloured red, carries lotus.

Amitayus (S): meditational deity, Tsepame; one of three deities of longevity, coloured red, holds nectar of amrita.

amrita (S): also soma, ambrosia of the gods, conferring immortality.

apsara (S): angel or nymph.

arhats (S): elders and contemporaries of Shakyamuni Buddha, sometimes known as the Sixteen Elders, first to achieve buddhahood.

Atisha: Buddhist master from Bengal (982–1054 CE), Jowoche; *see* Kadampa.

asura (S): demon.

Avalokiteshvara (S): patron deity of Tibet, Chenrezi; one of eight major bodhisattvas, coloured white, holds lotus, portrayed in many forms.

Azha: kingdom of the Tu-you-hun in northeastern Tibet conquered by Tibet in the seventh century CE.

Bal-po: old name for Nepal.

Balur/Bolor: old name for Gilgit, *see* Bru-sha.

bardo: state between death and rebirth; thus Bardo Thodol, Book of Dying.

Beyul: hidden land in Himalayas, revealed in terma.

bhural (Hindi): blue sheep, in Tibetan nawa.

bodhi (S): enlightenment; thus bodhisattva, one on the path to buddhahood who remains in the world to help others find salvation.

Bon: ancient pre-Buddhist religion of Tibet sometimes divided into three forms: revealed Bon; deviant Bon; and translated Bon.

Bru-sha: Gilgit region along the Indus river.

Buddha (S): awakened or enlightened one, applied to Gautama Shakyamuni after his enlightenment.

Buddhas of the Three Times: Dipamkara (of the past); Buddha Shakyamuni (of the present); and Maitreya (of the future).

Buddhas of the Five Families: the five Buddhas who together make up the buddha-body of perfect resource: Aksobhya, Amitabha, Amoghasiddhi, Ratnasambhava and Vairocana.

Buddha Shakyamuni: the historical Buddha, Gautama of the Sakya clan born in central India in the sixth century BCE. His teachings formed the basis of Buddhism as the Tripitaka.

Cakrasamvara (S): wrathful deity of the supreme yoga tantra, Demchog; Buddhist version of Shiva, coloured blue, four-faced, twelve-armed; shown in yab-yum union with his consort Dorje Phagmo.

chakstal: prostration

Chang-Tang (Jang-Thang): northern plain, this northern plateau of Tibet.

chang: barley beer.

Chenrezi: god of compassion, protector of Tibet; see Avalokiteshvara.

chhu: running water, river.

chod: offering but also 'cutting', a tantric system based on the Perfection of Wisdom rite, involving the visualising of total surrender to evil spirits or ghosts to acquire greater spiritual powers.

chodhung: conch horn.

chomay: butter lamp.

chorten: *see* stupa.

Chos: name by which the dharma is known in Tibet.

chuba: long-sleeved traditional coat tied at the waist.

da: arrow.

Dakini: female celestial beings of tantricism, personifying wisdom of enlightenment, khandroma.

Dalai Lama: reincarnate tulku of Gelugpa school, Tibetan Gyelwa Rinpoche; embodiment of Avalokiteshvara.

damaru: small narrow drum.

darchen: flagpole for prayer flags.

Demchok: *see* Cakrasamvara.

Deva (S): god, thus devi (goddess).

dharma (S): theory and practice of Buddhism, sometimes trans-lated as the 'Law'; known in Tibet as Chos.

Diamond Vehicle: Dorje Thegpa *see* Vajrayana.

dorje: diamond sceptre, male symbol used in trantric rites; *see* Vajra.

Dorje Chang: *see* Vajradhara.

Dorje Thegpa; Diamond Vehicle; *see* Vajrayana.

dre: demon.

dri: female yak.

drilbu: handbell used with dorje in tantric rites, feminine symbol.

Driza: see Gandharva.

drokpa: nomad.

Drolkar: White Tara; *see* Tara.

Droljang: Green Tara; *see* Tara.

Dro-shod: former name for headwater region of Tsangpo.

Drolma: *see* Tara.

drub-ne: power-place.

Drubchen: *see* Mahasiddha.

Dud: demons, (S) Raksha.

Dukhor: *see* Kalachakra.

Dzogchen: *see* Great Perfection.

dzong: citadel.

Eight Bodhisattvas: eight major bodhisattvas, often shown flanking Buddha Shakyamuni; they include Avalokiteshvara; Maitreya; Manjusri; and Vajrapani.

Four Guardian Kings: warrior kings who guard the four cardinal directions of temples.

Gandhara: name given to region and culture centred on what is today northern Pakistan and eastern Afghanistan; *see* Gandharva.

Gandharva (S): celestial beings, Driza.

garuda (S): mythological bird-man with bird's face and wings and human arms and limbs, Kyung; killer of snakes and king of birds, in Buddhism the mount of Vajrapani; said to hatch fully grown and resplendent, thus a symbol of the awakened mind.

gelong: monk.

Gelugpa: virtuous ones, indigenous school of Tibetan Buddhism founded by Tsong Khapa in the fifteenth century CE, acquiring political as well as spiritual powers from the Fifth Dalai Lama onwards.

gompa: monastery.

Great Perfection: concentrated tantric practice, Dzogchen; followed by Nyingma and Kagyu schools to obtain speedy enlightenment.

Greater Vehicle: Mahayana, system of Buddhism emphasising

compassion, the liberation of all beings based on the teachings of sutras and tantras, and the role of bodhisattvas.

Gu-ge: cave-land, one of three kingdoms in western Tibet, centred on the upper Sutlej valley, established after conquest of Shang-shung.

guru (S): religious teacher, lama.

Guru Rinpoche: popular name by which Padmasambhava is known in Tibet.

gyaltsen: victory banner, large object shaped like folded umbrella posted on monastery roofs.

gyu: *see* tantra.

harmika (S): square section of stupa above the dome.

Hinayana (S): *see* Lesser Vehicle.

Indestructible Vehicle: *see* Vajrayana.

Jampa: *see* Maitreya.

Jampelyang: *see* Manjusri.

Jowo: Precious One, a bodhisattva form of Buddha Shakyamuni as a young prince before he achieved enlightenment.

Kadampa: school of Tibetan Buddhism introduced into Tibet by the Indian master Atisha in the eleventh century CE.

Kagyupa: school of Tibetan Buddhism following the teachings of the Indian masters Tilopa and Naropa, introduced into Tibet by Marpa in the eleventh century CE.

Kailas: Indian name for Kangri Rinpoche.

Kalachakra (S): yogic tantra involving the wheel of time, Dukhor; brought to India and then Tibet from Shambhala in the eleventh century CE; also a wrathful deity symbolising the transmutation of the wheel of time.

Kangri or Gangri: Snow Mountain; thus Kangri Rinpoche, Precious Snow Mountain, also known as Kangri Ti-se, Yungdrung Gutseg and Kailas.

karma (S): the sum of one's actions extending through life-cycles, based on the Hindu and Buddhist laws of cause and effect.

Karma Kagyu: sub-school of Kagyupa, founded by first Karmapa tulku in the twelfth century CE, oldest succession of tulku lamas in Tibet.

Khandroma: *see* Dakini.

Khadak: ceremonial white scarf.

Kha-che: old name for Kashmir.

Khorlo: wheel, thus Wheel of Dharma, *see* Wheel; thus also khorlam, devotional circle around object of worship.

kiang: Asiatic wild ass, *Equus hemonius pallas*.

Kora: ritual circumambulation of sacred space: clockwise for Buddhists; counter-clockwise for Bonpo.

Kyung: *see* Garuda; thus Kyunglung, Valley of the Garuda.

kyilkhor: *see* mandala.

la: mountain pass.

lakhang: temple complex.

Langak Tso: Lake of Five Islands; also Rakas Tal.

Langchen Khambab: Horse-Mouth river, upper course of the Sutlej river.

lama: *see* guru.

lha: male deity, life-spirit; thus lha-mo, female deity; lha-ri, mountain spirit; lha-shing, tree spirit; lha-khang, house of spirit, Buddhist temple; lha-khor, hand-held prayer wheel; lha-tse, cairn of stones and prayer flags.

le: *see* karma.

Lesser Vehicle: (S) Hinayana, Tegmen, earliest system of Buddhism emphasising the four truths and related teachings through which individuals seek their own salvation.

Li-yul: Taklamakan desert region round Khotan.

lu: *see* naga.

lumo: female serpent spirit.

lung-ta: prayer flag activated by wind, literally 'wind-horse'.

Mahayana (S): *see* Greater Vehicle.

Mahasiddha (S): yogic master, enlightened beings, Drubchen.

Maitreya (S): the future Buddha, (Tibetan Jampo); one of the eight major bodhisattvas; coloured pale yellow, holds an orange bush.

mandala (S): a psycho-cosmogram; two- or three-dimensional symbol used as a focus for meditation; representation of the palace of a tantric deity.

Mapchhu Khambab: Peacock-Mouth River, upper course of the Karnali river.

Mapham Tso: Lake Unrivalled; also known as Yu Tso, Turquoise Lake, Manasarovar.

Manasarovar (S): Conceived in the Mind of God, Indian name for Mapham Tso.

mane: prayer; thus mane-do, prayer stone; mane-dong, prayer wall; mane-korlo, large prayer wheel, also known as dunkhor.

Manjusri (S): bodhisattva of wisdom, one of the eight major bodhisattvas (Tibetan Jampeyang); coloured pale green, holds a lily and a sword.

mantra (S); sacred formula; incantation associated with tantric deities leading to realisation, such as the six-syllable mantra of the bodhisattva Avalokteshwara *Om Mane Padme Hom*; also synonym for tantra.

Mar-yul: old name for Ladakh.

Meru (S): *see* Sumeru.

Milarepa: yogi and poet of Kagyupa school (c. 1040–1123), supposed conqueror of Naro Bonchung on Kangri Rinpoche.

Mi-nyag: kingdom connected with the Dong tribe, usually located north of Koko Nor.

Mu: sky-rope linking early Heavenly Kings of Tibet to heaven, also name of tribe of far western Tibet.

Naga (S): water-serpent deity or spirit, lu.

ne: place of pilgrimage; thus nekhor, a circuit around a pilgrimage site; nekhorpa, pilgrim.

ngapa: tantric yogi.

Ngari: region of far western Tibet.

nirvana (S): state of buddhahood, the attainment of freedom from the cycle of birth, suffering and death.

Nyenmo: female earth spirit or ogress.

Nyingmapa: earliest school of Tibetan Buddhism introduced into Tibet by Shantarakshita and Padmasambhava in the eighth century CE.

Orgyan: *see* Uddiyana.

Padmasambhava: better known as Guru Rinpoche (eighth century CE); popularly regarded as the founder of Buddhism in Tibet, co-founder of the Nyingmapa school, sometimes known as the Second Buddha.

Palbe: eternal knot, one of the eight auspicious symbols.

Palden Lhamo: wrathful protectress of Tibet.

Panchen Lama: Tulku lama, regarded as the emanation of Amitabha, linked with Dalai Lamas as power-brokers in later Tibetan history.

phuk: cave, thus drulphuk, meditation cave.

phurba: ritual dagger.

Rakas Tal: Demon Lake, Indian name of Mapham Tso.

ri: mountain.

Rinpoche: precious; honorific title.

Rinchen Zangpo: Great Translator based in Gu-ge (*c.* 958–1055), associated with the second diffusion of Buddhism in Tibet.

Sadak: earth spirit.

Sakyapa: school of Tibetan Buddhism founded in the eleventh century CE.

sangha (S): Buddhist monastic community.

sanghrama (S): monastery.

Sbalti: ancient Ladakh.

Senge Khambab: Lion-Mouth River, upper course of the Indus river.

Shakyamuni: clan name of the historical Gautama Buddha.

Shambhala: mystical land of paradise to the west of Tibet where the Kalachakra Tantra was first disseminated.

shan: Chinese term for mountain range.

shang: flat bell used in Bon ritual.

shang-shang: female fairy with bird's wings and tail.

Shang-shung (Zhang-zhung): 'Gateway', kingdom in far western Tibet associated with Mu tribe and Bon. Its capital was Kyunglung.

Shantarakshita: Indian guru from Nalanda monastery (eighth century CE); ordained the first Buddhist monks in Tibet and built Samye monastery.

shen: shamanistic Bon priest associated with blood sacrifices and death ceremonies.

Shenrab: 'best of shen', knowledge; thus Shenrab Miboche, legendary founder of Bon religion; see Tonpa Shenrab.

Shiva (S): Hindu yogic god of destruction and creation, whose home is Mount Kailas; consort of Parvati.

Sumeru (S): also Meru, the cosmic mountain at the centre of the universe.

Sutra (S): scriptures based on discourses of the Buddha delivered by Shakyamuni, expounding the causal path to enlightenment.

swastika (S): sun symbol associated with good fortune, in Tibetan yungdrung; the inverse swastika is associated with Bon.

Tajik: also Tag-Tzig, the region within or adjacent to the ancient land of Olmo-lungring; located near Persia, possibly comprising ancient Sogdia and Bactria, modern Tajikistan.

Tamchok Khambab: Horse-Mouth River, upper course of the Tsangpo river.

tanka: Tibetan painted scroll.

tantra (S): canonical texts which set out in symbolic language the means to achieve speedy liberation, often employing magic rituals, gyu.

tarcho: prayer flag, also darchen.

Tara: goddesses identified with compassion and redemption, Tibetan Drolma; feminine aspects of enlightenment, among the most popular of the twenty-one Taras are the Green (Droljang) and White (Drolkar).

terma: concealed treasures; sacred texts or objects, first hidden in the seventh century CE, concealed so as to be found in later centuries by treasure-finders; *see* terton.

terton: treasure-finder; *see* terma.

Three Ancestral Religious Kings: three kings of ancient Tibet revered by Buddhists: Songtsen Gampo (seventh century CE); Trison Detsen (eighth century CE); and Tri Ralpachen (ninth century CE).

Three Precious Jewels: Buddha, dharma and sangha, in Sanskrit Triratna. See also Tripataka.

tonpa: teacher, thus Tonpa Shenrab: *see* Shenrab.

torma: offering of cake made of tsampa, butter and sugar.

Tripitaka (S): 'Three Baskets', the earliest complete collection of Buddhist texts relating to Buddha's teachings, monasticism and scholasticism.

Triratna (S): *see* Three Precious Jewels.

tsampa: ground and roasted barley flour, eaten mixed with a little tea.

Tsang: region of west central Tibet centred on Shigatse.

Tsangpo: Great, thus name given to the great river of southern Tibet which flows into India as the Brahmaputra.

tso: water, lake.

Two Gatekeepers: the Doorkeepers of Buddhist temples: Hayagriva (west side); Vajrapani (east side).

tulku: incarnating lama.

U: central Tibet centred on Lhasa.

Uddiyana (S): Oddiyana or Orgyan, region usually identified as the Swat valley in northern Pakistan.

Uighurs: Turkish tribes on the northeast borders of Tibet who joined forces with T'ang Chinese against Tibet in the eighth and ninth centuries.

Ushnisha (S): growth or bun on top of the head of a Buddha.

vajra (S): sceptre-like ritual wand of tantric ritual, symbolising indestructible reality of buddhahood, dorje.

Vajradhara (S): bearer of the vajra, Dorje Chang; the tantric form of Shakyamuni Buddha.

Vajrayana (S): Indestructible or Diamond Vehicle, the aspect of Greater Vehicle emphasising the role of tantra and meditative techniques as a means of achieving enlightenment.

Vihara (S): Buddhist temple.

Vairocana (S): one of the five peaceful meditational Buddhas, Tibetan Mampar Nangze; coloured white, holds wheel, has many aspects.

Wheel of Dharma: cycle of teachings given by the Buddha Shakyamuni.

Wopame: *see* Amitabha.

Xian (Chinese): administrative centre, early capital of China.

yab-yum: tantric representation of male-female energies engaged in mystic sexual union.

Yaksha (S): demon.

Yantra: yogic exercise.

Yidam: Tutelary deity.

yogi, yogin (S): practitioner of intensive meditational exercises.

yu: turquoise.

Yungdrung: eternal, also swastika, associated with evolved form of Bon religion known as Yungdrung Bon; thus Yungdrung Gutseg, Nine Stacked Swastikas Mountain.

Zahor: Jallandhara, Indian hill country between Sutlej and
   Jumna rivers.
Zidak: protective deity of place.
Zhang-zhung: see Shang-shung.

Select Bibliography

S. A. M. Adshead, *Central Asia in World History*, 1993

Charles Allen, *A Mountain in Tibet*, 1982

R. P. Anand, 'The Status of Tibet in International Law' (*Quarterly Journal of the Indian School of International Studies*, Vol. 10, No. 4, 1969)

B. L. Bansal, *Bon: Its Links With Buddhism in Tibet*, 1994

S. Baring-Gould, *Curious Myths of the Middle Ages*, 1867

Samuel Beal (trans), *Buddhist Records of the Western World* (by Hsuan-tsang), 1884

—— *The Life of Hiuen-tsiang*, 1911

Ed Bernbaum, *The Way to Shambhala*, 1980

Heinz Bechert and Richard Gombrich (eds), *The World of Buddhism*, 1984

A. Bharati (ed), *The Realm of the Extra-Human*, 1976

A. D. H. Birar, *Mithrais Images in Bactria*, 1979

Martin Brauen, *The Mandala, Sacred Circle in Tibetan Buddhism*, 1997

Sir Olaf Caroe, *The Pathans*, 1958

Friar Giovanni di Plano Carpini, *The Story of the Mongols Whom We Call the Tartars* (Hildinger, 1996)

Martha Carter, 'Coins and Kingship: Kanishka and the Kushan Dynasty' (*MARG*, Vol. XLV, No. 4, 1994)

Victor Chan, *Tibet Handbook: A Pilgrimage Guide*, 1994

Graham Coleman, *A Handbook of Tibetan Culture*, 1993

Joe Cribb, 'Shiva Images on Kushan and Kushano-Sasanian Coin' (*Studies in Silk Road Coins and Culture*, 1997)

Hildegard Diemberger, 'Beyul, Khenbalung, the Hidden Valley of the Artemesia' (*Mandala and Landscape*, 1997)

Gyurme Dorje, *Tibet Handbook*, 1997

Keith Dowman, *The Sacred Life of Tibet*, 1997

Nevill Drury, *The Shaman and the Magician*, 1982

Franz-Karl Ehrhard, 'A "Hidden Land" in the Tibetan–Nepalese Borderlands' (*Mandala and Landscape*, 1997)

M. Eliad, *Shamanism*, 1972

K. Enoki, 'The Yueh-chih and Their Migrations' (*History of Civilisations of Central Asia*, Vol. II, 1994)

W. Y. Evans-Wentz, *Tibet's Great Yogi Milarepa*, 1928

—— *The Tibetan Book of the Dead*, 1957

Robert Fisher, *Buddhist Art and Architecture*, 1993

A. Foucher, *Notes on the Ancient Geography of Gandhara*, 1915

A. H. Franke, *Ladakh*

H. Giles (trans), *The Life of Hsuan-tsang* (by Hui-li), 1888

—— *The Travels of Far-Hsien, or Records of the Buddhist Kingdoms* (1887)

Richard Gombrich, 'The Evolution of the Sangha' (*The World of Buddhism*, 1984)

Lama Anagarika Govinda, *The Foundations of Tibetan Mysticism*, 1960

—— *The Way of the White Clouds*, 1966

Eric Haarh, 'The Zhang-Zhung Language' (*Acta Jutlandica*, Vol. 40, No. 1)

Janos Harmatta (ed), *History of Civilisations of Central Asia*, Vol. II, 1994

—— 'Religions of the Kushan Empire' (*History of Civilisations of Central Asia*, Vol. II, 1994)

M. Harner, *The Way of the Shaman*, 1980

Nancy Hatch and Louis Dupree, *The National Museum of Afghanistan Illustrated Guide*, 1974

Sven Hedin, *Trans-Himalaya*, 1909

—— *The Silk Road*, 1937

Herodotus, *The Histories* (Penguin, 1954)

James Hilton, *Lost Horizon*, 1933

J. R. Hinacle, *Studies in Mithraism*, 1994

John Hinnells, *Penguin Dictionary of Religions*, 1984

Oskar von Hinuber, 'Expansion to the North: Afghanistan and Central Asia' (*The World of Buddhism*, 1984)

J. Hitchcock and R. Jones, *Spirit Possession in the Nepal Himalayas*, 1975

H. Hoffman, *The Religions of Tibet*, 1961

—— *Zermig* (trans), 1961

—— 'Ancient Tibetan Cosmology' (*Tibet Journal*, Vol. II, No. 4, 1977)

—— 'An Account of the Bon Religion in Gilgit' (*Central Asiatic Journal*, Vol. III, 1969)

S. H. Hook, *Middle Eastern Mythology*, 1963

Toni Huber and Tsepak Rigzin, 'A Tibetan Guide for Pilgrimage to Ti-se' (*Tibet Journal*, Vol. XX, No. 1, 1995)

Siegbert Hummel, *The Lamaist Ritual Dagger* (Phurbu, 1952)

Christmas Humphreys, *Buddhism*, 1954

Nadia Julien, *The Mammoth Dictionary of Symbols*, 1996

Samten Karmay, *The Treasury of Good Sayings: A Tibetan History of Bon*, 1972

—— *The Great Perfection*, 1988

Ahmed Nabi Khan, *Gandhara: An Illustrated Guide*, 1994

Ashraf Khan, *Buddhist Shrines in Swat*, 1993

Jan Knappert, *Indian Mythology*, 1995

Per Kvaerne, *The Bon Religion of Tibet*, 1995

—— 'Tibet: The Rise and Fall of a Monastic Tradition' (*The World of Buddhism*, 1984)

—— 'Dualism in Tibetan Cosmogonic Myths' (*Silver on Lapis*, 1987)

—— 'Bon' (*The Encyclopedia of Religion*, 1987)

—— 'Cosmogonic Myths of Tibet' (*Mythologies*, Vol. II, 1991)

—— 'Who are the Bonpos?' (*Tibetan Review*, Vol. XI, No. 9, 1976)

B. I. Kuznetsov, 'Highest Deities of the Tibetan Bon Religion' (*Tibet Journal*, Vol. VI, No. 2)

—— 'Who Was the Founder of the Bon Religion?' (*Tibet Journal*, Vol. I, No. 1)

Etienne Lamotte, 'Mahayana Buddhism' (*The World of Buddhism*, 1984)

Larousse, *Encyclopedia of Mythology*, 1959

James Legge (trans), *A Record of Buddhistic Kingdoms*, 1886

B. A. Litvinsky, 'The Rise of Sasanian Iran' (*History of Civilisations of Central Asia*, Vol. II, 1994)

A. W. Macdonald, *Mandala and Landscape*, 1997

Tilo Majapuria, *Religious and Useful Plants of Nepal and India*, 1988

Sir John Marshall, *The Buddhist Art of Gandhara*, 1960

Dan Martin, 'Ol-mo-lung-ring, the Original Holy Place' (*Tibet Journal*, Vol. XX, No. 1, 1995)

Hemant Mishra, *Wild Animals of Nepal*, 1976

David Morgan, *The Mongols*, 1986

R. de Nebesky-Wojkowitz, *Oracles and Demons of Tibet*, 1956

Namkhai Norbu, 'Bon and Bonpos' (*Tibetan Review*, Vol. XV, No. 12, 1980)

—— *Gans Tisé i-dkar-chag: A Bonpo Story of the Sacred Mountain Tisé and the Blue Lake Ma-Pan* (Serie Orientale Roma, 1989)

Thubyten Jigme Norbu and Colin Turnbull, *Tibet: Its History, Religion and People*, 1969

Giacomella Orofino, *Sacred Tibetan Teachings on Death and Liberation*, 1990

Padma, 'The Mutual Infiltration and Influences of Buddhism and Bonism' (*Tibet Studies*, 1991)

Marco Polo, *The Travels* (trans. Robert Latham, 1958)

Swami Pranavananda, *Exploration in Tibet*, 1950

G. A. Pugachenkova, 'Kushan Art' (*History of Civilisations of Central Asia*, Vol. II, 1994)

B. N. Puri, 'The Kushans' (*History of Civilisations of Central Asia*, Vol. II, 1994)

Hanif Raz, *Taxila*, 1996

Charles Ramble, 'The Creation of the Bon Mountain of Kongpo' (*Mandala and Landscape*, 1997)

Sir Hugh Richardson, *Tibet and Its History*, 1962

Tsepak Rigzin, *Festivals of Tibet*, 1993

Nicholas Roerich, *Shambhala*, 1997

―――― *Altai-Himalaya*, 1930

―――― *Blue Annals*, 1949

Min Bahadur Shakya, *The Life and Contribution of the Nepalese Princess Bhrikuti Devi to Tibetan History*, 1997

Prof. Nicholas Sims-Williams, 'New Findings in Ancient Afghanistan' (lecture, 1997)

―――― with Joe Cribb, *A New Bactrian Inscription of Kanishka the Great*, 1996

Prof. Tadeus Skorupski (ed), *Indo-Tibetan Studies in Honour of Professor Snellgrove*, 1990

Prof. David Snellgrove, *Four Lamas of Dolpo*, 1967

―――― *The Nine Ways of Bon*, 1967

John Snelling, *The Sacred Mountain*, 1983

Sir Aurel Stein, *Ancient Khotan*, 1907

―――― *Serindia*, 1921

―――― *Archaeological Tour in Upper Swat*, 1930

Romila Thapar, *A History of India*, Vol. I, 1966

F. W. Thomas, 'The Zhang-Zhung Language' (*Journal of the Royal Asiatic Society*, 1933)

Prof. Robert Thurman, *Rituals and Symbols Revealed*, 1995

Chogyam Trungpa, *Shambhala: The Sacred Way of the Warrior*, 1995

Tsong-ka-pa, *Tantra in Tibet: The Great Exposition of Secret Mantra*, 1977

Prof. Giuseppe Tucci, *Indo-Tibetica*, 1932

—— *Rin-chen-bʒan-po and the Renaissance of Buddhism in Tibet around the Millennium*, 1988

—— *Secrets of Tibet: The Chronicle of the Tucci Scientific Expedition to Western Tibet (1933)*, 1935

—— *The Religions of Tibet*, 1980

—— *The Theory and Practice of the Mandala*, 1974

—— *Travels of Tibetan Pilgrims in the Swat Valley*, 1940

David Ulansey, *The Origins of the Mithraic Mysteries*, 1991

Arthur Versilius, *Song of the Cosmos*, 1991

Roberto Vitali, *Early Temples of Central Tibet*, 1990

—— *The Kingdoms of Gu-ge Pu-rang According to mNgar'-ris Rgyal-rabs*, 1996

Ernst Waldschmidt, *Gandhara kutscha Turfa*, 1929

Annabel Walker, *Aurel Stein: Pioneer of the Silk Road*, 1997

Frances Wood, *Did Marco Polo Go to China?*, 1995

Turrell Wylie, 'O-lde-spu-rgyal and the Introduction of Bon to Tibet' (*Central Asiatic Journal*, Vol. VIII, No. 2, 1963)

Yeshe De Project, *Ancient Tibet*, 1986

Index

Page numbers in *italic* refer to the black-and-white illustrations.